The Quakers in
English Society
1655–1725

ADRIAN DAVIES

CLARENDON PRESS · OXFORD

OXFORD

UNIVERSITY PRESS

Great Clarendon Street, Oxford OX2 6DP

Oxford University Press is a department of the University of Oxford.
It furthers the University's objective of excellence in research, scholarship,
and education by publishing worldwide in

Oxford New York

Athens Auckland Bangkok Bogotá Buenos Aires Cape Town
Chennai Dar es Salaam Delhi Florence Hong Kong Istanbul Karachi
Kolkata Kuala Lumpur Madrid Melbourne Mexico City Mumbai Nairobi
Paris São Paulo Shanghai Singapore Taipei Tokyo Toronto Warsaw

and associated companies in Berlin Ibadan

Oxford is a registered trade mark of Oxford University Press
in the UK and certain other countries

Published in the United States
by Oxford University Press Inc., New York

British Library Cataloguing in Publication Data

Data available

Library of Congress Cataloging in Publication Data

Davies, T. A.
The Quakers in English society, 1655–1725 / T. A. Davies.
(Oxford historical monographs)
1. Quakers—Great Britain—History—17th century. 2. Great Britain—Church
history—17th century. 3. Quakers—Great Britain—History—18th century. 4. Great
Britain—Church history—18th century. I. Title. II. Series.
BX7676.2.D39 2000 289.6′42′09032—dc21 99–045356
ISBN 0-19-820820-0

3 5 7 9 10 8 6 4

Typeset by Graphicraft Limited, Hong Kong
Printed in Great Britain
on acid-free paper by
Biddles Ltd, Guildford and King's Lynn

To my Mother
and in memory
of my Father

PREFACE

My interest in the Society of Friends arose out of curiosity about an early Quaker leader, James Nayler. A yeoman farmer and once a quartermaster in Cromwell's army, Nayler was notorious for having re-enacted Christ's last entry into Jerusalem at Bristol in 1656. A band of enthusiastic and largely female followers made up the procession, which strewed palms in his path and provocatively uttered the words 'Holy, Holy, Holy, Lord God of Israel' as they honoured their charismatic prophet. The event outraged contemporary opinion, which took Nayler to be proclaiming himself the new Messiah, a charge which was further encouraged by his wearing a beard and long hair in the manner of contemporary depictions of Christ. The accusations were forcefully denied, but Nayler was found guilty of the crime of 'horrid blasphemy' and sentenced by Parliament. As part of his punishment he had his tongue bored through with a hot iron, and his forehead branded with the letter 'B' as a reminder of his blasphemy.

The episode disconcerted me not only because of the terrible and inhumane punishment meted out to Nayler but also because hitherto I had thought of the Society of Friends as a group of sober Victorian nonconformists who were renowned for their enterprise in industry, concern for the poor, and an enlightened attitude to pacifism. This was a reputation very different from that of the sect in the 1650s, when MPs could describe followers as 'more dangerous than the most intestine or foreign enemies' or express the fear that they did 'contemn your magistracy and ministry, and trample it under their feet'.* This spurred me on to examine the relationship between Quakers and wider society, which is the main subject considered in this book.

The movement which emerged in the early 1650s quickly enraged the political and religious establishment with its anti-authoritarian tendencies. It was in time to temper dramatically that rebellious spirit which had accompanied its birth. Perhaps one reason was the persecution members were subjected to after the Restoration. Nevertheless, membership continued to grow until the turn of the century when, though the times were politically less troublesome and the movement more widely accepted, it was then beginning its long decline. It is the first seventy years of the movement

* *Diary of Thomas Burton*, ed. J. T. Rutt, 4 vols. (1828), i. 24–5, 26.

with which this study is concerned, a period during which the evolution of the movement was rapid and critical.

Many debts have been incurred during the writing of this work. Sir Keith Thomas, who supervised the Oxford doctoral thesis upon which this book is based, has provided many thoughtful insights and also shown a welcome patience as the various drafts slowly ground from the word processor. One of the privileges of studying early Quakerism is sight of the wealth of material left by the sect and those who wrote about it. Widely dispersed though these sources may be, and time-consuming to examine, I have none the less been greatly assisted by a number of archivists and institutions who by their kindness have eased the task considerably. Mention must be made of Malcolm Thomas, the Librarian, and the staff at the Friends' Library, London; Victor Gray, formerly the County Archivist, and the staff at the Essex Record Office, Chelmsford; Michael Sommerlad, formerly the Sub-Librarian, and the staff at the Essex University Library. At the time when they were consulted, the Colchester Borough Records were housed in the town's muniment rooms, at that time in Colchester Castle. Somewhat eerily, the reading area was the very room in which some three centuries earlier the young Quaker James Parnel had been confined while a prisoner of the Colchester authorities. Paul Coverley, Borough Archivist, and his staff were at all times welcoming and accommodating. I should also like to thank the staff of the Bodleian Library, Oxford, the British Library, the Guildhall Library, the former Greater London Record Office, and the Public Record Office, London.

A number of historians who have studied early Quakerism and the societies of East Anglia have also provided assistance. Hugh Barbour and Richard Vann early on discussed my research proposal and gave valuable advice. Alan Macfarlane, John Walter, Keith Wrightson, Bill Clifftlands, and Janet Gyfford generously discussed the fruits of their own research in Essex. As the study took an anthropological slant—on the matter of Quaker clothes, language, and bodily deportment—I benefited from the comments of Roy Porter, John Walter, Lesley Smith, and Peter B. Clarke at the Centre for the Study of New Religious Movements. Papers which now constitute various chapters in this book were given at seminars convened by the late Bob Scribner and Michael Hunter at the Institute of Historical Research, London, Sir Keith Thomas at St John's College, Oxford, Michael Hawkins at the University of Sussex, David Allen at Birmingham University, and at the Friends' Historical Society Conferences at Reading and London. These were occasions which provided helpful criticism and gave me pause for thought. Professor Ken Carroll has been a good friend over many years and I am grateful for the interest he has shown in my work. Later drafts of the book were read and commented upon by Sir Keith Thomas, John Walsh, John Walter, Lesley Smith, William Lamont, Ken Carroll, Peter B. Clarke, Roy Porter, Ross Wordie, John Davies, and Gareth Lloyd Jones. I should also like to thank Vivian Davies, Frances Fletcher, Ted Milligan, and Len Weaver for many kindnesses. Sylvia Carlyle at Friends' House alerted me to the existence of illustrations critical of the sect and helped to search them out. All errors and omissions in the book, however, remain my own. Dates are given in the modern style. So as to give a flavour of the period I have retained the original spelling in quotations; however, on a few occasions I have made slight amendments so as to assist clarity. Also thanks to Eirlys Jones.

In order to follow the daily lives of Quakers and others in local society I have created a nominal index of Friends which is based upon information derived from Quaker and other sources. The index amounts to over thirty thousand entries and has proved an invaluable tool for this study. The nature of the sources from which the index was compiled and their usefulness are discussed in Appendices I and II at the end of the book.

CONTENTS

IV. QUAKERS AND THE WORLD

LIST OF FIGURES

LIST OF TABLES

ABBREVIATIONS AND CONVENTIONS

BARMM	Barking Monthly Meeting Minutes
Baxter, *Autobiography*	*The Autobiography of Richard Baxter*, ed. N. H. Keeble, rev. edn. (1975)
Besse, *Sufferings*	Joseph Besse, *A Collection of the Sufferings of the People Called Quakers*, 2 vols. (1753)
Braithwaite, *Beginnings*	William C. Braithwaite, *The Beginnings of Quakerism*, 2nd edn. (1955)
Braithwaite, *Second Period*	William C. Braithwaite, *The Second Period of Quakerism*, 2nd edn. (1961)
CBR	Colchester Borough Records
COGMM	Coggeshall Monthly Meeting
COGTW	Coggeshall Two Weeks Meeting
COLTW	Colchester Two Weeks Meeting
Crisp, *Works*	Stephen Crisp, *A Memorable Account of the Christian Experiences, Gospel Labours, Travel and Sufferings of that Ancient Servant of Christ, Stephen Crisp* (1694)
Davies, 'The Quakers in Essex'	T. A. Davies 'The Quakers in Essex, 1655–1725' (unpub. Oxford D.Phil. thesis, 1986)
ERO	Essex Record Office
EUL	Essex University Library (for individual categories of documents see Bibliography)
FHL	Friends' House Library
Fox, *Journal*	*The Journal of George Fox*, ed. John L. Nickalls (1952; reissued 1975)
FPT	Norman Penney (ed.), *The First Publishers of Truth* (1907)
GL	Guildhall Library
GLRO	Greater London Record Office
HBR	Harwich Borough Records
JFHS	*Journal of the Friends' Historical Society*
Josselin, *Diary*	*Diary of Ralph Josselin, 1616–1644*, ed. Alan Macfarlane (1976)
MMS	Minutes of Meeting for Sufferings
MYM	Minutes of Yearly Meeting

Parnel, *Collection*	James Parnel, *A Collection of the Several Writings given Forth—from the Spirit of the Lord, through the meek Patient, and Suffering Servant of God, James Parnel* (1675)
Penn, *Writings*	William Penn, *The Peace of Europe, The Fruits of Solitude and Other Writings*, ed. Edwin B. Bronner (1993)
PRO	Public Record Office
Vann, *Social Development*	Richard T. Vann, *The Social Development of English Quakerism, 1655–1755* (Cambridge, Mass., 1969)

Place of publication here and in the notes is London unless otherwise indicated.

Introduction

The Quaker religion . . . is something which it is impossible to overpraise. In a day of shams, it was a religion of veracity, rooted in spiritual inwardness, and a return to something more like the original gospel truth than men had ever known in England.

William James, *The Varieties of Religious Experience* (1902, repr. New York, 1985), 7.

though they are the least literate of the English sects, they possess more ample collections of their own church history than any other Christian church, or even than any monastic order. If the Acts of the Apostles had been fully and faithfully recorded as the acts of the Quakers, what a world of controversy and confusion would have been avoided.

Robert Southey, *Letters from England by Manuel Alvarez Espritella* (1807), iii. 76.

I had the curiosity to visit some Quakers here in prison: a new phanatic sect, of dangerous principles they shew no respect to any man, magistrate or other, and seem a melancholy proud sort of people, and exceedingly ignorant.

Ipswich, 9 July, 1656.
The Diary of John Evelyn, ed. E. S. de Beer (Oxford, 1955), iii. 179.

The Society of Friends is the most intensively studied of the sects which emerged in the years of religious ferment spanning the Interregnum. According to Friends, the Quaker movement was unique in the history of the Christian church because it had returned to the authentic gospel path trodden by Christ and his apostles. As proof of its historic mission, Friends recorded much of the sect's progress and this evidence has proved an invaluable source for historians. There are surviving letters, polemical works, autobiographies, diverse manuscript evidence, and much more, and through them the historian can become privy to the mental world and every-day lives of the ordinary men and women who joined the sect. As a result scores of histories about the movement, sympathetic and otherwise, have appeared since George Fox first preached the Quaker gospel in 1652.[1]

---

[1] The best general account of the sectarian milieu remains Christopher Hill's, *The World Turned Upside Down: Radical Ideas During the English Revolution* (Harmondsworth, 1975).

Up to 1900 most histories of the Society were written almost exclusively, and thus narrowly, from the perspective of the hagiographer.[2] But early in this century there was a scholarly and impressive narrative of the movement by the Quaker historian William C. Braithwaite,[3] and since then others have brought to light new evidence on Friends' social origins, political ideology, relations with the legal system, the Quaker family, and other aspects.[4] However, this work differs in major respects from the studies of Quakerism so far available. The central objective of this book is to consider the social consequences of religious belief. In particular it sets out to discover what the relationship was between converts to and followers of the Quaker faith on the one hand, and the others with whom they shared their everyday lives in local society on the other. It is the extent of the fissures which opened up in society as a result of Quakerism which is here my chief concern.

On the surface it seems that contemporaries were deeply shocked at the provocative beliefs and conduct of early Quakers and especially the degree to which Friends were prepared to disrupt communal harmony. The explanation for this is that the Quaker religion was all-embracing, for attaining salvation and satisfying God's will on earth were achieved not only by avoidance of church worship, ritual, and dues but also by the manner

Recommended studies of non-Quaker sects include B. S. Capp, *The Fifth Monarchy Men: A Study in Seventeenth-Century English Millenarianism* (1972); Gerald Aylmer (ed.), *The Levellers in the English Revolution* (1975); Christopher Hill, Barry Reay, and William Lamont, *The World of the Muggletonians* (1983); A. L. Morton, *The World of The Ranters: Religious Radicalism in the English Revolution* (1970); and J. C. Davis, *Fear, Myth and History: The Ranters and the Historians* (Cambridge, 1986).

[2] Besse, *Sufferings*; William Sewell, *The History of the Rise, Increase and Progress of the Christian People Called Quakers*, 2 vols. (1712); Thomas Clarkson, *A Portraiture of Quakerism*, 3 vols. (1806).

[3] Braithwaite, *Beginnings* and *Second Period*. An earlier, scholarly account of the movement is provided by J. S. Rowntree, *Quakerism: Past and Present* (1859).

[4] There are numerous works of relevance, but among the most important are Alan Cole, 'The Social Origins of the Early Friends', *JFHS* 48 (1957), 99–118 and his 'The Quakers and the English Revolution', *Past and Present*, 10 (1956), 39–54. repr. in Trevor Aston (ed.), *Crisis in Europe* (5th impression, 1975), 341–58; Vann, *Social Development*; Hugh Barbour, *The Quakers in Puritan England* (New Haven, Conn., 1964); Hill, *The World Turned Upside Down*, chap. 10; Barry Reay, *The Quakers and the English Revolution* (1985); Craig Horle, *The Quakers and the English Legal System, 1660–1688* (Philadelphia, 1988). Also of importance are recent local studies which help put this monograph in context: Nicholas Morgan, *Lancashire Quakers and the Establishment, 1660–1730* (Halifax, 1993); David Scott, *Quakerism in York, 1650–1720*, University of York, Borthwick Paper, 80 (1991); Helen Forde, 'Friends and Authority: A Consideration of Attitudes and Expedients, with Particular Reference to Derbyshire', *JFHS* 54 (1978), 115–25; and Michael Mullett (ed.), *Early Lancaster Friends*, Centre for North-West Regional Studies, University of Lancaster, Occasional Paper, 5 (1978).

in which members went about their daily lives, even by their language, dress, and bodily carriage. The words of Richard Baxter, the 'Presbyterian' divine, are surely proof enough of the reasons why the earliest Quakers were regarded with loathing and contempt by the clergy and many god-fearing citizens. They describe a sentiment that was not uncommon and suggest a reputation very different from that enjoyed by the movement in its later quietist phase. Quakers may be considered to have been godly puritans who took puritan doctrine and its social message to an extreme. Writing about the emergence of Quakerism from the vantage point of the 1690s, Baxter outlined the heresies of the new religion:

They make the light which every man have within him to be his sufficient rule, and consequently the Scripture and ministry are set light by . . . they pretend their dependence on the Spirit's conduct against set times of prayer and against sacrament, and against their due esteem of Scripture and ministry; they will not have the Scripture called the word of God; their principal zeal lieth in railing at the ministers as hirelings, deceivers, false prophets, etc., and in refusing to swear before a magistrate, or put off their hat to any, or say 'You' instead of 'Thou' or 'Thee', which are their words to all . . .[5]

Except when proselytizing, Quakers were wary of the consequences of what they termed the 'pollution' which arose from mixing with outsiders and consciously tried to limit involvement with the 'world', a word by which Friends meant people, values, and institutions external to the sect. Questions for consideration here are not only what were the consequences both for individual Quakers and the wider community of conversion to this new religion but also how they changed over time. Despite the evident hostility encountered by Friends and their own sense of uniqueness, they did not constitute a wholly segregated group in local society.

The consensus hitherto has been that the uncompromising stance of Quakers led to their being isolated and marginalized in local society.[6] To be sure, there was a clear tension in relations between Quakers and the world throughout the period covered by this study; followers were treated with hostility and sometimes violence and were never to be accepted fully as members of local society. None the less, the contention here is that the view of Quakers as isolated and marginalized is exaggerated since it is determined too much by a study of records in which Quakers became visible only at points of conflict. The Friends did indeed form an alternative

---

[5] Baxter, *Autobiography*, 73–4. For a thoughtful perspective on Baxter's religious position see William Lamont, *Richard Baxter and the Millennium* (1979).   [6] See Chap. 14 below.

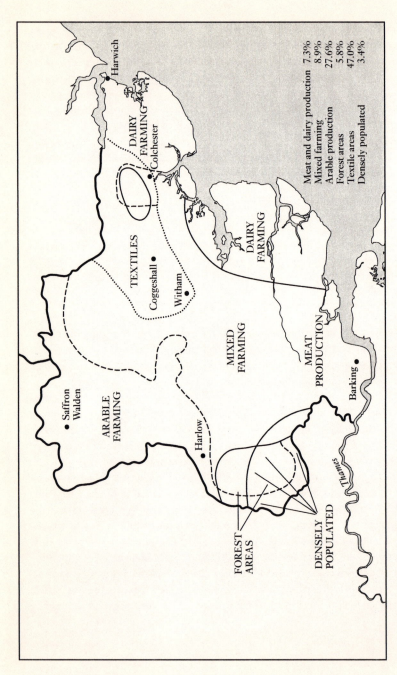

Map of Essex Showing Distribution of Quakers, *c.*1655–1725 According to Land Use

The following labels appear on the map:

Harwich

DAIRY FARMING
Colchester

TEXTILES
Coggeshall
Witham

DAIRY FARMING

Saffron Walden

ARABLE FARMING

MIXED FARMING

MEAT PRODUCTION

Harlow

Barking

Thames

FOREST AREAS

DENSELY POPULATED

Meat and dairy production   7.3%
Mixed farming   8.9%
Arable production   27.6%
Forest areas   5.8%
Textile areas   47.0%
Densely populated   3.4%

community, and were often disliked or even hated, but a historiographical concentration upon the records generated by the movement has tended to place an excessive emphasis upon the exclusion of Quakers.[7]

To assess the degree of Quaker separation, the movement has been placed within the fuller context which can be provided by detailed examination of additional local records. For this reason the study was located in Essex, a county rich in Quaker and other sources, and spans the years from 1655 to the first quarter of the eighteenth century. However, it is not strictly a history of Essex Quakerism which is presented here but as much a study of themes and topics in the history of the movement which utilizes the county's and other relevant sources for insight and elucidation. Even so, it is suggested that Essex, the county to which James Parnel first brought the Quaker gospel in 1655 and where the movement was moderately successful, provides a fresh and different perspective on the movement's first seventy years; most studies of the movement have concentrated on the north-west where Quakerism first arose under the leadership of George Fox and acquired its largest following.

A concentration upon ordinary Friends by the creation of a nominal index of Quakers in the county is critical to this study. This permitted, for example, a better appreciation of the size and geographical distribution of the movement over the decades, an important insight into the social profile of the movement, and a means by which the previous dissenting allegiances of those who became Quakers could be traced. But most of all it facilitated a close examination of the characteristics of Quaker society and the degree to which the Friends were alienated from or integrated into the surrounding society of their townships and parishes. Gradually the pattern of daily relations between Quakers and others in local society became clear. For example, vestry minutes revealed the pattern of parochial office-holding among Quakers, Colchester court books provided evidence of the apprenticeship practices of Quaker masters, and an examination of wills identified the nature of the concern among ordinary Quakers for the parish poor. The evidence suggested that local society was far less divided by sectarianism than has been hitherto assumed.[8]

---

[7] See also on wider sectarianism Christopher Hill, *Society and Puritanism in Pre-Revolutionary England* (1969), 475–7.

[8] Davies, 'The Quakers in Essex', chap. 7; Scott, *Quakerism in York*, 5–6, 24, 28–9; Bill Stevenson, 'The Social Integration of Post-Restoration Dissenters, 1660–1725' in Margaret Spufford (ed.), *The World of Rural Dissenters, 1520–1725* (Cambridge, 1995), 360–87; W. J. Sheils, 'Oliver Heywood and his Congregation', in id. and Diana Wood (eds.), *Voluntary Religion, Studies in Church History*, 23 (Cambridge, 1986), 261–77 reached conclusions similar to my own though based upon the activities of a far less extreme group of dissenters.

However, it also became clear that this was only half the story, for, while there was a good deal of social interaction between Quakers and the world, the relationship between the two was not static. Indeed, it would be a serious error to assume that the nature of the integration of Friends and local society in the 1650s and 1660s remained constant. The study identifies key periods of change in Quaker relations with the world: these are the mid-1670s and the early 1690s. Certain factors stand out as pre-eminent in determining a particular approach at one time or another. The first of these was the attitudes of the wider community towards Quakerism; the second was the will of the Society as expressed initially by its leaders and subsequently by the corporate body; and finally there was the perspective of ordinary Friends. Of course, there are always exceptions to the pattern but these factors combined at times differently to form a sectarian dynamic which determined strongly the way in which Quakers interrelated with the world.

An interest in the relations of Quakers and others in local society also encouraged me to adopt a perspective different from that which is normal in sectarian studies. Sociologists have made us aware of common factors in sectarian evolution such as the significance of charismatic leadership, the effect of organizational growth on sectarian development, sectarian relations with the world, and the tendency of sects to be transformed into denominations.[9] Many of these factors explain developments in early Quakerism. The temper of Quakerism did cool over time, and there are signs of this change early on. Within a decade, for example, the movement in Essex shed some of its more offensive behaviour, as followers were no longer encouraged to run naked through the street calling people to repentance or to disturb parish assemblies. By 1670 the Society had developed an effective disciplinary organization which in part had the purpose of keeping followers in line. By then a personal relationship with God, and a trust in the leading of the light in every Friend—the hallmark of the earliest Quakerism—were not sufficient to justify individual behaviour; this had instead to be tested by the corporate will of the group. By the

A number of American studies of Quakerism provide helpful comparative material. See, for example, Jonathan M. Chu, *Neighbors, Friends or Madmen: The Puritan Adjustment to Quakerism in Seventeenth-Century Massachusetts Bay* (Westport, Conn., 1985) and C. G. Pestana, *Quakers and Baptists in Colonial Massachusetts* (New York, 1991).

[9] Bryan Wilson, *The Social Dimensions of Sectarianism; Sects and New Religious Movements in Contemporary Society* (Oxford, 1990), 105–28 and his *Religion in Sociological Perspective* (Oxford, 1982), chap. 4.

first quarter of the eighteenth century the Society had assumed features which were consistent with the religion having moved to the status of a denomination.

None the less, one must be cautious of too strict an adherence to sociological models of sectarian change, since they encourage the neglect of important factors in the movement's local genesis and evolution and place an undue emphasis upon the words and actions of those who led the movement at a national level. Local Quakers had a significant role in the development of the movement and appear not to have been merely the passive bystanders often implied in sociological theory. Of course, this study is heavily dependent on the writings of the legendary Quaker figures who wrote about their early missionary experiences: often they alone provide evidence on important matters. None the less, while incorporating this valuable source and accepting the significance of their role, a definite attempt has been made to understand the force of the sect's development from the viewpoint of the grass roots: why members felt drawn to the movement and how they promoted its success. Indeed, the attitudes of ordinary Friends were to be crucial in accounting for the evolution of the Society in the county of Essex and the pattern of integration which developed there.

The methodology here is such that the book can be read both as a narrative account of various topics, separated under chapter headings, and at the same time as an exploration of issues of integration and alienation. Each chapter engages with topics which are familiar to historians of Quakerism and seventeenth-century society and the significance of the new evidence gathered here is assessed. The work of other historians of the early modern period has sometimes been relied upon for comparative evidence to explain what was distinctive about early Quakerism. There is not always a consensus as to what was typical in seventeenth-century society; and where disagreements exist they have been signalled in the text or the notes.

When this book was begun it was my intention to write a social history of the movement and that is what I have done. However, as the research and writing progressed, and the areas of interest expanded, the project became bigger than I had anticipated. Whether it was in the matter of theology, religious sects, the body, literacy, the nature of community, etc., I greatly appreciated the work of those from different fields of study who provided me with a wider scholarly context through which to approach these subjects. Where applicable I have drawn upon the insights provided by related disciplines, most notably those of the sociologists on modern

religious sectarianism[10] and the anthropologists on ideas of purity and attitudes to natural symbols.[11]

By comparison, of course, the tools of the historian are limited,[12] but
the output of historians influenced by these disciplines has proved fruit-
ful and they too have stimulated me to consider early Quakers in a light
rather different from that which is customary. Particularly important in
this respect was the work of Peter Burke on perception and communication[13] and John Bossy's model study of another dissenting movement, the
English Catholic Community.[14] Many of the themes explored in this work
will be familiar to those who know the work of Margaret Spufford, and I
have benefited from the many insights she has provided about the nature
of village life in the sixteenth and seventeenth centuries.[15] From a rather
different perspective but no less significant was Geoffrey Nuttall's analysis of the different emphases attributed to the Holy Spirit by the Quakers
and Puritan divines[16] which, though first published over fifty years ago,
has proved a most valuable companion as I have travelled the highways
and byways of Quaker history. My interest in the seventeenth century was
stirred by the work of Christopher Hill and Keith Thomas and this study
owes an intellectual debt to them.[17]

To begin there is an examination of the impact of the first Quakers.
Historians have made us aware of the religious milieux of the 1650s—
the Ranters, Baptists, Muggletonians, and other sectarians with whom
Quakers vied for converts—but what was special about Quakerism and what
made it hated by so many contemporaries?

---

[10] For instance, Bryan Wilson, a number of whose essays are now conveniently brought
together in *The Social Dimensions of Sectarianism*. See also T. F. O'Dea and Janet O'Dea
Aviad, *The Sociology of Religion*, 2nd edn. (Englewood Cliffs, NJ, 1983).

[11] Mary Douglas, *Purity and Danger: An Analysis of the Concepts of Pollution and Taboo*
(1979), and ead., *Natural Symbols: Explorations in Cosmology* (Harmondsworth, 1973).

[12] E. E. Evans-Pritchard, *Essays in Social Anthropology* (1962), 59.

[13] Peter Burke, *The Art of Conversation* (Oxford, 1993); id., *The Fortunes of the Courtier*
(Oxford, 1995); id., *The Historical Anthropology of Early Modern Italy: Essays on Perception
and Communication* (Cambridge, 1987); id., *Varieties of Cultural History* (1997); and id. (ed.),
New Perspectives on Historical Writing (Oxford, 1991).

[14] John Bossy, *The English Catholic Community 1570–1850* (1975).

[15] See especially Margaret Spufford, *Contrasting Communities: English Villagers in the
Sixteenth and Seventeenth Centuries* (Cambridge, 1974), *passim* and as editor, *The World of
Rural Dissenters*.

[16] Geoffrey F. Nuttall, *The Holy Spirit in Puritan Faith and Experience*, 3rd. edn.
(Chicago, 1992).

[17] See especially Hill, *The World Turned Upside Down*, and Keith Thomas, *Religion and
the Decline of Magic: Studies in Popular Beliefs in Sixteenth- and Seventeenth-Century England*
(Harmondsworth, 1973).

PART I

Holy Subversives

I

Spiritual Warriors

this Court doth take notice from divers partes of this Country that many idle, sedi-
tious and evill disposed persons doe travaile . . . from place to place propagating
and spreading certaine desparate and damnable opinions and Delusions derogat-
ory to the honor of God and destructive to mens soules, subverting the principles
of Christianity and seducing and withdrawing many from their due Obedience to
the good Government of this Nacion.

Essex Quarter Sessions Order Book (Order Against Quakers), Midsummer
Session, 1656.[1]

Go ye into all the world, and preach the gospel to every creature.

Mark 16: 15.

The object of the next four chapters is to account for the chorus of disapproval that greeted the new sect of Quakers wherever it appeared. The
argument is that Friends' spiritual rebirth lay at the root of the hostility
they encountered in local society, for it led them to propound beliefs inimical not only to the Church and its ministry but also to a whole range of
social behaviour which was officially and popularly sanctioned. Religious
conversion led Quakers to defy the norm in matters of church attendance, tithe payments, community rituals, and civility by action which to
Quakers seemed clearly sanctioned by the Gospel, but which was considered extremely provocative at the time.

While members of the community were always to a degree fearful of
the sect, there was none the less a gradual acceptance of the movement
and its followers from around the early 1670s. This can partly be
explained by a greater familiarity with Quaker ways on the part of local
society and a more accommodating attitude on the part of Friends to outsiders. However, between Quakers and the clergy there was always distrust, even when the tension had eased towards the end of the seventeenth

---

[1] *Essex Quarter Sessions Order Book, 1652–1661*, ed. D. H. Allen (Chelmsford, 1974), 88;
see also Plate II.

PLATE 1. *The Quakers Fear* (n.p., 1656). Bodleian Library, Wood 401, fo. 165ᵛ

century. The doctrinal views of Friends, clear refusal to accept church authority, and above all the Quaker challenge to the legitimacy of tithe payments were bound to promote an atmosphere of suspicion and sometimes hatred between churchmen and Quakers.

Of course, not everyone was hostile to the new movement; otherwise there would have been no conversions to the new religion, nor would the county of Essex have harboured several thousand Quakers during the period of this study. It was James Parnel, the young evangelist, who first brought the Quaker message to Essex (see Plate 1). Shortly after his release from Cambridge gaol he crossed into the county in June 1655.[2] Despite his youthfulness—his opponents derisively nicknamed him the 'Quaking boy'—his ministry was quickly effective.[3] Among the first converts were Robert Ludgater, a Coggeshall fellmonger, and William Talcot, a stapler from Colchester. More conversions followed and soon Parnel was able to rely upon a network of sympathizers across the northern half of the county. Some of these converts were men of wealth and influence. They included

[2] *FPT*, 91.   [3] Parnel, *Collection*, pp. xxi–xxii.

the former mayor of Colchester, John Furly, and John Isaac, a wealthy tanner from Halstead.[4]

Parnel's initial success did not go unnoticed. Within weeks leading Friends travelled to the county to give him support. George Fox preached at Coggeshall and Colchester during July and two itinerant Friends, Richard Hubberthorne and Edward Burrough, were also known to be active in the county.[5] The presence of the Quakers was noted by the minister at Earls Colne, Ralph Josselin, who entered in his diary: 'this corner begins to feel the quakers, some of their heads it is said are among us.'[6] Parnel was not, however, to witness the fruits of his evangelizing. Within a year of his arrival in the county he died while incarcerated in Colchester goal.[7] The loss of a charismatic leader like Parnel did not lessen the Quakers' appetite for proselytizing. In 1656 a foothold was established in Harwich and over the next decade many prominent Friends, among them Josiah Cole, Charles Marshall, and Sam Cater, traversed the county in search of converts.[8]

The success of Quaker evangelists began to worry the authorities in the county. In part their anxiety stemmed from what they knew of Quakers through Parnel's preaching and writing. His attack on magistracy and the judge who tried him,[9] along with the apparently subversive content of his teaching, must have caused alarm.[10] Equally worrying was his claim to speak with a voice as infallible as that of the prophets and his supposedly self-confessed identification with Christ.[11] One hostile pamphleteer described Parnel's followers as his 'Disciples',[12] and after his death rumours spread that some Quakers travelled to Colchester to witness his resurrection (see Plate 1).[13] What must have seemed to contemporaries dangerous and blasphemous fantasies were exacerbated by the Quaker habit of interrupting ministers during church services. It was only a matter of time before the county authorities took stern action against Friends. They did so in 1656, when an order at Quarter Session[14] instructed justices, constables, and

---

[4] *FPT*, 96–7; Parnel, *Collection*, pp. iv–v.

[5] Fox, *Journal*, 213; FHL, Caton MS 3/119; Swarthmore MS 1/351 (21 June 1656); Besse, *Sufferings*, i. 190.　　　　　　　　　　　　[6] Josselin, *Diary*, 350.

[7] Henry Glisson, *A True and Lamentable Relation* (1656), 5–6; Josselin, *Diary*, 367; Besse, *Sufferings*, i 192.

[8] George Fox, the younger, *A True Relation of the Unlawful and Unreasonable Proceedings of the Magistrates of Harwich in Essex* (n.p., 1660), 1; *FPT*, 102.

[9] Parnel, *Collection*, 246, 283–4.　　　　[10] See Chap. 4 below.

[11] Parnel, *Collection*, p. xiii; W.P., *An Answer According to Truth* (1655), 19; Glisson, *A True and Lamentable Relation*, 4.　　　　　　　　　　　　　　　[12] Ibid., 5.

[13] Josselin, *Diary*, 367.

[14] *Essex Quarter Sessions Order Book 1652–1661*, ed. D. H. Allen, 88.

church wardens to prevent Friends from travelling to meetings and to fine and gaol those who harassed the clergy.[15] In 1656 justices at Saffron Walden placed the visiting George Whitehead and some local Quakers in the stocks in the hope that humiliation might deter them.[16] Ultimately such measures proved ineffective. For some time the Quakers continued to interrupt church services and their numbers still grew. From a thousand and a quarter Quakers in the county over the period 1655 to 1664, the figure rose by more than six hundred in the next decade. The membership peaked over the ten years up to 1684, when it had over two thousand followers.[17] Probably more draconian measures were necessary to stop the Quakers spreading their particular gospel. Even such action as that might have been ineffective, for the success of Quakerism lay in more than the commitment and quality of its leaders; it depended as much upon its appeal to ordinary men and women for whom it filled a spiritual void. Once Quakerism had taken proper root, it would prove very difficult to eradicate.

PRIESTS AND PROPHETS

I have not yet had freedom to leave these parts, for here is a harvest and but few labourers; a war is begun in this nation, and but few on our part to manage it . . . Our heart will be more enlarged to hear that the war prospers in England. Write and let us know, that we may partake with you in rejoicing; and assuredly you may praise the living God on our behalf.

Edward Burrough to Margaret Fell, 5th 11m 1655 Waterford, FHL, Swarthmore MS 3/16.

some of these hereticall Antichrists have said, that it were no great matter, if all the Bibles in *England* were burned . . .

John Bewick, *An Answer to a Quakers Seventeen Heads of Queries* (1660), 162.

Quakers . . . most likely to be the thriving Sect; the Principles of it being such that they put no rules to the conscience, but only breathed the air and lived in the Regions of *Enthusiasm*. It was a *Trojan* horse of all heresies, every man might be of this comprehensive Religion with a Salvo to his own . . .

J. Price, *The Mystery and Method of His Majesty's Happy Restauration* (1680), 31.

[15] FHL, Great Book of Sufferings, i. 414.
[16] FHL, Swarthmore MS 4/191; EUL, EQ 22, 7–8. For other examples of Friends in the stocks see FHL, Great Book of Sufferings, i. 319, 407, 413–14; Besse, *Sufferings*, i. 193.
[17] See Chap. 12 below.

Religious antagonism towards Quakers stemmed primarily from what was considered to be the undue weight attached by the sect to the significance of the Holy Spirit: in Quaker parlance the 'inner light'. The Friends were part of a tradition of Protestant thinkers who gave a special prominence to the workings of the Spirit, but unlike Puritans and some other reformers Quakers did not accept that such experience needed the safeguard of tradition and the weight of biblical authority behind them.[18] As a result, they were branded as heretics and religious fanatics; by championing the primacy of the indwelling light they brushed aside doctrines and institutions that were considered the bedrock of the Christian faith. In both their religious and their social doctrines the early Friends were in many respects the most extreme of godly Puritans.

Quakers believed that all mankind possessed a divinely implanted inner light which had a potential saving power. This was certainly comforting to some and surely helped swell the ranks of the movement, but it also directly challenged the influential doctrine of predestination, which advanced the notion that all men were either preordained to reach heaven or doomed to eternal perdition.[19] In a dispute at Thaxted, Essex in 1669, Quaker George Whitehead met his Congregationalist opponent Stephen Scandrett to argue the case, roundly denying the Calvinist assertion that Christ had 'died only for a few or for a small number, Elected from Eternity'.[20] George Fox, one of the founders of early Quakerism, belittled those who argued this as 'pleaders for sin'. He expounded his views in a famous passage in his *Journal*:

For I saw that Christ had died for all men . . . I saw that the grace of God, which brings salvation, had appeared to all men, and that the manifestation of the Spirit of God was given to every man to profit withal.[21]

The prevailing view in the seventeenth century was that all men were imbued with a degree of natural light as part of God's creation, but that this was of itself insufficient to guarantee salvation. After the Fall man was so mired in sin as to be unable to discern the will of God. When redemption was delivered it was through the supernatural workings of the Spirit, whose latent presence was drawn out through study of the Bible. Spirit and Bible together could deliver salvation but even then only partially:

[18] Nuttall, *Holy Spirit*, 5–7, 42–4. This section on Quaker theology owes much to Dr Nuttall's work. See also Barbour, *The Quakers in Puritan England*, 25–9.

[19] Bernard M. G. Reardon, *Religious Thought in the Reformation* (Harlow, 1981), chaps. 7 and 8.

[20] Quoted in William Allen, Robert Ludgater, *et al.*, *The Glory of Christ's Light Within* (1669), 44–5.   [21] Fox, *Journal*, 34.

that outcome lay in the hands of God, not man.[22] Opponents said that Quakers' errors derived from their failure to distinguish between the natural and the divine light. John Stalham, the vicar of Terling, Essex, warned his parishioners in 1657 that 'Quakers adore their own light and magnify natural light, as it were the Gospel saving light, this is from the perverse principles of their fleshy wisdom'.[23] Quakers argued that since mankind was partially saved, only obedience to the inner light was needed to bring this seed to fruition. The proposition shocked many, for its implication was that pagans, heathens, and even the Turks might be saved even though they possessed no knowledge of the scriptures or Christ. Worse, it was objected by some that under this doctrine even those who were sinners might be redeemed.[24]

If Quaker radicalism had stopped here, the outcry might not have been so fierce: already some of the 'Arminians' in the church had begun to undermine the notion of predestination. But the divergence came over issues larger than free will and determinism, for Quaker theology seemed to destroy the need for the scriptural revelation or even the atonement of Christ. If, as Quakers claimed, the natural light carried with it the potentiality for saving grace, what then was the point of the historic incarnation, or Christ's death and resurrection, which constituted the turning point, the crucial dividing-line of history. Ralph Josselin, the vicar of Earls Colne, Essex, noted the Quaker heresy and remarked ruefully in his *Diary* in January 1657 how 'my heart was up for our crucified christ, against the imaginary christ of the Quakers'.[25] Quakers did not deny the significance of the earthly mission of Christ, though their belief in an inner light inevitably diminished the importance which they assigned to it. Thomas Comber, the Dean of Durham, spoke for many when in 1678 he published a critique of the Quaker position:

a man may be a Quaker Christian without the express knowledge of *Christ in the outward*, either of his Name, Nature, Laws or Offices. The great *Mogul* hath this Religion as much as *George Fox*. This lays aside all that Jesus was, Did, Taught and Suffered.[26]

The Quaker devotion to the light also led Friends to espouse their most controversial doctrine, which reappraised the significance of the scriptures.

---

[22] Nuttall, *Holy Spirit*, 20–30, 161–2.
[23] John Stalham, *Marginall Antidotes* (1657), 1.
[24] Nuttall, *Holy Spirit*, 160–1.   [25] Josselin, *Diary*, 388 (Jan. 1657).
[26] Thomas Comber, *Christianity No Enthusiasm; or, The Several Kinds of Inspirations and Revelations Pretended by the Quakers* (1678), 52–3.

In their view the indwelling light displaced the Bible as the cornerstone of the Christian faith. This dethronement of the scriptures found its most extreme representation in reports that Quakers set fire to Bibles at assemblies for worship as testimony to the power of the Spirit within. One Quaker was said to have 'burnt the Bible' and advised another to read it no more but to 'hearken the light within him'. Bristol Quaker Dennis Hollister was reported in 1658 to have said at a Baptist assembly that 'Scripture was the greatest blind and plague to mens soules, this day in *England*'.[27]

The Friends did not dismiss the Bible as a source of authority; but they held that it possessed no superior authority which limited the inspiration of the indwelling light. They were convinced that the Spirit which guided them was the same as that which inspired those who wrote the original scriptures. It followed that the Word could not be accepted as ruler over the Spirit. Moreover, Quakers went further in challenging orthodoxy by suggesting that it was now the inner light which should test the Word and not vice versa.[28] This change in emphasis shocked contemporaries. Ralph Josselin noted his anxieties about this doctrine in his *Diary* in 1656. He wrote in hope that the 'lord awaken those thereby, that give heed to the light of their own spirits, and will not put themselves under direction of word and spirit'.[29] Later, in 1678, the Anglican Churchman Thomas Comber remarked in a somewhat wry tone that 'There are no need of Teachers or Scriptures, if all receive immediate Instruction . . . Though all Bibles were burnt a Quaker light would *verbatim*, write a new one . . . '.[30] It was inevitable that biblical authority would be diminished as a result of the prominence Friends gave the Spirit (see Plate 2). Opponents were quick to signal the real dangers inherent in the Quaker position and their repugnance at this error. In the late 1660s doubts about Friends' teachings inspired one priest to warn the recently converted Oliver Sansom that he would 'set a Fagot to the Heretick's Tail'.[31]

There were further troubling repercussions to the Quaker emphasis on the Spirit. If the Bible was denigrated as the yardstick by which the leading of the Spirit was to be judged, how then could one discern whether the inspiration was genuinely divine or mere mad whimsy? Ralph Josselin

---

[27] William Grigge, *The Quakers' Jesus* (1658), 45, 50; John Bewick, *An Answer to a Quakers Seventeen Heads of Queries* (1660), 162. In 1657 a number of 'intemperate' Kent Quakers were reported by the Society to have burnt their Bibles, thus giving the 'world' an opportunity to reproach 'truth'. FHL, Swarthmore MS 4/414; Howard H. Brinton, *Friends for 300 Years* (repr. Wallingford, Pa., 1988), 32–4.   [28] Nuttall, *Holy Spirit*, 27–8.
[29] Josselin, *Diary*, 367 (11 Apr. 1656).   [30] Comber, *Christianity No Enthusiasm*, 65.
[31] Oliver Sansom, *An Account of many Remarkable Passages of the Life of Oliver Sansom* (1710), 29–30 (*c*.1664).

PLATE 2. From Francis Bugg, *Quakerism Drooping* (1703), p. 85

voiced this concern, complaining that 'an infallible spirit once granted them what lies may they not utter, and what delusions may not poor man bee given up unto'.[32] A number of renegade Quakers published accounts of their periods of membership which were critical of the movement on this score. In retrospect they concluded that when among the Friends they acted not under the inspiration of the Holy Spirit but under some diabolical influence, and they recounted instances of their sometimes bizarre and terrifying behaviour to back up their case. These reports were often recycled in pamphlets by enemies of the movement.[33] Quakers replied that the indwelling spirit was capable of discerning whether an act was evil or not, and in any case the collective behaviour of others under the light acted as a touchstone by which they could test whether individual leadings were authentic.[34] However, opponents were not to be convinced easily by the Quakers' claim. Richard Baxter warned people against the naïve doctrine of illumination which Quakers propounded.

[32] Josselin, *Diary*, 350 (29 July 1655).

[33] The two main personal accounts suggesting Quaker delusion under the light are John Toldervy's *The Foot Out Of The Snare* (1656) and John Gilpin, *The Quakers Shaken* (1653). The incidents recounted there are repeated in, for instance, Thomas Welde, *The Perfect Pharisee* (Gateside, 1653), 26; Ephraim Pagitt, *Heresiography*, 5th edn. (1654), 138; Ralph Farmer, *The Great Mystery of Godliness and Ungodliness* (1655), 87; and Richard Blome, *The Fanatick History* (1660), 72–3. [34] Nuttall, *Holy Spirit*, 44–6.

all sober Christians should be the more cautious of being deceived by their own imaginations, because certain experience telleth us, that most in an age that have pretended to prophecy, or to inspirations or revelations, have been melancholy, crack-brained persons, near to madness, who have proved deluded in the end.[35]

Under the influence of the indwelling light, which directly linked man and God, Friends dispensed with the ordinances and set prayer, and argued that a state of sinless perfection could be reached on this earth. Indeed, some thought Quakers claimed for themselves an infallibility. The root of Quakerism appeared to some critics as that which inspired the libertine sect of Ranters. Uncomfortable parallels were drawn between the two as similar exponents of what might easily develop into antinomianism. The Baptist Thomas Collier noted of Quakers in 1657 that 'theirs are but the principles of the old Ranters have no Christ but within, no Scriptures to be rule . . . have no ordinances, no law but what men found to be so, no condemnation for sin but in the conscience'.[36]

Not only did the sect advance theological heresies, but the doctrine of the inner light in particular imperilled the very foundation of the church or any clerical hierarchy. Following through the doctrine of the priesthood of all believers, they maintained that those who followed the guidance of the inner light were capable of being ministers of God, albeit of a 'mechanic' sort, no matter what their education or position in the social hierarchy. This notion was deeply shocking to the clerical and social elites. Moreover, according to Friends, the conventional route to the priesthood, an education at the Universities of Oxford or Cambridge, was unnecessary.[37] The novel twist which Quakers gave the doctrine of the Spirit appeared to anticipate for many the onset of religious anarchy. In the Quakers' religious principles there lay the seeds of a future cataclysm. Frightened contemporaries drew uncomfortable parallels with the religious fervour of the Münster Anabaptists which had resulted in religious and social anarchy in the town in 1533–4. The unpalatable truth, critics said, was that if Quakerism remained unchecked there would be destruction and carnage on a similar scale.

The spectre of social revolution was to hang over the Quaker movement, with fear of the repetition of such an outrage in England often alluded to by hostile pamphleteers.[38] The claims of some Quakers that they had

[35] Quoted ibid., 56–7.
[36] Thomas Collier, *A Looking Glass for the Quakers* (1657), 7, 16.
[37] Thomas Aldam, *False Prophets and False Teachers* (1652), 3.
[38] For instance, Richard Blome, *Questions Propounded to George Whitehead and George Fox* (1659), 24, 10; Grigge, *The Quakers' Jesus*, 12.

wrought miracle cures gave weight to these fears of a movement out of control. During the 1650s James Nayler, for instance, was said to have raised a certain Dorcas Erbury from the dead and George Fox described how he worked cures by the laying on of hands. Some mocked the apparent ability of Quakers to turn water into wine or to cast out evil spirits at their conventicles.[39] There were obvious drawbacks to putting one's faith in the extraordinary powers of the early leaders: widely quoted was the supposed example of the Quaker who deliberately drowned himself in the expectation, erroneous as it turned out, that he would be restored to life.[40] Though the allegations of opponents need to be treated with caution, some Friends none the less did believe that they were blessed with an extraordinary power to heal. This gave added force to the allegations that they attributed to themselves a divine or Christ-like status.[41] Here was yet more evidence of Quaker delusion, though issuing from the mouths of opponents.

Antipathy towards the Quaker movement is often put down to its attack on the magistracy and the disruptive behaviour of members in the local community, both of which are indeed important reasons for explaining the bitterness and hostility the sect encountered in local society. However, it is significant that the authors of pamphlets critical of Friends rarely failed to mention what they considered the blasphemies and doctrinal errors that vitiated the Quaker faith (see Plate 3). Indeed, many of those who put pen to paper couched their objections to the sect mainly in terms of the repugnance Quaker religious doctrine inspired.

QUAKERS AND THE PARISH CLERGY

'So you have no priests?' I asked. 'No, my friend', said the Quaker, 'and we are all the better for it. God forbid that we should dare to order somebody to receive the Holy spirit on Sunday to the exclusion of the rest of the faithful. Heaven be praised, we are the only people in the world who have no priests. Wouldst thou wish to deny us such a happy privilege?'

Voltaire, *Letters On England*, tr. Leonard Tancock (1734; repr., Harmondsworth, 1980), No. 2, p. 27.

preacht at Gains Colne the quakers nest, but no disturbances, god hath raised up my heart not to feare, but willing to beare, and to make opposicon to their wayes in defence of truth, it is an evil that runs much in all places.

Josselin, *Diary*, 348 (3 July 1655).

[39] Pagitt, *Heresiography*, 140; Braithwaite, *Beginnings*, 247; George Fox, *George Fox's Book of Miracles*, ed. H. J. Cadbury (1948).   [40] Blome, *Questions Propounded*, 17.
[41] Francis Higginson, *A Brief Relation of the Irreligion of the Northern Quakers* (1653), 2; Christopher Wade, *To All Those Called Quakers* (1659), 4.

PLATE 3. From Francis Bugg, *Quakerism Drooping* (1703), p. 75

The depth of Quaker conviction guaranteed disruption to religious and social life in the parish. Given the particular religious views of Friends, there was no reason why the church and its authority should be permitted respect. And particularly reprehensible in Friends' eyes was the supposedly arrogant expectation of the Church that Quakers and others in the parish should be compelled to attend church and provide maintenance for the clergy. These were the ingredients which were to precipitate bitter conflict in the parish community. The Quakers' inner light also disposed of the Church's ordinance and prayers of which the clergy were the chief guardians. There had always been disputes about the exact purpose and meaning of the sacraments among English Protestants, but they were accepted by many at least as 'Badges and Pledges of Christian Communion and Fellowship'.[42] Quakers would have none of this, dismissing the rites as superstitious and thus useless.

By contrast, Friends' worship was distinguished by an extreme simplicity and consisted of a silent congregation in which the guidance of the spirit was sought. Sometimes this was a prelude to an ecstatic awakening as members fell into violent paroxysms under the influence of the divine inner light, as befitted the sobriquet of Quaker.[43] This was far removed from the ordered sobriety of normal parish worship. In the Quakers' design the clergy and conventional church service were thus denied any purpose or relevance. Moreover, in their manner of worship Quakers seemed to question the validity of existing social arrangements. Seating in church most often corresponded to the gradations within the social hierarchy; men might be separated from the opposite sex, and young women from their seniors. The well-to-do were positioned in the front of the church, the poor to the rear.[44] Ralph Josselin recalled on one occasion how two male Friends provocatively sat in seats reserved for the maids and, having been ejected, the wife of one complained that they should be allowed to sit where they liked.[45] Given blatant Quaker disregard of church authority and social niceties, it is not surprising that local ministers were often the main agents of prosecution, exerting pressure upon magistrates and the mob to act against Friends in local society.[46]

---

[42] Ralph Farmer, *Satan Inthron'd in his Chair of Pestilence* (1657), 52.

[43] Higginson, *A Brief Relation*, 15–16.

[44] Thomas, *Religion and the Decline of Magic*, 180–1. But see also Margaret Aston, 'Segregation in Church', in W. J. Sheils and Diana Wood (eds.), *Women in the Church, Studies in Church History*, 27 (1990), 283–94.   [45] Josselin, *Diary*, 377 (17 Aug. 1656).

[46] Parnel, *A Shield of the Truth* (1655), To the Reader; [Anon.], *A True and Faithful Relation of the Proceedings of the Magistrates from the People of God (called Quakers) in Colchester* (1664), 4; Crisp, *Works*, 65, 85; *FPT*, 103.

So great was Quaker disrespect that the sect nicknamed the clergy 'hireling ministers'. A common Quaker practice during the 1650s was to speak at parish assemblies after divine service had ended or even on occasion to interrupt worship or church rituals in progress. 'Thou . . . art a deceiver,' remarked John Sewell in 1658, a Quaker yeoman from Gestingthorpe, Essex, to the priest after he had witnessed a baptismal service, 'prove it from the words or by the words that children ever were baptised by sprinkling water upon them'.[47] On another occasion in October 1657 Mary Brady, a Chelmsford Quaker, interrupted Nathaniel Raven, the minister of Felsted parish, after his sermon and 'with a loud voice [did] say . . . "You are a false prophet, and I come to admonish you to repent"'.[48] Quaker suffering books note thirty-nine occasions in the 1650s when Essex Quakers were arrested for disturbance in church; this is surely an underestimate of such activity since in the main it is instances which resulted in imprisonment that are recorded.

It was not only in church services that Friends challenged clerical authority. They added fuel to the flames of ministerial hatred by personally vilifying local ministers when the opportunity arose. Ralph Josselin, for instance, was more than once subjected to the lash of the plain-speaking Quaker tongue when going about his business in the parish. In his *Diary* for 31 August 1656 he noted that Quaker Robert Abbot remarked of him to another 'there cometh your deluder'. On 8 September he related how 'Quakers . . . pitifully scorne the Ministers. [O]ne said . . . woe to the false prophet'. On yet another occasion, 31 October 1656, he recounted being 'In the lane set upon by one called a quaker, the lord was with my heart that I was not dismayed'.[49]

The appearance on church doors of scurrilous libels denouncing ministers and the heckling of ministers by Quakers as they passed in the street also appear to have been common. 'Serpent', 'liar', 'deceiver', 'children of the Devil', 'hypocrite', 'dumb dog', 'scarlet coloured beast', 'Babylon's merchants', and 'sodomites' is a list, but not an exhaustive one, of the names tossed at the clergy by embattled Friends.[50] There are plenty of instances from Essex and elsewhere of provocative Friends seeking to undermine the authority of the local minister. At Sherburn in Yorkshire, for example, George Owston was presented at the Church Courts in 1670 for

[47] ERO, Q/Sb 2/100.   [48] ERO, Q/SR 373/121, 370/100.

[49] Josselin, *Diary*, 379, 380, 384.

[50] FHL, Great Book of Sufferings, Part I (1657), 408; Thomas Welde, *The Perfect Pharisee* (Gateside, 1653), 44; Richard Baxter, *The Quaker's Catechism* (1655), To the Reader; Joshua Miller, *Antichrist in Man, the Quaker's Idol* (1656), 17, 20.

'shutting the door upon parishioners, taking away the key, and, tying up the bell rope'.[51] In Earls Colne Quaker Henry Abbott, called upon to pay a rate in 1656, replied that he would rather give money to see the church pulled down and laid in the highway.[52] Some clergy would certainly have shrugged off the activities of Quakers as those of deluded zealots but even the most sweet-tempered would have agreed that they were an unwelcome nuisance.

After 1660 the Church relied on the restored system of ecclesiastical courts to subdue Quakers in local society but in reality these fared little better than the parish clergy. Friends ignored the courts, arguing that these bodies had no legitimate claim to summon or discipline them. Some Barking Quakers were reported in 1666 by the ecclesiastical court to be 'bold and impudent' in that they said that they had no 'care for any Eucharistical power',[53] and Boxted Friends mischievously let it be known to church officials in 1663 that they would attend the ecclesiastical court, if it could be proved that the clergy were 'the true ministers and the church the true church'.[54] On the rare occasions that citations to attend were observed, the court and its officials were left in no doubt as to the contempt in which they were held, with Quakers sometimes laughing dismissively at verdicts brought against them, or cocking a snook at the court's authority by wearing their hats when judgements were recorded.[55] The comportment of a Mayland Friend provides further evidence of Quaker disdain of clerical authority. Summoned to the court in 1678, Jonas Roberts described his local incumbent as one who 'teaches nothing but lies, and those who come to the parish church of Mayland will be damned, for the minister of the Church of England is a minister of Satan'.[56]

On Essex Quakers excommunication seems to have been imposed with little effect. Friends spent long periods without seeking absolution, to the manifest displeasure of officials. The church courts reported that John Aylett of Great Leighs had been excommunicated in 1670 for five or six years; Phineas Barnard of Mountnessing by 1685 for ten years; two Shalford Quakers, John Dawson and John Cutt, for twelve years by 1667, and Peter Petchey, a blacksmith from East Ham, had been excommunicated in 1684

[51] Quoted in Jean E. Mortimer, 'Thoresby's "poor deluded Quakers": The Suffering of Leeds Friends in the Seventeenth Century', *The Thoresby Society: The Leeds Historical Society*, 2nd ser., 1 (1990), 40.   [52] Josselin *Diary*, 366.

[53] ERO, D/AEA 44, fo. 82^v (June 1666); D/ACA 55, fo. 119^r (May 1664).

[54] EUL, COLMM 35, 150.

[55] ERO, D/ACA 55, fos. 61^{r-v} (Nov. 1663); D/AEV 13, fo. 65^r (July 1683).

[56] Quoted in Felix Hull, 'More Essex Friends of the Restoration Period', *Essex Review*, 57 (1948), 61.

'by his own confession for twenty years'.[57] Against the recalcitrant the courts might issue writs of *de excommunicato capiendo* which resulted in prosecutions in the civil courts. A successful prosecution by a plaintiff could result in Quaker imprisonment until evidence of conformity to the doctrines of the established Church was given. However, for the period up to 1685 it has been possible to discover only nineteen occasions when a writ issued for excommunication and imprisonment was used against Essex Friends.[58]

The courts were handicapped by clerical disagreement as to what was the best course for neutralizing dissent. Some churchmen advocated a tough stand. At Wivenhoe parish, Essex in 1664, for example, churchwardens suggested that the Quakers and Anabaptists 'be made examples of'.[59] At Tillingham in the same county it was argued that the failure to present nonconformists 'did very much embolden them to commit the vile or worse offence'.[60] This hard-nosed approach was disregarded by others who felt it would only confirm the dissenters in their cause. Instead, there was advocated a policy of reclaiming sectaries for the church whereby ministers and officials sought to win over Quakers and other dissenters by meeting and discussing their errors with them.[61] A similar policy had been pursued by the pre-Civil War courts and the lever of excommunication had usefully served this end. But such a strategy was ill-suited to countering a post-Restoration dissent which was well embedded in the community, organized and fiercely determined to resist pressure to conform. It is difficult to imagine what measures other than the most draconian would have been effective against Quakers and other dissenters.

Despite the taunts of opponents that Quakers had undermined the authority of the Bible, few were so knowledgeable about the holy text. This familiarity made Friends aware that their experiences were similar

[57] ERO, D/AEV 44, fo. 220ᵛ (June 1669); fo. 242ʳ (May 1670); D/AEV 13, fo. 128ᵛ (June 1685); D/AMV 3, fo. 122ᵛ; D/AEV 13, fo. 48ʳ (July 1684).

[58] Besse, *Sufferings*, i. 206, 201, 208; GLRO, D/LC 324, fo. 237ʳ (1682); FHL, Book of Cases, i. 8; MSM ii. 123; Great Book of Sufferings, i. 401, 399.

[59] GL, MS 9583, Bundle 2 (Sept. 1664), Wivenhoe.

[60] GL, St Paul's Archives, Churchwardens' presentments (unlisted) (3 June 1671).

[61] GL, MS 9853, Bundle 2 (Sept. 1664). See also Witham, Sheering, Great Henny, Kelvedon, Great Leighs. Thomas Turner, the Archdeacon of Essex, noted in his visitation book in 1684 that the curate of Hockley was to have 'discourse with the seven Anabaptists in his parish', *Transactions of the Essex Archaeological Society*, 20 (1930–1), 229. See also *Bishop Fell and Nonconformity*, ed. Mary Clapinson, Oxfordshire Record Society, 61 (1986), pp. xxxi–xxxiii; Sansom, *An Account of many Remarkable Passages*, 13; Richard Davies, *An Account of the Convincement, Exercise, Travels of that Ancient Servant of the Lord* (1844), 98 on the sympathetic attitude of the Bishop of St Asaph.

to those of the early apostles and the prophets of the Old Testament. Like
them, Friends believed that they were infused with an outpouring of the
Holy Spirit, and some even believed that they were the New Testament
Church. A result was that Quakers began to imitate the behaviour which
they read about in the Bible.[62] Dressed in sackcloth and ashes and sometimes with faces blackened, Quaker evangelists paraded through English
towns and parishes imploring their inhabitants to seek repentance. In 1655,
in Colchester, Martha Simmonds, soon to be the notorious consort of James
Nayler, 'was moved to walke in sackcloth barefoote with her hayre spread
& ashes upon her head, in the toun in the frosty weather, to the astonishment of many'.[63] Another of their antics, commentators observed, was
to run unclothed or barely attired through the streets, thus signifying to
those who witnessed them a spiritual nakedness and the need to repent.[64]
The boldness of Quakers was to know no bounds. In 1667 Solomon Eccles
performed a most extraordinary 'witness' which was captured by the pen
of the contemporary diarist Samuel Pepys:

To Westminster hall, where the Hall full of people to see issue of the day, the
King being to come to speak to the House today. One thing extraordinary was this
day, a man, a Quaker, came naked through the hall, only very civilly tied about
the privities to avoid scandal, and with a chafing-dish of fire and brimstone upon
his head did pass through the Hall, crying, 'Repent! Repent!'[65]

Gaol might be the reward for acting out these 'signs' and 'wonders',
though when questioned about their motives Friends quoted biblical precedent in justification. Eccles, for instance, who was much given to prac-
tising 'signs' (on separate occasions he burned his violin and covered
himself in his own dirt as a sign to the people), considered himself to be
guided by the same spirit as that which inspired Isaiah and Ezekiel.[66] The
example of the Old Testament prophets and a passage in Revelation where
it was noted that the Lord appointed two witnesses to prophesy in sackcloth and ashes gave obvious encouragement for these Quaker activities.

---

[62] T. L. Underwood, *Primitivism, Radicalism, and the Lamb's War: The Baptist–Quaker
Conflict in Seventeenth-Century England* (New York, 1997), 5; Kenneth Carroll, 'Quaker
Attitudes towards Signs and Wonders', *JFHS* 54 (1977), 76, *passim*; and id., '"Sackcloth"
and "Ashes" and other Signs and Wonders', *JFHS* 53 (1975), 314–25.

[63] Quoted in "*Letters to William Dewsbury and Others*, H.J. Cadbury (ed.), (1948), 41.

[64] Kenneth Carroll, 'Early Quakers and "Going Naked As A Sign"', *Quaker History*, 67
(1978), 76–9.

[65] Samuel Pepys, *The Shorter Pepys*, ed. Robert Latham (Harmondsworth, 1987), 814
(29 July 1667).

[66] Carroll, '"Going Naked As A Sign"', 80–1; Braithwaite, *Second Period*, 245–6.

Disruption of parish worship by Quakers ceased on the whole in the early 1660s, but efforts by the sect to poach a minister's flock and to maintain their own separate meetings for worship continued, and this heightened the animosity felt by the Church, though Friends naturally saw evangelism as a legitimate opportunity to win new souls for God. Most Friends also persisted in refusing to pay tithes and church rates for several decades. In the parish of Wakes Colne, Essex, the minister and churchwardens were disturbed by the actions of Robert Walford, who in the early 1660s encouraged villagers to absent themselves from church and castigated those who ignored his counsel, saying that going to church on the Lord's day was 'going to serve the devil'.[67] At High Easter in the same county the churchwarden complained in 1665 that neighbours fell out when Friends first appeared in the parish, and at Great Bursted during the 1670s the distress of parishioners was evident when the campaign waged by the Quaker Thomas Turner in partnership with his spouse led to familial disagreements, with husband and wife being turned against one another.[68] Quaker evangelism seemed disagreeable because it threatened the ideal of communal harmony which was broadly recognized as the cornerstone of parish life.[69] While it was accepted as inevitable that parochial relations would at times be upset by the vicissitudes of daily life the provocative behaviour of Friends was a source of much criticism and a major reason for hostility towards the movement in the local community.

The danger that the sect posed to the parochial consensus constituted one of the major contemporary objections to the movement. An interesting feature of the anti-Quaker literature was the advice given to parishioners on how to resist the Quaker menace. It was suggested by some that Friends should be isolated in the parish by being subjected to a form of 'social apartheid'. Joshua Miller, for example, argued in 1655 that no familiarity or courtesy was to be shown them and certainly no welcome into the family home.[70] In the event of a family being divided by the religion, Ralph Farmer advised in 1660 that a husband prohibit a wife's attendance at the sect's assemblies; if the husband favoured the Quaker faith, Sam Eaton suggested in 1654 that a wife should shun Friends brought to the family

---

[67] GL, MS 9583, Bundles 2–11 (Sept. 1664); ERO, D/ACA 55, fo. 119 (May 1664); William Prynne, *The Quakers Unmasked* (1655), 27.

[68] ERO, D/AMV 2, fo. 155ᵛ; D/AEA 44, fo. 280ʳ⁻ᵛ.

[69] Martin Ingram, *Church Courts, Sex and Marriage in England, 1570–1640* (Cambridge, 1987), 30–2.

[70] Miller, *Antichrist in Man*, 29–30; [Anon.], *The Querers and Quakers' Cause* (1653), 19.

home in order to avoid ensnarement.[71] In addition, attendance at public worship, a regard for the scriptures, and the company of good Christians were thought further antidotes to the Quaker infection.[72]

Sometimes, as a result of their religious inclinations, Quakers were publicly humiliated by being placed in the stocks or beaten, surely a sign of communal disapproval of their antisocial conduct.[73] To realize how serious was the Quaker incursion into parish life it must be recognized that the activities of some recent deviant subcultures like 'Mods and Rockers', 'Hippies', 'Rastas', 'Rudies', and 'New Age Travellers',[74] which are or have been a reason for disquiet and negative comment, were as nothing besides the impact of Friends who tried deliberately and publicly to change the world by fervent preaching and winning over people to the cause. No wonder the epithet 'Quaker' was a reason for trembling among the clergy and linked with subversion.

Though Quaker behaviour was viewed as disruptive to parish life it needs to be considered against the background of the spiritual awakening which converts to the sect had undergone. The profound religious conversion they had experienced was akin to that witnessed in the present day by members of evangelical and charismatic churches who describe themselves as having been 'born again'.[75] Having cast off the carnal man, Friends wished others to share the liberating experience of the 'truth' which had enlightened them. The significance of this changed personal state is revealed by those Friends who warned that the names given them in baptism were not representative of their reborn state. However, Friends did not go so far as followers of some modern sects and cults and adopt different names altogether.[76] In 1654 Richard Hubberthorne, one of the early Quaker evangelists,

---

[71] Samuel Eaton, *The Quakers Confuted* (1654), 65; Ralph Farmer, *The Lord Craven's Case Stated* (1660), 38.

[72] Ralph Hall, *Quakers Principles Quaking* (1656), Epistle to the Reader.

[73] EUL, EQ 22, 8.

[74] Stan Cohen, *Folk Devils and Moral Panics: The Creation of the Mods and Rockers*, 2nd. edn. (Oxford, 1980). Ted Polhemus has a wide-ranging look at recent subcultures in *Street Style* (1994). See also Paul E. Wallis, *The Profane Culture* (1978); Peter B. Clarke, *Black Paradise: The Rastafarian Movement* (Wellingborough, 1986); Eileen Barker, *New Religious Movements* (1989).

[75] See, for example, Andrew Walker, *Restoring the Kingdom: The Radical Christianity of the House Church Movement* (1985).

[76] Thomas Welde, *A Further Discovery* (Gateside, 1654), 7, quoted Nayler as referring to himself as 'by the world called James Nayler'. See also Parnel, *A Trial of Faith* (1654), 8. Geoffrey F. Nuttall's 'Reflections on William Penn's Preface to George Fox's Journal', *JFHS* 57 (1995), 115–16 discusses the importance of names, anagrams, and puns to early Friends and Hugh Ormsby-Lennon also considers the phenomenon in 'From Shibboleth to Apocalypse: Quaker Speechways during the Puritan Revolution' in Roy Porter and Peter

recalled his conversion and the impulse that followed upon it to spread the Quaker gospel:

and the trumpet of the Lord was sounded within me and the earth did tremble, and the vials of the wrath of the Almighty were poured down upon me . . . the foundation of wisdom and earthly knowledge was shaken . . . And, the terrors of the Almighty being upon me, my acquaintance and familiars stood afar off me, for they knew not the power of the Lord, nor the judgements of my God . . . And by this Word was I called to go and declare it, as I had received it from the Lord, to those who lived in the same heathenish nature, without the knowledge of God, and to declare the judgements of God against sin and ungodliness, as they were made manifest in me.[77]

Friends were themselves to face fierce verbal and sometimes physical assault but they persisted in their campaigns because they believed that the end of the world was close at hand. There was an expectation that the present earthly and sinful age was to be replaced by a new heavenly kingdom over which Christ would rule for a thousand years.[78] It was time for urgent repentance. The approach of the 'Second Coming' was widely debated in the seventeenth-century Church, and indeed by many Christians over the centuries,[79] though few apart from Quakers interpreted it in so extreme a fashion. There are disagreements among historians over quite what Quakers expected in the millennium, but a consistent theme[80] is the representation of Christ's earthly kingdom in which individuals were personally transformed by accepting the spirit of God. The outward, physical coming of Christ was not forgotten, but Quakers emphasized to a greater degree the importance of an inward judgement and the presence of Christ in the here and now.[81] Indeed, John Bunyan, the leading Baptist and a fierce

Burke (eds.), *Language, Self and Identity: A Social History of Language* (1992), 92–4. I owe the point on naming customs of some modern religious movements to the kindness of Peter B. Clarke, King's College, London.

[77] Quoted in Hugh Barbour and Arthur O. Roberts (eds.), *Early Quaker Writings* (Grand Rapids, Mich., 1973), 159.

[78] V. N. Olsen, *John Foxe and the Elizabethan Church* (Berkeley, Calif., and Los Angeles, Calif., 1973); William M. Lamont, *Godly Rule: Politics and Religion, 1603–1660* (1969); Christopher Hill, *Antichrist in Seventeenth-Century England* (Oxford, 1971).

[79] Norman Cohn, *The Pursuit of the Millennium: Revolutionary Millenarians and Mystical Anarchists of the Middle Ages* (1970). For the importance of millenarian thought in a later period see J. F. C. Harrison, *The Second Coming: Popular Millenarianism 1780–1850* (1979).

[80] Bryan W. Ball, *A Great Expectation: Eschatological Thought in English Protestantism to 1660* (Leiden, 1975), 195–7, 204–10; T. L. Underwood, 'Early Quaker Eschatology' in P. Toon (ed.), *Puritans, the Millennium and the Future of Israel* (1970), 96–9, 101.

[81] Ball, *A Great Expectation*, 203–4; Hill, *Antichrist in Seventeenth-Century England*, 144–5.

opponent of Quakerism in the 1650s, sought to discredit the sect on this count.[82]

Provocative language and aggressive evangelism were thought to be the only ways to break the malign hold of the Church and the world on man in his fallen state. A total conviction of the fundamental truth of Quakerism explains the extraordinary zeal with which Friends set about their missionary campaigns and why they were undeterred by fierce opposition. All in all, Friends' aggressive proselytizing and disregard for communal norms earned them a reputation as God's awkward squad. Indeed, the profound spiritual rebirth experienced by Friends and the disruptive social consequences which followed on from that differentiated them markedly from other dissenters.

QUAKERS AND TITHES

Oh, the vast sums of money that are gotten by the trade they make of the selling the Scriptures, and by their preaching from the highest bishop to the lowest priest! . . . the Scriptures were given forth freely, and Christ commanded his ministers to preach freely . . .

Fox, *Journal*, 39.

The Quakers began to make a great stir among us, and acted the parts of men in raptures, and spake in the manner of men inspired, and everywhere railed against tithes and minister.

Baxter, *Autobiography*, 97.

The battle between Quakers and clergy was joined most bitterly over the issue of clerical maintenance. Refusal to pay tithes in particular was a signal to the clergy that Friends were in earnest, for disabling ministers from gaining a livelihood was one of the most effective methods of undermining the Church and its clergy. After all, tithes were a valuable (and for most clergy the chief) source of income.[83] Moreover, it is important to recognize that while eccentric Quaker behaviour in the parish and personal invective against the clergy were modified after the Restoration, the

---

[82] John Bunyan, *A Vindication of the Book called, Some Gospel-Truths Opened* (1657), 42.
[83] On tithes see Eric J. Evans, '"Our Faithful Testimony": The Society of Friends and Tithe Payments, 1690–1730'; *JFHS* 52 (1969); Morgan, *Lancashire Quakers and the Establishment*, chaps. 5–6; Barry Reay, 'Quaker Opposition to Tithes, 1652–1660', *Past and Present*, 86 (1980).

majority of Friends still resisted tithe payments through the seventeenth century and this was a serious and continuing challenge to the authority of the ministry.

There were several objections to payment, but the basic argument of Friends was that tithes, first established under Jewish law, were no longer legitimate because they were abolished under the new covenant when Christ came to the earth. The subsequent reimposition of tithes was considered an act of apostasy brought about by the 'popish' church. The commitment of Friends was such that they would rather go to gaol than pay the tax. Josselin noted of the local Quaker Robert Abbot in 1657 that he could not offer his tenth, since to do so would 'deny Christ come in the flesh'. In the following year, John Staffold interrupted the minister at Weathersfield, saying 'Beware of such as he is, for they go in sheep's clothing but inwardly they are ravening wolves'.[84]

Quakers declared that a ministry that lacked spiritual authority deserved neither respect nor funding from the laity. The arguments between Quakers and the Church have often been considered and the concern here is more to assess the divisions that emerged in local society because of Quaker convictions. There is evidence of the conduct of both parties in local tithe disputes in the petitions made by the clergy to the Exchequer court for redress. Though little used, the documents are immensely valuable because they provide a unique insight into the behaviour of clergy and Quakers in the parish setting and also reveal how others in local society viewed these conflicts. From the records it is clear that the number of Quakers who refused to pay tithes was considerable and, it seems, Friends were absolutely determined to resist attempts by the clergy to get their dues. Ecclesiastical records confirm the unyielding Quaker position. For example, when Quaker Thomas Brown from Rochford, Essex refused in 1666 to pay his tithe, the church court presentment noted that 'he has been frequently presented'.[85] The Pollard brothers, both Quakers from Steeple, were reported by officials to be 'witholding of tithe from the minister there' in 1662, and William Hockley, a Friend from Thaxted, refused to pay the minister his tithe in 1669 giving him 'reviling words' instead.[86] The clergy's response to this resistance was equally determined. The vicar of Boxted, Samuel Doughty, surely represented a

[84] Josselin, *Diary*, 418; ERO, Q/SR 376/15; M. G. F. Bitterman, 'The Early Quaker Literature of Defence', *Church History*, 42 (1973), 211–14.

[85] ERO, D/AEA (Archdeaconry of Essex, Acts), 44, fo. 96ᵛ.

[86] ERO, D/ABA (Bishop of London's Commissary in Essex and Herts., Acts), 10, fo. 13ᵛ; D/AMV (Archdeaconry of Middlesex Visitation), 4, fo. 8ʳ (Jan. 1668).

general clerical sentiment when, in a submission to the Exchequer court in 1672, he described Quakers as:

Men of evil and perverted dispocicion in principals, & contriving all manner of waies not only the defaming of your orator, but impoverishing, [being] contemptible as much as in them lyes [to] the whole clergy of England.[87]

For the clergy, much was at stake in the outcome of these disputes. A Quaker victory, ministers claimed, denied them the financial support necessary to perform the full range of their clerical duties.[88] Fear of a gradual slide into poverty was another often-voiced complaint, as was the neglect of parochial duties which would be a consequence of Quaker campaigns.[89] At Epping the rector grumbled in 1669 that such was Quaker success that he was in danger of being foreclosed on his debts.[90] There was also a widespread concern that the Quakers' success in evading tithe payments might encourage other parishioners to try their luck. Edward Hayward complained in 1681 that many parishioners followed the example of Quakers and declined to produce payments.[91]

On occasion, communal resistance to tithe payment was determined by more than the bandwagon which Friends had set in motion. There is evidence that Quakers and other inhabitants sometimes colluded to frustrate a minister's efforts to gather tithes. During the 1650s, for example, Friends and other villagers at Hadstock removed the book detailing tithe payments, thus disabling the rector, Thomas Watkins, from claiming his dues.[92] At Little Walton in 1670, Friends drove cattle into neighbouring parishes at tithing time, subsequently suggesting that any request for payment was therefore void.[93] In 1675 the Quaker Samuel Parminter was ringleader of a group of villagers who refused to pay tithes at Belchamp Otten.[94] The reasons for resisting payment may have differed, but the joint action of parishioners certainly weakened the chances of the incumbent getting his dues. The reason for communal support may have been that Friends were tapping into a general anti-clerical sentiment when waging their tithe campaigns. There is some evidence that new followers had been

---

[87] PRO, E112/398/265.

[88] On the failure of the clergy to satisfy their pastoral duties of encouraging religion and learning in the parish on account of Quaker activity see PRO, E112/396/7 (1657); E112/398/265 (1683); E112/398/261 (1683).

[89] PRO, E112/397/144 (1669); E112/396/4 (1662); see also E112/396/7 (*c.*1657).

[90] PRO, E112/397/172.

[91] PRO, E112/400/427, Edward Hayward (1681); E112/398/259 (1672), Joseph Powell of South Halstead.   [92] PRO, E112/299/122 (1659).

[93] PRO, E112/397/181 (1670).   [94] PRO, E112/399/340.

involved in tithe disputes prior to their joining the movement,[95] and the Quaker stance would certainly have appealed to many in their ranks who disliked the prospect of handing over their hard-earned gains to what they considered a self-indulgent clergy.

Quakers sought to portray themselves as the blameless victims of clerical tyranny in respect of tithe demands, though the underhand tactics they sometimes employed suggest that they were not as innocent as they wanted others to believe. In fact, Friends pursued a variety of subterfuges to avoid payment. The most vulnerable of their victims were recently appointed incumbents who were perhaps unfamiliar with the tithing practices in a parish. When Friends at Great Coggeshall, which harboured the second largest Quaker population in Essex, refused tithe payment in 1685, the local incumbent petitioned the Exchequer and described how they carried on,

sometimes pretending noe Tithes are due in kind within the said parish, but some *Modus Decimandi* in lieu of tithes, and at other times alledging there is some real composicion for all Tithe within the said parish and at other times that he hath paid your orator or given satisfaction for the same. Whereas in truth there is not any such *Modus Decimandi* or composicion but Tithes are really due in kind and noe satisfaction has been given to your orator for the Tithe.[96]

For local Friends the end of avoiding tithe payments appears to have justified the means. Of course, resilient clergy could get their dues, but to do so involved delay and possible court appearances. There is indirect evidence that some clergy did not press their claims against Friends or at least waited a considerable time before seeking a legal remedy.[97] This may have indicated a difficulty in proving a case or reluctance on their part to prosecute inhabitants over whom they had some spiritual oversight. There may even have been some connivance at tithe payment, though there is little hard evidence of this practice among Friends until the last decade of the seventeenth century. In the 1690s laws were passed which enabled the clergy to recover tithes more easily and the Quakers' stance on tithes no longer posed such a challenge to the clergy.[98] However, some still persecuted

---

[95] Reay, 'Quaker Opposition to Tithes, 1652–1660', 100–4; Davies, 'The Quakers in Essex', 29.   [96] PRO, E112/579/64.

[97] This is implied by the intervals between the dates at which the clergy became parochial incumbents and their prosecuting Quakers for tithe payments. This is also sometimes evident from Suffering records. For example, William Shepherd of Wickham St Paul's had a claim for eight years' tithe against him in 1682. EUL, EQ 22, 18.

[98] Eric J. Evans, ' "Our Faithful Testimony": The Society of Friends and Tithe Payments, 1690–1730', 106–21.

Quakers relentlessly until they were driven into poverty.[99] And the Society remained determined that its members should avoid the payment of clerical dues despite a waning of commitment on their part.

Quakerism carried in its train more than aggressive proselytizing in the parish and disrespect of clerical authority. The new faith also undermined a wide spectrum of social behaviour that the Church sanctioned. During the seventeenth century religious belief and social behaviour were closely linked.[100] Quaker rejection of the Church's spiritual authority was to have profound social repercussions within local society.

[99] EUL, EQ, 22, 10 (1660). The case of Robert Levitt, who was relentlessly harassed by the authorities. See also Table 13, p. 184.

[100] For a stimulating discussion of the transformation of England's religious culture at this time see C. John Sommerville, *The Secularisation of Early Modern England: From Religious Culture to Religious Faith* (New York, 1992). See also Peter Berger, *The Sacred Canopy: Elements of a Sociological Theory of Religion* (repr. New York, 1990).

2

The Quaker Tribe

Here is a People in our City, that Men call *Quakers*, that in their life differ from us, and if we pipe to them, they will not Dance, and if we Mourn, they will not lament, they will neither Rejoyce in that in which we Rejoyce nor Grieve at that at which we Grieve, but . . . they differ from us.

> Stephen Crisp's description, *c.*1672–5, of how outsiders perceived Quakers. *Works*, 333–4.

I asked a Quaker friend to describe the essence of his faith. 'No pomp', he replied, 'under any circumstance'.

> Edward Stevenson quoted in *Reader's Digest* (June 1982), 67.

In their daily lives Friends practised a form of 'tribalism' which led to a disregard of worldly customs and associations. Recollections in Quaker diaries and journals and the criticisms levelled by opponents of the sect indicate that after conversion the importance to members of family, neighbours, and everyday acquaintances was diminished. John Kelsall, of Dolobran in Montgomeryshire, wrote in 1703 that he could find no 'peace or satisfaction or fellowship with any' except among Quakers.[1] When William Penn returned from Ireland in 1667 Pepys remarked that 'he was a Quaker again, or some very melancholy thing; that he cares for no company, nor comes into any'.[2] And William Edmundson, recalling fellow converts to the new faith in the 1650s, noted that 'the world and the things of it were not near our hearts . . . we were glad of one another's company'.[3] Predictably, the traditional network of familial and parochial ties ceased to exercise as great an influence over Friends as over other members of

---

[1] John Kelsall, 'A Journal of the historical account of the chief passages, concerns and excercise of my life', 72 (*c.*1703), FHL, MS vol. S, 193–4.

[2] *The Illustrated Pepys. Extracts from the Diary*, ed. Robert Latham (1978), 168, quoted by David Blamires, 'Quakers Observed in Verse and Prose', in id., Jeremy Greenwood, and Alexander Kerr (eds.), *A Quaker Miscellany for Edward H. Milligan* (Manchester, 1985), 17.

[3] William Edmundson, *A Journal of the Life, Travels and Sufferings, and Labour of Love in the Work of the Ministry* (Dublin, 1715), 26 (*c.*1655). For other examples of this sectarian tendency see also *A Journal of the Life of Thomas Story*, ed. William Alexander (York, 1832), i. 108, 105 (*c.*1691); Josiah Coale, *The Books and Diverse Epistles of the Faithful Servant of the Lord, Josiah Coale* (1671), 10; Farmer, *The Lord Craven's Case Stated*, 2.

local society. Any group of like-minded people, whether religious or otherwise, is bound to shift the focus of its loyalties to some extent.[4] But this impulse was accentuated by Friends' wish to avoid what they considered the dangers posed by worldly contamination.[5] James Parnel expressed this as a reason for Quaker exclusiveness in 1655. He wrote that:

purity and impurity cannot agree together and it is our desires to keep ourselves unspotted of the world, for that which is unclean defiles, and from that we are separated, who are the Sons and the Daughters of the living God.[6]

The fear of spiritual defilement was so great that the Society issued a stream of instructions warning followers of the dangers which accompanied mixing with the spiritually impure, that is those not under the guidance of the inner light. Many contemporaries detected a 'them' and 'us' mentality among Quakers. For instance, one anonymous critic of the movement wrote in 1681 that Friends especially spurned those who received or favoured the Anglican sacrament.[7] The Gateshead divine, Thomas Weld, a former minister of the Essex parish of Terling, remarked in 1653 that Quakers separated from others on account of the 'conceit' of 'their own unsurpassing holinesse'.[8] The elders in the Society did indeed warn members against friendships of the world and too close an attachment to non-Quaker relatives.[9] The expectation was that the children of members should attend Quaker schools so that they might then be isolated from the dangers of worldly contagion. At home parents were advised, where necessary, to prohibit offspring from associating with non-Quaker children for the same reason.[10] Though the intention of these measures was to enable Friends to live their daily lives in the context of Quaker purity, this would have been interpreted by contemporaries as showing contempt for existing social arrangements. The admonitions of the sect were heeded by members. So noxious were the customs of the world thought to be that

---

[4] Sam Fussell, *Muscle: Confessions of an Unlikely Bodybuilder* (1992), provides an unusual and amusing view of a subculture. Another unorthodox perspective is to be found in Charles Sprawson's *Haunts of the Black Masseur: The Swimmer as Hero* (1992), 134–7.

[5] A useful comparative perspective on ideas of religious purity is provided by the essays in Walter E. A. Van Beek (ed.), *The Quest for Purity* (Berlin, 1988).

[6] Parnel, *A Shield of the Truth* (1655), 38.

[7] [Anon.], *Five Important Queries* (1681), 1.   [8] Welde, *The Perfect Pharisee*, 48–9.

[9] William Dewsbury, *The Life of William Dewsbury* (1836), 110 (*c*.1655); Thomas Rawlinson, *Light Sown for the Righteous* (1657), 84; Ambrose Rigge, 'A True relation of Ambrose Rigge by way of a Journal', in *Constancy in the Truth Commended* (1710), 348 (*c*.1702); John Whiting, *Persecution Exposed* (1715), 53–4; Higginson, *A Brief Relation*, 27.

[10] EUL, EQ 26, 49 (1710), EQ 26, 52 (1724); FHL, MYM, ii. 338 (1701), MYM, iv. 149 (1710).

John Kelsall described how, after mixing with outsiders, he felt compelled to cleanse his body, thus removing symbolically the spiritual dirt and impurity which had rubbed off on him. He wrote in 1714:

my spirit would be wounded by them and I found by Experience that I had need of washing when I came from amongst them, though lawful occasion sometimes led me there, my very heart would [be] as it were sick with the smell and fume of vanity, irreligion and prophaneness that abounded among them, and the same would pretend to religion and talk thereof but they were ever like Heathens never retaining any right notion or Ideas of true Religion.[11]

Kelsall's actions were probably extreme but they are none the less indicative of the feeling among some Quakers that every opportunity should be taken to avoid worldly pollution. Indeed, the desire of Friends to escape the world was to have other significant and practical repercussions on the way that they lived their daily lives in the local community.

Sect members harboured feelings of repugnance at church rituals because they were thought merely superstitious and thus useless. As a result Friends spurned participation in the rites of passage. The religious significance of these rituals was, of course, immense, because they marked God's oversight of the stages of man's progress on earth. But their social function was also important in that they expressed the changed relations of individuals to one another in local society. Failure to acknowledge the rites of passage was taken as a slight to Church authority and a breach of those social rules which met with general acceptance in local society.

While baptism marked the admission of an infant into the Church, it also possessed social significance in that it gave formal recognition to a child as a member of local society. Quaker repudiation of this ritual was taken as a reproach to accepted church and communal practice.[12] There were further worrying consequences for relations between Friends and the local community. There was an expectation among some that parochial midwives would baptize a child if its life seemed at risk. This precaution was unacceptable to some Quaker communities and as a result local midwives and other parish women were denied the opportunity to assist Quaker women during labour. In their place Essex Friends appointed women of

---

[11] FHL, Kelsall's Journal, 161–2; Keith Thomas, 'Cleanliness and Godliness in Early Modern England' in Anthony Fletcher and Peter Roberts (eds.), *Religion, Culture and Society in Early Modern Britain: Essays in Honour of Patrick Collinson* (Cambridge, 1995), 62–6.
[12] On the rites of passage see David Cressy, *Birth, Marriage, and Death: Ritual, Religion and the Life-Cycle in Tudor and Stuart England* (Oxford, 1997); Thomas, *Religion and the Decline of Magic*, 40–2; Allen, Ludgater, *et al.*, *The Glory of Christ's Light Within*, 35; Parnel, *A Shield of the Truth*, 12; ERO, QSb 2/100 (1658).

some standing in the religious community. At Earls Colne it was Ann Burton, the wife of Samuel the tallow chandler, who acted as the Quaker midwife in 1663 and after.[13] At Barking in the 1680s Elizabeth Mortimer, a Quaker widow and active member of the women's meeting for some twenty years, assisted Quaker women during confinement.[14] The advantage of a Quaker midwife was that she could be relied upon not to use the baptismal ceremony nor adorn the newborn with ribbons, a practice disapproved of by Friends.[15]

The Society's marriage practice also put Friends at odds with prevailing social mores. From the start, the Quaker 'tribe', mindful of the need to avoid spiritual impurity, insisted that marriage should be endogamous and that the marriage procedure itself be accomplished under the direction of the local Quaker business meeting. That the betrothal, publication of intention, and marriage ceremony itself were completed without official sanction was a matter of grave disquiet to the Church and local society. The establishment of a new household added a potential burden on parish resources, and there was an expectation that it should also fulfil important social and religious obligations in the interest of the wider community.[16] That is in part why the Church and neighbourhood wished to exercise control over those who entered the matrimonial state. There was a further concern: the sect's insistence that marriages be accomplished between Quakers alone lessened in some cases the already limited supply of eligible partners within a parish. Demographic studies indicate that at this time a substantial number of people never married and that among those who did so the mean age at first marriage was relatively high.[17] The presence of the Quaker sect in a parish could then result in a significant depletion in the number of partners available for matrimony. This must

[13] ERO, D/ACA 55, fo. 60ᵛ (Nov. 1663).

[14] ERO, D/AEV 13, fo. 47ᵛ (July 1684), fo. 16ʳ (May 1684).

[15] On the activities of Quaker and other midwives see 'At a Meeting of the Midwives in Barbados', 11th 12 m 1677', *JFHS* 37 (1940), 22–4; Phyllis Mack, *Visionary Women: Ecstatic Prophecy in Seventeenth-Century England* (Berkeley, Calif., and Los Angeles, Calif., 1992), 345–7; Thomas Forbes, 'The Regulation of English Midwives in the Sixteenth and Seventeenth Centuries', *Medical History*, 8 (1964), 238; Antonia Fraser, *The Weaker Vessel: Woman's Lot in Seventeenth-Century England* (1985), 507. See also Cressy, *Birth, Marriage, and Death* who suggests that baptism by women was rare in the seventeenth century (117–23, chaps. 5–8).

[16] For the role of the community in marriage formation see John Gillis, *For Better, For Worse: British Marriages, 1660 to the Present* (Oxford, 1985), 6, 12; Patrick Collinson, *The Birthpangs of Protestant England: Religious and Cultural Change in the Sixteenth and Seventeenth Centuries* (1988), 87.

[17] Ingram, *Church Courts*, 129–30; E. A. Wrigley and R. S. Schofield, *The Population History of England, 1541–1871: A Reconstruction* (Cambridge, 1989), 233–4, 256.

have been a cause of resentment in local society, though some Essex parishioners in the late seventeenth and eighteenth centuries attempted to circumvent this obstacle by feigning conversion to Quakerism in the hope of finding a match.[18]

The upshot of Quaker disregard for Church authority and accepted practice was that members were treated by some as outcasts. It was said that their marriages were void since they were accomplished without spiritual or legal authority. The church records reflect these sentiments with presentments, for example, for couples being 'unlawfully married' in 1670, and 'clandestinely married' in 1684.[19] Sometimes court officials queried, as in February 1663, 'by what authority' Friends were joined.[20] The hostile reaction to the sect is most apparent in the status accorded to Quaker unions and the offspring they produced. Having rejected clerical and communal sanction, sect members were accused of living immorally. The partners were thought little better than fornicators. Presentments of Quakers in the court records mirror these sentiments; for example, 'for living with a woman he called his wife' in 1662; 'for lying with a woman before marriage' in 1663; and 'for committing fornication together' in 1668. At Fordham in 1665 John Lee and Thomas Lee were said to 'have two wenches that they live with as their wives'.[21] Quaker defiance of the norm may account for the allegation that Friends were excessive fornicators and adulterers, mostly with one another.[22] Under the guise of the Spirit, Quakers were supposedly led to indulge the flesh. William Prynne added spice to the unsubstantiated speculation when in 1656 he described in a teasing and admonishing tone how some Friends had 'lately taken shaking with their female proselytes between the sheets in a warm bed'.[23] There was also a much-quoted story of a female Friend who went to the bed of a co-religionist's husband because the Lord had instructed her to do so.[24]

---

[18] PRO, RG6 1554a, 110 (1722); EUL, COLTW I, 16 (1698); FHL, BARMM II, 7th 12 m 1694/5; ERO, T/A 261/1/1 (1721).

[19] See, for example, ERO, D/ACV 6 (Nov. 1670 and July 1671), Maria Brown's unlawful marriage to Thomas Perry; D/ABV 2, fo. 141ʳ (July 1684), Thomas Smith and his wife of Braintree.

[20] ERO, D/ABA 11, fo. 175ᵛ, Thomas Cockerill and his wife of Colchester; D/AMV 2, fo. 12ᵛ (22 Feb. 1663), Zachariah Child and his wife of Felsted.

[21] ERO, D/AMV2 (15 Dec. 1662), Henry Feast of Roydon; D/ACA 55, fo. 37 (13 Oct. 1663), Isaac Downes of Boxted; D/AMV 4, fo. 7ʳ (11 Jan. 1668); D/ACA55, fo. 89 (Mar. 1665).

[22] Higginson, *A Brief Relation*, 30; [Anon.], *The Querers and Quakers' Cause* (1653), 24.

[23] William Prynne, *The Quakers Unmasked* (1655), 23–6; Richard Davies, *An Account of the Convincement*, 70.

[24] Henry Hallywell, *An Account of Familism* (1673), 111; Lord Say and Sele, *Folly and Madness Made Manifest* (1659), 7.

Some Quaker parents were summoned to the courts on the grounds that, as they had not been married in church, their issue was illegitimate. There were several presentments in the 1660s and 1670s for 'having a bastard child', 'a child born out of wedlock', and 'having many children together yet unmarried'.[25] In 1679 Michael Jackson of Quendon was presented at the church court for 'begetting a bastard child on the body of Mary Bull'.[26] At Wimbish in 1684 the incumbent wrote 'bastard' next to the names of Quaker children in the parish burial register.[27] The siring of illegitimate children was thought the most reproachful of all the conventional sexual misdemeanours[28] and the imputation of bastardy on Quaker children was an indication of the seriousness of the offence. Some of the popular literature critical of the sect picked up the themes described here. *The Quaker Wedding*, which was published in 1670, referred to the Quakers' 'Brothel bed' and the 'bastards' which would issue from it.[29] The behaviour of Quakers, of course, was not to be changed by church bullying or general criticism and they could be assured that in common law at least their unions were recognized as valid.[30] Nevertheless, the repeated ridicule to which Quaker marriages were subject suggests the degree to which Friends had transgressed community norms.

The final and most important of the rites of passage, that surrounding burial, was also disregarded by Friends. Early on the sect had encouraged members to avoid the established burial rite and to facilitate this had acquired alternative burial grounds. The purpose of Quaker yards was to enable Friends to bury their dead free from the Anglican ritual and to avoid the 'idolizing' to which they felt church grounds were too much subject.[31] Any ground which was untainted by the pollution associated with the rite might serve the purpose. At Halstead in 1664, for instance, it was reported at the Bishop's court that 'several persons called Quakers have taken a piece of land and do bury the dead in the same, slighting the church'.[32] Friends also resorted to the use of gardens, orchards, or dis-

---

[25] ERO, D/AMV4, fo. 162^r, Roydon (Nov. 1670), D/AMV, 4 fo. 136^r, Thaxted (1665); GL, MS 9583, Bundle 2, Thaxted (Sept. 1664); St Paul's Churchwardens Presentments (Unlisted) (14 May 1684), Belchamp Otten—Robert Parminter and Elizabeth Blomfield.
[26] ERO, D/ACV 7.   [27] ERO, D/P 313/1/2 (3 Mar. 1684).
[28] Ingram, *Church Courts*, 166, 261–3; Wrigley and Schofield, *The Population History of England*, 233–4.   [29] [Anon.], *The Quakers' Wedding Bed* (1671).
[30] Horle, *The Quakers and the English Legal System*, 234–8.
[31] *Somersetshire Quarterly Meeting of the Society of Friends, 1668–1699*, ed. Stephen C. Morland, Somerset Record Society, 75 (1978), 20.
[32] GL, MS 9583, Bundle 2, Halstead (Sept. 1664); see also ERO, D/AMVI (15 Dec. 1662), Henry Feast of Roydon.

used ground to achieve their goal.[33] The lengths to which Quakers were prepared to go to avoid interment in the parish yard were interpreted as a sign of Quaker contempt for the Church and custom in local society.

Quaker disdain for the parish burial rites was complained about and there were numerous reports to this effect in the church courts: 'not buried by a minister of the Church of England', or 'not burying the dead according to the rites of the church'.[34] According to the ecclesiastical powers, a decent burial had not occurred and in particular the absence of the appropriate ceremony was tantamount to denying the deceased any respect. Indeed, there are entries in parish burial registers penned by local incumbents which refer to Quakers as being 'buried like an ass' or 'buried like a dog'.[35] For the clergy, of course, it was not merely a personal slight or failure to pay proper respect to the church that occurred when Quakers refused to bury the dead according to the established ritual. There was also a loss of burial fees; Friends were often prosecuted for non-payment, though no service had been performed.[36]

Ceremonies ancillary to the interment were also spurned by the sect. Early on in the movement's history, Friends were reluctant to partake in the communal feasting, drinking, or the exchange of gifts which normally accompanied the burial rite. Analyses of funeral rituals in pre-industrial societies suggest that their function was in part to ease the sense of loss suffered by the bereaved by assisting reintegration into local society. 'Funeral rituals', one authority has remarked, 'reunite all the surviving members of the group with each other . . . in the same way that a chain which has been broken by the disappearance of one of its links must be re-joined.'[37] They had a greater importance after the Reformation because the doctrine of predestination and the rejection of the idea of purgatory transformed the burial ceremony into a rite which marked the passage of the deceased from this world to an already decided fate in the next.[38] Quaker revulsion

---

[33] ERO, D/AMV 1 (Dec. 1662); D/AMV 2, fo. 5ʳ (1664), Wimbush; D/ACA 55, fo. 362ᵛ (July 1669), Great Chishall; EUL, EQ 26, 229 (1718); FHL, London Middlesex and Quarterly Meeting, ii. 71 (1705), MYM, v. 216 (1717).

[34] GL, MS 9583, Bundle 2, Burnham and Braintree in 1664. See also ERO, D/AMV 2, fo. 34ʳ (Apr. 1664) at Castle Hedingham.

[35] 'Notes and Queries', *JFHS* 21 (1924), 94; C. E. Whiting, *Studies in English Puritanism from the Restoration to the Revolution, 1660–1689* (1968), 449–50.

[36] For instance, EUL, EQ 22, 29 (1698), in which John Freeman of Great Sampford is distrained at the behest of the local incumbent for non-payment of his wife's burial fees. See also ERO, D/AMV 3, fo. 122ʳ (May 1667), for the case of John King of Sible Hedingham.

[37] The words are those of the social anthropologist Arnold Van Gennep, quoted by Clare Gittings, *Death, Burial and the Individual in Early Modern England* (1984), 159.

[38] Ibid., 40–2; Thomas, *Religion and the Decline of Magic*, 721–3.

at these important communal events was considered the more deplorable because it disregarded the needs of those who had suffered loss and it seemed also to challenge the rules which regulated and gave cohesion to the rhythms of daily life in the seventeenth century. That there was a profound disapproval of Quaker practice is evident from those extraordinary occasions in the 1650s when Quaker burials were disrupted and the corpses either forcibly interred in the parish graveyard or left unburied in the street.[39]

The authority of the Church was diffuse and penetrated deeply into the social fabric. Quaker doctrine challenged not merely the Church and its rituals but also a wide spectrum of social behaviour which the Church sanctioned. Moreover, it was not only the social elites who despised the movement, for the Quaker assault was also directed at many aspects of plebeian culture which were condemned by Friends because they were tinged with paganism or showed too great a regard for human satisfaction. Quakers did not approve of sport or entertainment like football and cockfighting; they were also dismissive of excessive drinking and the use of common language which were out of keeping with Quaker purity. At times of licensed disorder in the community Quakers might become the butt of popular disapproval and ribaldry. Some of the popular literature of the time was written with the intention of lampooning the principles of Friends and would have met with a positive response from the lowest ranks in society.[40] Quaker ideals were inimical to plebeian culture as much as to the values of the wealthy and propertied. Friends constituted a godly minority in local society whose behaviour and convictions jarred sharply with the expectations and assumptions which regulated daily life in the parish community.

---

[39] George Fox, the younger, *A True Relation of the Unlawful and Unreasonable Proceedings of the Magistrates of Harwich in Essex* (n.p., 1660), 2; Braithwaite, *Second Period*, 132.

[40] Reay, *The Quakers and the English Revolution*, chap. 4.

3
Body Language

Not to respect Persons, was and is another of their Doctrines and Practices, for which they were often Buffeted and Abused. They Affirmed it to be *sinful* to give flattering titles, or to use Vain Gestures and give Compliments of Respect.

William Penn, *A Brief Account of the Rise and Progress of the People, Call'd Quakers* (1694), 43–4.[1]

To meet Quakers at any Time, they will not speak a word, They are so pure and holy, no speech They can afford. They say they take God's name in vain if that they say God Speed. So they be dumb cause no bad word shall from their lips proceed.

A Lecture for all Sects and Schismatics to read (*c.*1680)

The human body, in short, is as much a historical document as a charter or a diary or a parish register . . . and it deserves to be studied accordingly.

Keith Thomas, Introduction to Jan Bremmer and Herman Roodenburg (eds.), *A Cultural History of Gesture* (Oxford, 1991), 2.

The body is the intermediary between the individual and society and thus a critical factor in how people seek to identify themselves to others. However, it is only recently that attitudes to the manner in which the body is used—whether it be in speech, acts of civility, dress, or bodily carriage—have been recognized as important and worthy of historical inquiry.[2] The presentation of the body was of as much concern to Quakers as to their seventeenth-century contemporaries.[3] Indeed, responses to the body

[1] The tract is reprinted in Penn, *Writings*, 283.

[2] A pioneer in the field was Norbert Elias, *The Civilising Process: The History of Manners*, tr. Edmund Jephcott (repr. Oxford, 1978). The book was first published in 1939. Also important for the present discussion is the work of Mary Douglas, *Natural Symbols*, chap. 5.

[3] There are a number of recent works which have been helpful in exploring attitudes to the body in the early modern period. See, for example, Joan Wildeblood and Peter Brinson, *The Polite World: A Guide to English Manners and Deportment from the Thirteenth to the Nineteenth Century* (1965); Roger Chartier (ed.), *A History of Private Life III: Passions of the Renaissance* (1989), 167–207; Jan Bremmer and Herman Roodenburg (eds.), *A Cultural History of Gesture* (Oxford, 1991); Anna Bryson, 'The Rhetoric of Status: Gesture, Demeanour and the Image of the Gentleman in Sixteenth- and Seventeenth-Century England', in Lucy Gent and Nigel Llewellyn (eds.), *Renaissance Bodies: The Human Figure in English Culture c.1540–1660* (1990), 136–53; Richard Sennett, *The Fall of Public Man* (Cambridge, 1974), esp. chap. 4.

language of Quakers reveal a great deal about general attitudes to civility and bodily control at that time, and the unusual body language of Friends is a crucial factor in explaining the hostility they encountered in local society.

Much advice was given in the early modern period about the correct use of the physical body.[4] There was an expectation that social status should be accorded the appropriate respect in society whether the recipient was superior or inferior, friend or neighbour. The principal method of acknowledging a person's status in daily life was through the medium of the physical body. The garments which clothed the human form, modes of address and terminology, bodily gestures such as a kiss, bow, embrace, or curtsy, and even the human carriage itself constituted elaborate signals which imparted important information about a person's position in the social hierarchy. Differences in social standing were thereby more easily recognized and the appropriate formalities executed. To put it boldly the intention was that the use of the body in personal intercourse should closely mirror social relations. And though the correct use of the body was principally the concern of courtly culture, and to a lesser degree of the provincial elites in society, there was none the less a wider expectation that people should be favourably disposed to one another during social interaction. These were all expectations which Quakers were to flout openly. There was another important aspect of contemporary attitudes to bodily styles which was to affect the way Quakers were viewed in that the gestures and deportment of the body were thought by contemporary moralists to signify a person's inner nature.[5]

The Society of Friends encouraged members to adopt a distinctive bodily style whether it was in speech, dress, or bodily gestures. Quakerism was not a purely negative culture with the expectation only that followers should not behave like others. A certain degree of uniformity enabled Friends to differentiate themselves from the rest of society and thus enhance their own sense of identity. Most important was the view that Quaker bodily style was related to Friends' experience of spiritual rebirth and the path to heavenly perfection which then opened before them.

By heeding the inner light Friends believed that they could achieve a state of innocence reflecting that of man in his prelapsarian days. Quaker

---

[4] Books influential in determining attitudes to civility were Erasmus's *De Civilitate morum puerilium*, which was first published in 1530, and Castiglione's famous *Book of the Courtier* published two years earlier. These texts were frequently referred to and served as models for other works of this sort. See the comments in Chartier (ed.), *Passions of the Renaissance*, 168; J. R. Woodhouse, *From Castiglione to Chesterfield: The Decline in the Courtier's Manual* (Oxford, 1991), 14–15, 17, 18: Burke, *The Fortunes of the Courtier*, chap. 5; Anna Bryson 'Concepts of Civility in England, c.1650–c.1685' (University of Oxford D.Phil. thesis, 1984). [5] Chartier (ed.), *Passions of the Renaissance*, 170.

dress, speech, and the rejection of ordinary courtesies were all outward, tangible symbols which indicated the degree to which individual Quakers had been inwardly successful in reaching that goal. The measure by which that goal was reached was the degree of attachment shown to the Quaker doctrines of plainness and simplicity. Ambrose Rigge of Reigate declared that though a legitimate use of clothes was to provide adequate warmth and modesty for the body they also served as a 'monitor of our Apostacy'.[6] The plain Quaker garb which George Emmot assumed on his conversion in the 1650s made him seem, he thought, 'not worldly but all spiritual'.[7] John Gratton, a Derbyshire Friend, wrote in his Journal that the new Quaker language he learned after being won over to Friends in 1671 was a reflection of his having entered the kingdom of heaven.[8] What outsiders interpreted as Quaker perversity were viewed by the sect as signs of progress to heavenly perfection and indicative of inward spiritual growth. Moreover, Friends were aware that failure to conform to the outward symbols of the faith might reflect a falling away on the part of members and they were fearful of the consequent danger to their spiritual health. These Quaker testimonies also served implicitly as a reproach to those in the world who remained still in a fallen state.

Membership of the Quaker sect required that the passions associated with the human will should be extinguished. James Parnel wrote in 1655: 'hearken to that in your Conscience which raiseth Desires after Righteousness, and which showeth you the vanities of your Lives.'[9] There are many echoes of this sentiment in the works of other Friends. Published recollections often reflect upon the consequences of accepting the Quaker faith. Thomas Rawlinson noted that many Quakers had given up 'the Glory and the Pleasures of this Life', a self-denial which could include separation from husband, wife, children, or other kindred and sometimes the loss of houses, lands, and livings.[10] William Crouch, who was described as 'being Risen with Christ and having his Affections set on things about [that] he might live as a Pilgrim and Stranger here as to the things of this World', wrote of the worldly pleasures from which it was necessary to abstain to qualify as a Quaker. The list included gay clothes, whatsoever encouraged vanity, gestures, motions, salutations, or obsequious practices which in society were considered good manners or breeding.[11]

---

[6] Ambrose Rigge, *Constancy in the Truth Commended*, 255.
[7] Quoted by Reay, *The Quakers and the English Revolution*, 36.
[8] John Gratton, *A Journal of the Life of that Ancient Servant of Christ* (1720), 44, 48.
[9] Parnel, *Collection*, 7.   [10] Rawlinson, *Light Sown for the Righteous*, 16.
[11] William Crouch, *Posthuma Christiana: or, a Collection of Some Papers of William Crouch* (1712), 9, 10, 153.

At the end of the seventeenth century William Penn argued for temperance not only in eating, drinking, and apparel but in furniture, gain, parsimony, sleeping, company, watching, and 'every passion of the mind, love, anger, joy, sorrow, resentment'.[12] Conversion to Quakerism was to have profound effects on adherents in areas of personal and social life which one would barely have imagined and these in turn were to have significant repercussions upon the interpersonal relations between sect members and others in local society. Some outsiders judged the Quaker obsession with plainness and simplicity to be comic or faintly ridiculous; others felt that obsession to be an indication of Quaker vanity. Indeed, critics of the movement argued that these testimonies were attempts to deceive and were the Devil's work, being in reality a cover for Quaker pride, lust, and covetousness (see Plate 4).

Concern with the testimonies of plainness and simplicity was evident from the earliest years of the Society whether it was in the matter of dress, speech, or bodily deportment. But it was given a renewed emphasis in the 1690s; the toleration granted Friends in worship and relative freedom from persecution removed a distinctive characteristic of the movement which had given members a cohesion and a sense of their own uniqueness. As a result, the movement placed a new significance on the testimony of plainness as being the badge of membership. Moreover, a decline in the sect's numbers and attempts to revive Quaker fortunes encouraged some leaders to identify to an extraordinary degree adherence to these testimonies as tantamount to real commitment. Perhaps ironically, what had once divided the sect from society was to be a matter of controversy among Friends themselves. These symbols of purity had, some Friends said, become too rigidly identified as the measure of allegiance and thus ignored what they saw as inward and genuine spiritual growth.[13]

None the less, given the disruptive nature of the Quaker incursion into local society and the sect's dismissive attitude to the rules of civil behaviour, it is with some justice that contemporaries throughout the period considered the attitudes of Friends in this respect to be 'rude', 'arrogant', 'conceited', and 'clownish'.

GREETINGS AND SOCIAL ENCOUNTERS

when they depart from a house they use no civil salutes; so that their departure and going aside to ease themselves are almost undistinguishable. It is the opinion

---

[12] Penn, *Writings*, 116.
[13] Braithwaite, *Second Period*, 512–15; Morgan, *Lancashire Quakers*, 259–63, 269.

PLATE 4. From William Jones, *Work for a Cooper* (1679), frontispiece. The print is thought to be of Quaker Thomas Wynne.

of many honest men who have observed the ways of this society, that there are none professing Christianity more irreligious than they are, Ranters excepted . . .

    Francis Higginson, *A Brief Relation of the Irreligion of the Northern Quakers* (1653), 29.

Friends were determined not to comply with the social practices which regulated interpersonal behaviour. They rejected conventional forms of address outright, and, along with notions of honour and breeding, the customs governing the circumstances of greeting and departing were considered marks of Lucifer and sinful.[14] The extent of Quaker perversity is revealed by the sect's repudiation of even the most basic greetings. To address somebody with the words 'Good Speed' or 'Good Morrow' was wicked in Friends' eyes. There were several reasons for this attitude. True to their reputation of being excessively sincere and sticklers for blunt and honest speaking, Friends asked what was 'Good' about the day? They claimed that it would be incorrect to salute those who were not under the guidance of the divine inner light. Moreover, the day could quite literally not be considered a good one when so many remained under the power of darkness. And to conform to worldly practice would in any case merely feed the human appetite for pride and vanity. Friends argued that only God was worthy of such human regard. James Parnel had written in 1655 that 'amongst those who were redeemed out of the word there was no superior but only Christ the Head'.[15]

By contrast, the sect believed that members' personal behaviour should be characterized by modesty and self-effacement. The scriptural injunctions to simplicity and plainness in all things were crucial in determining the comportment of Friends in this respect. Indeed, the meaning of the word 'plainness' was understood among Friends in the seventeenth-century more as being sincere and truthful in one's actions,[16] principles to which Friends held fast and which were consequently a source of much antagonism to them. The sect was wary of all forms of address because it was distrustful of the hypocrisy which it felt inevitably accompanied them. For many at this time, manners were considered only social rituals which eased the process of face-to-face interaction; they might have little to do with true sincerity or a person's genuine feeling for another.[17] Quakers' apparent lack of manners and extreme stress on honesty and humility in personal matters, an attribute of their being reborn, put them sharply in conflict with prevailing social practice. True respect, Quakers argued, came inwardly from the heart, not through outward speech or gestures. George Fox expressed this sentiment in 1657 when he wrote:

The customs, and manner, and fashion of this world, which is practised amongst people in the World, when they meet one with another, they will say how do you

---

[14] Parnel, *A Shield of the Truth*, 21.   [15] Ibid., 23, 21; Penn, *Writings*, 285.
[16] Howard H. Brinton, *Quaker Journals: Varieties of Experience Among Friends* (Wallingford, Pa., 1972), 48–9.
[17] Peter Burke, *The Historical Anthropology of Early Modern Italy*, 13, 233–5.

Sir, doff the Hat, scrape a Leg, make a courchy [curtsy]. I am glad to see you well
. . . when they are past them, with the same tongue wish evil to them . . .[18]

Puritans had earlier expressed grave reservations about servile obedience to the rules of etiquette for similar reasons,[19] but Quakers were unusual
in the depth of their convictions and the degree to which they were prepared to stick to them in daily life. An additional obstacle to the Quaker
acceptance of normal social conventions was the sect's requirement for equality of respect. No man was to be given special honour; that was due to
God alone. What then seemed civilized and cordial behaviour, such as the
removal of the hat or bodily gestures which signalled civility and good neighbourliness, was denounced by Friends as constituting a 'worshipping' of
man.[20] Some Friends were anxious even that jokes, laughter, certain facial
expressions or vocal intonations should not be permitted among members since they distorted the countenance, thereby indicating that Quakers
did not possess a noble and religious disposition. Certain tones of voice
or facial gestures which might be interpreted as good manners were to be
spurned.[21] Thomas Ellwood, for instance, recalled how after joining
Friends in the 1650s he wanted the 'visible character of gravity' which
affected his countenance to be noticed.[22] The lives of Quakers were God-
centred, since the expectation was that all human action upon earth should
satisfy the divine will. The experience of rebirth was to have profound implications for the personal and social habits of those who joined the sect.
Quakers broke with a whole range of well-regarded formalities the purpose of which was to ease interaction at a personal level. The refusal to
use the deferential second person plural to superiors was widely remarked
upon. The elder, William Edmundson, recalled in his Journal that the use
of the familiar 'thee' and 'thou' seemed 'strange things to people and few
could suffer them to be used'.[23]

The general response to Friends was one of incomprehension. We saw
earlier how interruption of public worship and disruption of communal

---

[18] George Fox, *Concerning Good-Morrow, and Good-Even; the World's Customs* (1657), 1–2,
14.

[19] Richard L. Greaves, *Society and Religion in Elizabethan England* (Minneapolis, 1981),
522–5.

[20] Blome, *The Fanatick History*, 87; Parnel, *Collection*, 446; William Tomlinson, *Seven
Particulars* (1657), 6–7; [Anon.], *The Papists Younger Brother; or the Vileness of Quakerism
Detected* (1679), 44; Toldervy, *The Foot Out of the Snare*, 15.

[21] Edmundson, *Journal*, p. xv; Crouch, *Posthuma Christiana*, 153; Stuart Sutherland 'What's
in a Smile?', *Falmer*, 18, University of Sussex (1991), 4–5.

[22] Thomas Ellwood, *The History of the Life of Thomas Ellwood* (1714), 41.

[23] Edmundson, *Journal*, 12.

harmony blackened the sect's reputation. The rejection of communal mores regarding the rules of personal contact also brought followers into disrepute. One critic concluded in 1671 that a tenet of Quakerism was that 'to be *religious*, one is obliged to be *uncivil*'.[24] Remaining silent when acknowledgement was anticipated was a strong reason for dislike of Quakers. Indeed, silence was as important an element of communication as speech in daily life and the appropriateness of each was determined by custom and the social importance of the person being addressed.[25] The neighbours of the Lincolnshire Friend John Whitehead were irritated at the lack of courtesy he showed them and they delivered a stern rebuke, complaining that he failed to distinguish between the way he responded to them and animals which grazed in the village.[26] Ralph Josselin reacted with puzzlement at Quaker custom; when writing in his *Diary* in April 1656 he remarked that it was 'strange for persons to bee silent, not to speak when saluted or spoken unto'.[27] Silence too was the reason for the imprisonment of the Colchester Friend Edward Grant in 1657. He would not join in reciting with others at appropriate moments of a church service thus incurring the anger of the congregation and a gaol sentence.[28]

Formal gestures of greeting or parting serve in social terms as symbols of inclusion and by refusing to recognize the niceties of daily life Quakers implicitly seemed to state that other parishioners were not worth social recognition or of any significant note.[29] They were considered to have snubbed their fellow parishioners. Though it is true that Quaker behaviour sometimes elicited only a puzzled response, failure to acknowledge neighbours or acquaintances in a conventional manner was often a reason for taking deep personal offence. Most trenchant in criticism was Francis Higginson. He cavilled at the 'savage incivilities' of Friends, describing how:

None of the Quakers will give common respect to Magistrates, or to any Friends or old Acquaintance. If they meet them by the way, or any stranger, they will go or ride by them, as though they were dumb, or as though they were beasts rather than men, not affording a Salutation, or Resaluting though themselves be saluted.[30]

[24] R.H., *The Character of a Quaker in his True and Proper Colours* (1671), 2.

[25] Burke, *The Art of Conversation*, 128–41.

[26] John Whitehead, *The Written Gospel Labours of that Ancient and Faithful Servant of Jesus Christ* (1704), 145.   [27] Josselin, *Diary*, 366.

[28] EUL, EQ 22, 7.

[29] On greeting ritual see Raymond Firth, 'Verbal and Bodily Rituals of Greeting and Parting', in J. S. La Fontaine (ed.), *The Interpretation of Ritual: Essays in Honour of A.I. Richards* (1974), 1–38; Michael Argyle (ed.), *Social Encounters: Readings in Social Interaction* (Harmondsworth, 1983).

[30] Higginson, *A Brief Relation*, 28; William Haworth, *The Quaker Converted to Christianity* (1674), 64; Francis Harris, *An Answer to Some Queries* (1655), 18.

However, the anxiety which Friends generated at times of face-to-face contact may have been alleviated somewhat by their substituting the use of the handshake, kiss, and the salutation 'Friend' when meeting. We know that this was the practice among followers[31] and it may have extended on occasion to outsiders. Of course, the handshake was a feature of civil behaviour in general, but used on its own, as it was by the sect, it constituted a brutal reproach to existing customs since it implied a levelling principle.[32]

HOLY LANGUAGE

Speak properly, and in as few words as you can, but always plainly; for the end of speech is not ostentation but to be understood.

William Penn, More Fruits of Solitude (1702), No. 122.[33]

a Quaker is a *Canting* thing that *Cozens* the world by the *purity of his clothes*, a few *Close-stool faces and whining expressions.*

R. H. The Character of a Quaker, in his True and Proper Colours (1671), 17.

Friends used what amounted to a private language in their everyday discourse which marked them out in local society.[34] The distinctive speech pattern of Quakers was frequently remarked upon. John Brown wrote in 1678, for instance, that Friends spoke 'ordinarily in a dialect peculiar to themselves'[35] and an anonymous observer noted of members earlier in 1672 that their language was but 'phrases' by which members practised '*new Minted Modes* of Speaking'.[36] Richard Gough, the yeoman and historian of the parish of Myddle, Salop, when troubled by the arrival of the sect in his parish, was alert to the peculiar speech style of these sectarians. He noted of a new convert in the parish that 'He came home the next day a

---

[31] Welde, *The Perfect Pharisee*, 32–3.

[32] Herman Roodenberg, 'The "Hand of Friendship": Shaking Hands and other Gestures in the Dutch Republic', in Jan Bremmer and Herman Roodenburg (eds.), *A Cultural History of Gesture* (Oxford, 1991), 176–9.   [33] Quotation from Penn, *Writings*, 74.

[34] The following pages owe much to Richard Bauman's *Let Your Words Be Few: Symbolism of Speaking and Silence among Seventeenth-century Quakers* (Cambridge, 1983), *passim*. Also useful were Hugh Ormsby-Lennon's 'From Shibboleth to Apocalypse: Quaker Speechways during the Puritan Revolution', 72–102 and Nigel Smith, *Perfection Proclaimed: Language and Literature in English Radical Religion, 1640–1660* (Oxford, 1989).

[35] John Brown, *Quakerisme: The Path-way to Paganisme* (Edinburgh, 1678), 88; [Anon.], *Quakers are Inchanters* (1655), 75; Blome, *The Fanatick History*, 67.

[36] R.H., *Plus Ultra, or the Second Part of the Character of a Quaker, in his True and Proper Colours* (1672), 3.

perfect Quaker in appearance, and had got their canting way of discourse as readily as if he had been seven years apprentice'.[37]

Quaker language was unusual for more than the strange cadences that characterized its delivery, for sect members also adhered to a distinctive vocabulary when speaking. For example, any terms which had 'popish' overtones were excised from the Quaker 'lexicon' so that words like Candlemas, Lady Day, or Christmas did not figure in Quaker speech at all. The use of 'Saint' was also shunned and the derisive term 'steeple house' substituted for church. Friends thus referred in conversation or in print to towns such as St Albans or St Edmundsbury as Albans or Edmundsbury, and a further linguistic peculiarity was that St Paul's Churchyard became in Quaker parlance Paul's Yard, and Grace Church Street, Gracious Street. The conventional names for days of the week and months of the year were also rejected because of their pagan associations. Friends substituted numerals in their place so that Sunday became 'first day' and March—under the Julian Calendar—'first month'. They also avoided words that were purely ornamental, honorific, or, as they saw it, simply misleading.[38] Terms which might indicate respect of youth to the aged and titles such as 'Master', 'Mistress', or 'Sir', 'Your Majesty', 'Reverend', 'Your Humble Servant', 'Your Honour', etc. were forbidden because they were symbols of deference and thus violated the Quaker principle of equality.[39] These are the speech and language characteristics which would have been encountered when meeting Quakers socially. It is worth emphasizing the importance of these practices in distinguishing Friends in local society. They also earned Friends the reproach of the social elites, who feared that Quakers intended to overthrow the social order.

The sect went further in an attempt to purify Quaker speech by limiting the opportunities for and regulating the nature of the discourse entered upon by members. Quakers recognized that verbal communication was an essential part of social interaction and one that could not be avoided in daily life. The difficulty was that the everyday necessity to resort at least partially to natural language frustrated the Quakers' wish to be free of worldly pollution. Quakers believed that the language of humanity, given at the Fall, was a snare set by the Devil which would corrupt and distract from the guidance of the Spirit. It had therefore to be used with

---

[37] Richard Gough, *The History of Myddle*, ed. David Hey (Harmondsworth, 1981), 172.
[38] Parnel, *A Shield of the Truth*, 2; T. E. Harvey, 'Quaker Language', Supplement 15, *JFHS* (1928), 7, 8–9; Maurice A. Creasey, ' "Inward and Outward": A Study of Early Quaker Language', Supplement 30, *JFHS* (1962), *passim*; Brinton, *Friends for 300 Years* (repr. Wallingford, Pa., 1988), 132–3.   [39] Brinton, *Friends for 300 Years*, 133.

caution.[40] It appears that in discourse some Quakers mainly concerned themselves with 'weighty' matters, being mostly 'the things of God'.[41] To overcome the difficulties inherent in the use of natural language Quakers used as few words as possible when communicating in speech. Leading figures in the movement encouraged ordinary Friends in this practice. William Dewsbury, for instance, advised sect followers against using 'many words, at all times' and Edmund Burrough concurred that 'it is better to speak little'.[42] In 1664 William Bailey warned Quakers against the use of too many words in conversation and particularly cautioned on the manner of delivery. Friends were not to be intemperate, quick, or loud in discourse. And 'rash' or 'passionate' words were also to be avoided by mothers speaking to their children since it was feared that this might plant an evil seed which could lead to imitation in adulthood and thus dishonour to God.[43] Prior to his joining the Quakers Thomas Ellwood recalled a visit to the newly converted Isaac and Mary Penington. His remarks are revealing in that they show the profound effect which religious conversion had on the personal behaviour of followers, especially regarding speech habits. He described:

So great Change, from a Free, Debonair, and Courtly sort of Behaviour (which we formerly had found them in), to so strict a Gravity as they now receive us with, did not a little amuse us, and disappoint our Expectation of such a pleasant Visit as we used to have, and had now promised ourselves . . . We stay'd Dinner, which was very handsome, and lacked nothing to recommend it to me, but the want of Mirth and pleasant Discourse, which we could neither have with them, nor, by reason of them with one another amongst ourselves; the Weightiness that was upon their Spirits and Countenances keeping down the lightness that would have been up in us.[44]

Some contemporaries thought that the 'peculiar dialect' of Quakers was deliberately employed to bolster a sense of group identity. Richard Blome wrote in 1660 in his pamphlet *The Fanatick History* that 'Their Language to themselves *peculiar* so that by it they may be known'.[45] And an

[40] Bauman, *Let Your Words Be Few: Symbolism of Speaking and Silence among Seventeenth-century Quakers*, 29–30.

[41] Edmundson, *Journal*, p. xv.   [42] Quote in Bauman, *Let Your Words Be Few*, 22.

[43] Ibid., 22–3; Crisp, *Works*, 418.

[44] Thomas Ellwood, quoted in Mary Penington, *Experiences in the life of Mary Penington (written by herself): c.1652–1682* (1911; reissued 1992), 11.

[45] Blome, *Fanatick History*, 67; R.H., *The Character of a Quaker*, 2; Jonathan Swift, *A Critical Edition of the Major Works*, ed. Angus Ross and David Woolley (Oxford, 1984), 156–7. For the distinctiveness of Quaker speech in a later period see Elizabeth Isichei, 'From Sect To Denomination among English Quakers', in Bryan Wilson (ed.), *Patterns of Sectarianism: Organisation and Ideology in Social and Religious Movements* (1967), 168.

anonymous pamphleteer said of a Quaker in 1671 that his '*Religion is not to speak like his Neighbour*'.[46] Since Friends could not live in geographical isolation and thus were unable to avoid some social involvement, their peculiar speech, dress, and manners allowed them to demonstrate their separateness and affirm the boundaries between them and other inhabitants of local society. Linguists have observed that groups who seriously question conventional values and try to assert a counter-identity often develop an alternative language which undermines normal forms of speech. The sect seems to have possessed its own particular argot, and, while not necessarily inventing a wholly new vocabulary, was prepared to substitute expressions or words consistent with the tenets of Quakerism for those applied in conventional usage.[47]

Though Quakers thought their speech pure and agreeable, others disapproved. So unpopular was the habit of 'theeing' and 'thouing' that George Fox and the Colchester Friend, Benjamin Furly, were drawn to attempt a defence of Quaker practice which drew on biblical precedent and examples of such use in other languages.[48] Moreover, what Friends judged plain and simple speech was derided by some as 'nonsensical whining' or 'uncouth, strange words and gibberish language'; others jested that Quaker speech was incomprehensible without the aid of a 'Quaker lexicon'.[49] These critical perceptions were damaging to the reputation of the Society, for in the seventeenth century it was accepted that a man's speech was symptomatic of his innermost nature.[50] A Quaker's abnormal delivery and incomprehensibility revealed to contemporaries not an inner grace, the quality most sought after, but a temperament which was unruly and too easily subject to personal whim. Quaker language reinforced the view that the character of Friends was eccentric and for that reason not to be trusted.

---

[46] R. H., *The Character of a Quaker*, 2.

[47] M. A. K. Halliday, *Language as Social Semiotic: The Social Interpretation of Language and Meaning* (1978), chap. 9 on 'Antilanguages'; Burke, *The Historical Anthropology of Early Modern Italy*, chap. 7.

[48] George Fox, Benjamin Furly, and John Stubbs, *A Battle-Door for Teachers and Professors to learn Singular and Plural* (1660).

[49] [Anon.], *The Quaker's Art of Courtship* (1687), 4–5; Haworth, *The Quaker Converted to Christianity*, 53; Christopher Fowler and Simon Ford, *A Sober Answer to an Angry Epistle* (1656), 16.

[50] Fenela Ann Childs, 'Prescriptions for Manners in English Courtesy Literature 1690–1760, and their Social Implications' (University of Oxford D.Phil. thesis, 1984), 167–8; Bryson, 'The Rhetoric of Status', 145; Michael Argyle, *Bodily Communication*, 2nd edn. (1988), 8.

FASHIONING THE BODY

I took off from my Apparel those unnecessary Trimmings of *Lace, Ribbands,* and *Useless Buttons*: which had no real Service; but were set on only for that which was by mistake called *Ornament,* And I ceased to wear *Rings.*

> Thomas Ellwood, *The History of the Life of Thomas Ellwood* (1714), 26.

We are told with truth, that meekness and modesty are the rich and charming attire of the soul: and the plainer the dress, the more distinctly, and with greater lustre, their beauty shines.

> William Penn, *Some Fruits of Solitude* (1693), No. 77.[51]

The expectation of the Society was that members' dress should be free of ornament and extravagance. Modesty should prevail and nothing that smacked of vanity or the satisfaction of human pride was permitted. Fashionable accessories such as lace, ribbons, cuffs, hatbands, and points were not to be worn by Friends. There were also warnings against the use of cross pockets in men's coats, broad hems on cravats, and overfull skirted coats.[52] It appears that by and large Friends followed the guidance that they were given. An account left us by Benjamin Bangs, a Stockport Friend, in his Journal is revealing about the adherence of members to the Society's prescriptions regarding dress. Bangs recounts that, prior to conversion, he found his way to a Quaker meeting by tailing Friends whom he had seen and identified in the street because of their 'habit' and 'sober behaviour'.[53] Voltaire, recalling a meeting with an elderly Quaker in his famous *Letters on England*, noted that the Friend wore a coat with no pleats at the side and no buttons on the pockets or sleeves. He added that a large hat with a flat brim covered his head.[54] Contemporaries were aware that Quaker dress reflected an important part of Quaker comportment in the world and was part of a wider set of symbols and behaviour regarding Quaker self-presentation. Ralph Farmer noted in 1660:

Witness their *morose* and severe carriage and *conversation,* their *demure* looks, their *abstinences* in meat and drink, the pulling off their Points, Laces and Ribbons from

---

[51] From Penn, *Writings,* 32.

[52] Amelia Mott Gummere, *The Quaker: A Study in Costume* (repr. New York, 1968), 18, 32, 141; Janet Mayo, *A History of Ecclesiastical Dress* (1984), 111–12.

[53] Benjamin Bangs, *Memoirs of the Life and Convincement of that Worthy Friend* (1757), 16–17.

[54] Voltaire, *Letters on England* tr. Leonard Tancock (1734; repr. Harmondsworth, 1980), 23.

their *cloaths*, their separating and withdrawing from the society and familiarity of all others.[55]

However, though distinctive, Quaker dress did not constitute a uniform in the sect's early years. It was only in the late seventeenth and eighteenth centuries that there was a concern for uniformity of style. For the earliest Friends, dress was characterized merely by modesty and the absence of ornament.[56]

Quaker prohibitions regarding dress were disapproved of by others in part because they violated important social conventions. At this time the quality and style of clothes were important indicators of occupation and social position. The dress of aristocracy, clergy, lawyers, and merchants was significantly different, the purpose being that gradations of social status could thus be recognized and the appropriate respect paid. Until the seventeenth century these social rules were given legal force by sumptuary laws which in theory designated what were the appropriate forms of dress for different social classes.[57] While these no longer applied in the time of the Quakers, there was still a general belief that dress should signal social distinction. The Society simply disregarded these ideals; Quaker George Emmot, a gentleman from Durham, removed the fine trappings commensurate with his status and instead adopted a sober garb, substituting a piece of string for a hatband.[58] Richard Blome complained in 1660 that Quaker ministers wore 'any mean habit . . . no Lace, Cuffs, Hatbands & . . . inveighing against gluttony, drunkenness, pride, covetousness &c'.[59] Even at times of mourning Friends shunned the appropriate dark clothes since they too were considered to reflect too great a concern for human self-esteem.[60] In reply to an inquiry about Quaker dress in the early eighteenth century Voltaire was told: 'Others wear the badges of their dignities, but we those of Christian humility'.[61]

---

[55] Farmer, *The Lord Craven's Case Stated*, 2.

[56] Joan Kendall, 'The Development of a Distinctive Form of Quaker Dress', *Costume*, 19 (1985), 58–61; FHL, MYM, i. 270 (1691).

[57] Christopher Breward, *The Culture of Fashion* (Manchester, 1995), 26–7, 54–6; James Laver, *A Concise History of Costume* (1973), 72, 86, 103, 232; Sennett, *The Fall of Public Man*, 65–72.

[58] Quoted by Reay, *The Quakers and the English Revolution*, 36.

[59] Blome, *Fanatick History*, 68; Jonathan Clapham, *A Full Discovery and Confutation* (1656), 52; Thomas Welde remarked upon the 'meanness' of Quakers' apparel in *The Perfect Pharisee*, 53.

[60] Kendall, 'The Development of a Distinctive Form of Quaker Dress', 58–61; Lou Taylor, *Mourning Dress: A Costume and Social History* (1983), 96. See the will of Richard Barwell of Witham, ERO, D/DR/126, No. 9, in which he instructs that no black clothes are to be worn at his funeral.   [61] Voltaire, *Letters on England*, 26.

Among the articles of clothing it is use of the hat for which Quakers are most renowned. Failure to remove it before judges, magistrates, and clergy in particular earned Friends a reputation as social radicals. The parson in the parish of Abberton in Essex would not countenance Quaker practice and beat the Friend James Potter in the street when he refused to raise his hat in acknowledgement.[62] Moreover, that Friends remained covered in church was taken as behaviour that was contemptuous of the ministry and its doctrines. A Thaxted Friend, Samuel Fann, and seven other Quakers were cited to the Archdeacon's Court in 1664 for 'irreverent behaving himself in Church . . . by sitting with his hat on his head in sermon time'.[63] A most remarkable account of the bitterness which could arise as a result of refusal to use the hat in an acceptable manner is to be found in the account of Thomas Ellwood's life. There Thomas recounts how his father was so enraged by his failure to remove his hat that he first confiscated his headgear in order to stop further insult, then refused to speak to him, and eventually disowned him.[64]

The ferocity of the attack mounted by Friends during their first decade against the very idea of fashion must have turned people against them. James Parnel furiously lambasted 'Proud, Lustful ones', and their 'proud Attire, inventing New Wayes. Fashions to make yourselves glorious in the Sight of Men that they may worship and honour you'.[65] But concern about dress was to remain a continuous theme in Quaker writing. While by the end of the seventeenth century it had become a shibboleth by which loyalty might be measured, Friends consistently protested that the great concern shown for rich and splendid attire was a cause of poverty for others. However, Friends no longer preached the message in so aggressive a manner.

WALKING IN THE LIGHT

For one to be humble in his Carriage among his Neighbours today, surly, dogged and proud tomorrow; courteous in his Salutes today, Brutish and unmannerly to morrow, affable and discoursing now, presently dumb, silent, morose; . . . in one day his whole Garb, Carriage, Love, Words, Gestures will be changed.

William Haworth, *The Quaker Converted to Christianity* (1674), 64.

---

[62] EUL, EQ 22, 8.   [63] ERO, D/AMV 2, fo. 42ʳ (May 1664).
[64] Ellwood, *History of the Life*, 47–9, 54–60; on the declining significance of the hat in social etiquette during the twentieth century see Alison Lurie, *The Language of Clothes* (Feltham, 1982), 179.   [65] Parnel, *Collection*, 427.

The manner of a person's walking or posture is nowadays not seen as important or as being noticeably different from that of others, though descriptions of different types of carriage such as the term 'military bearing' suggest that distinctive bodily styles still exist. In recent times a fluid social structure has meant that strict attention to well-mannered behaviour, whose use in the past corresponded to the gradations in the social hierarchy, is no longer considered to be as important. Human posture, gestures, and carriage in general no longer carry the acute social messages which they once did.[66] However, the body and the physical actions associated with it were given much greater prominence in the socially stratified seventeenth century.

Quaker social doctrine was to have a marked effect on the bodily style of members in a way that has not been addressed, for Friends developed an array of gestures and a gait which were consistent with their religious principles. Some followers recollected that after conversion they consciously set out to alter their style of walking. John Gratton, for instance, described how his attempt to master Quaker deportment was like that of a child learning to walk, and Thomas Ellwood recounted that once having joined the Friends he reformed his bodily carriage along with his clothes, gestures, and speech.[67] That these considerations were of wide concern is suggested by the injunction from Yearly Meetings in London and Dublin which advised adherents on the importance of achieving acceptable bodily styles. Indeed, in the 1650s George Fox advised schoolmasters to monitor the carriage and gestures of children to ensure that they were in keeping with the Quaker way.[68]

The expectation of the Society was that Quaker deportment should broadly be consistent with Quaker ideals. This is evident from what we know of Quaker instructions regarding plainness and simplicity, the statements from the Society, and the recollections of Friends. The divine Francis Harris referred in 1655 to the peculiar Quaker body language when he described Friends as having 'dumb and silent gestures'.[69] Francis Duke

---

[66] Argyle, *Bodily Communication*, 213; R. Firth, 'Verbal and Body Ritual', 17; Keith Thomas, 'Yours', in Christopher Ricks and Leonard Michaels (eds.), *The State of the Language: The 1990s edition* (1990), 454–5.

[67] John Gratton, *A Journal of the Life of that Ancient Servant of Christ* (1720), 44 quoted by Bauman, *Let Your Words Be Few*, 50; Ellwood, *History of the Life*, 41.

[68] FHL, MYM, i. 270 (1691); FHL (Swanbrooke House, Dublin), QM1C1 (Books for Recording ye Progress of Friends Sent from ye Quarterly Meeting) (8th of the 10th 1692). I owe this reference to the kindness of Kenneth Carroll. George Fox, *A Warning to All Teachers of Children which are called School-masters and Schoolmistresses* (1657), 2–3.

[69] Harris, *An Answer to Some Queries*, 18.

of Westminster in London observed in 1660 in a more caustic vein that Friends' carriage was 'sneaky, surlie, silent, dumb,' and 'scurvie'.[70] There are few good, clear accounts of Quaker deportment and it is therefore difficult to get an exact description. One useful observation was made by an anonymous writer in 1689, who wrote that sober-minded Friends were 'stiff, blunt and inflexible' with a posture that was 'ordinarily with their arms folded upon their breasts, their hats somewhat of a large size . . . a walk slow, stark and severe, and out of that posture they will not put themselves'.[71] No concession was made to conventional mores. In the eighteenth century Voltaire wrote on meeting a Quaker that he 'kept his hat on while receiving me and moved towards me without even the slightest bow'.[72] Most contemporary critics judged that Quaker deportment seemed unnecessarily sober by comparison with the body language of others. It was not that Friends refused to execute bodily gestures with the necessary grace and precision; their bodily movements were so limited that they seemed hardly to use recognizable gestures at all. Evidence of this is provided by William Crouch, a prominent London Friend, who noted in his autobiography popular reactions to Quaker speech and gestures:

But among all the Calamities and Sorrowes they endured, it is great Grief to see and understand their *Religion*, *Behaviour*, and *Actions* to be so *Execrably* and *Maliciously Defamed* and Reviled: for so they were every where in *Libells* and *Verses*, *Base* and *Reproachful Pictures* described and designed by the vilest Sort of men. There was scarce a *Talkative*, *Prating*, or *Babling* Fellow, that loved to talk and act *Comically*, but must reduce his Discourse and Gesture to Ridicule the Sincerity and Simplicity of the *Quakers*.[73]

Quaker body language was widely thought strange, and the dismissive response it met certainly suggests that to refrain from the appropriate bodily gestures was interpreted as a discourteous social act. However, the advantage to Friends of a simple deportment was that it did not feed the pride of others nor compromise Quaker sincerity. 'Grave', 'sober', 'serious' are the words which recur in descriptions of Quaker bodily style by Friends and others. Quaker deportment also revealed a supposed manliness and gravity which to Friends were indicative of a noble and religious mind.[74]

---

[70] Francis Duke, of Westminster, *An Answer to some of the Principle Quakers* (1660), 53.

[71] [Anon.], *The Quaker's Art of Courtship*, 28.

[72] Voltaire, *Letters on England*, 23; Clapham, *A Full Discovery and Confutation*, 49.

[73] Crouch, *Posthuma Christiana*, 187.

[74] For example, see Isaac Penington, *Memoirs of the Life of Isaac Penington*, ed. J. Gurney Bevan (1831), 56–7; Edmundson, *Journal*, p. xv.

Just as accent and dress distinguished the well-to-do in the seventeenth century so did bodily posture. 'Walk,' James Cleland remarked in 1607 in a courtesy book, 'as becometh one of your birth and age'.[75] So great was the requirement to walk with grace and ease, the qualities desired by a gentleman, that these skills were often learned at the hands of a dancing master. Indeed, many of the bodily postures of the period would be familiar to us nowadays only in the positions associated with classical ballet. Another popular courtesy manual written in 1678 described how a gentleman had to learn how 'to keep his body in good posture where he stands, sitteth or walketh'. Also necessary was:

> how to come in or go out of a Chamber where is Company; he must be taught how to carry his head, his hands, and his toes out, all in the best way, and with the handsome presence. In a word, how to do things with a *Bonne Grace*, and in the finest and most genteel manner that a person is capable of. But nature and art must concur to give a man a fair presence, which for certain is a great advantage. A Master teaches the steps, but the Grace, the carriage and the free motion of the body must chiefly come from use.[76]

Such accomplished deportment differentiated gentlemen from rustic folk. But it is little surprise that the sober Quaker gait was viewed unsympathetically in this context. It was taken as a deliberate snub to acceptable codes of civility. To Jonathan Clapham a Friend's gait was 'so morose and clownish as to deny civility and humanity towards man'.[77] Quaker deportment was also threatening, because it challenged the notion of social distinction and thus the validity of the social hierarchy that it represented. In 1678 John Brown, for instance, remarked with astonishment at the deportment of 'civilly educated' Friends, who 'yet turning Quaker can so suddenly and perfectly imitate and follow their rude and rustick carriage as if they had never seen civility with their eyes'.[78]

Failure to obey the rules of civility posed a further problem. It was argued that because of their posture members were hardly distinguishable from God's brute creatures and that by implication they sought deliberately to

---

[75] James Cleland, *Hero-paideia* (1607) quoted in Wildeblood and Brinson, *The Polite World*, 180.

[76] Jean Gailhard, *The Complete Gentleman* (1678) quoted ibid., 179–80. For a recent important and scholarly assessment of the deportment and gestures of gentlemen in the seventeenth century see Anna Bryson, 'The Rhetoric of Status', 137–8; on an earlier period see Georges Vigarello 'The Upward Training of the Body from the Age of Chivalry to Courtly Civility', in Michel Feher, Ramona Naddaff, and Nadia Tazi (eds.), *Fragments for a History of the Human Body, Part II* (Cambridge, Mass., 1989), 148–9.

[77] Clapham, *A Full Discovery and Confutation*, 66.

[78] Brown, *Quakerisme: The Path-way to Paganisme*, Epistle to the Reader.

mock his human creation.[79] Quaker deportment was also at odds with the drive for the use of standard gestures, which was in turn part of a movement for reform encompassing education, discipline, and civility. It was argued that since bodily gestures and deportment reflected the disposition of the soul, control of the outward body would have a beneficial effect on the inner self.[80] Friends' comportment hardly satisfied the aspirations of commentators in this respect; their ecstatic convulsions at meetings for worship had already aroused the suspicion that they were not fully human because under the influence of the spirit they were reported to have barked like dogs, roared like bulls, and swarmed like bees.[81] Quaker bodily carriage now added to this distrust since a Friend had, it was said, a 'strange kind of apish postures, sometimes like the swine looking and bending to the earth'.[82] Puzzled contemporaries sought explanations that could account for this behaviour and most thought that it was due to Friends' lacking the power of reason, the very quality which distinguished man from beast. To deride Quakers as deluded was a common jibe: the epithets 'giddy-headed' and 'sick-brained'[83] were common terms of abuse. One opponent wrote in 1660 that Quakers were 'mad and fitter for bedlam than sober company'.[84] However, critics differed as to the exact reasons why members had lost their sanity, with some being convinced that Quakers were too willing to be guided by sensuality, while others felt they were diabolically possessed or under the malign influence of witchcraft.[85] Whatever the cause, the danger for Friends was that they might forfeit any claim to humanity and the compassion that went with it. If Friends persisted in behaving like animals, good reason might be seen for them to be treated as such.

Not all members of the parochial community or the social elites subscribed to the rules of etiquette described here, and many in the lower echelons would have been ignorant of or indifferent to what were considered

---

[79] Miller, *Antichrist In Man*, 29.

[80] Chartier (ed.), *Passions of the Renaissance*, 172, 174.

[81] [Anon.], *Quakers are Inchanters* (1655), 75; Harris, *Some Queries*, 9.

[82] Miller, *Antichrist In Man*, 29; Haworth, *The Quaker Converted to Christianity*, 53.

[83] John Faldo, *A Vindication of Quakerism No Christianity* (1673), Preface; [Anon.], *The Papist's Younger Brother*, 132; John Deacon, *The Grand Impostor Examined* (1656), 4; Samuel Hammond, *The Quakers' House Built Upon Sand* (1658), 3; British Library, Stowe MS 175 (c.1666), 'The State of Nonconformity in England'. I owe this reference to the kindness of Dr Bill Clifftlands.

[84] EUL, EQ 22, 2; R.H., *The Character of a Quaker*, 7; Duke, *An Answer to some of the Principle Quakers*, 7; William Jones, *Work for a Cooper* (1679) 5.

[85] Ellis Bradshaw, *The Quakers' Whitest Divell Unvailed* (1654), 6; Say and Sele, *Folly and Madness Made Manifest*, 4; [Anon.], *The Quaker's Art of Courtship*, 28.

the appropriate forms of deference. So complex and diverse was seventeenth-century society that it was difficult for the rules of civility to be enforced effectively or with common assent across the social spectrum. The anthropologist, Mary Douglas, has argued that the political and physical body can closely reflect one another,[86] but this could not easily be achieved in a society as complex as that of seventeenth-century England. Such an outcome was possible perhaps only in closed, small-scale communities. Nevertheless, the intention at least was that the manipulation of the body in social interaction should reflect social relations. Not all rank-and-file Quakers subscribed to the Society's prescriptions on civility, dress, and speech.[87] A number of weighty Friends occasionally murmured about rank-and-file indifference to Quaker principles, and as the seventeenth century progressed attitudes to what was considered acceptable changed as the movement itself became more institutionalized. None the less, judging by the sect's disciplinary records, there is no evidence to suggest widespread failure to adhere to Quaker doctrine. Indeed, some members were quick to report to the local meeting those who ignored Quaker guidance on certain of these matters.[88]

The sect's open and vocal repudiation of the social rules which governed interpersonal behaviour has not been given sufficient prominence as a reason why the sect met with so much hostility in local society. Indeed, even those critics, many of them ministers, who agreed with Quakers' reservations about the contemporary emphasis on formality as being excessive and who shared some of the Quaker principles regarding simplicity in clothes and gesture (see Plate 5), also objected to Quaker extremism in these matters, which they felt violated customs upheld by the scriptures and natural law.[89]

---

[86] Douglas, *Natural Symbols*, 93–112.

[87] For evidence that some Quakers compromised with worldly standards see FHL, Kelsall's Journal, 20, where he berates some Friends for speaking in a worldly manner, and Hugh Ormsby-Lennon, 'From Shibboleth to Apocalypse', 99–100. On attitudes to dress see Kendall, 'The Development of a Distinctive Form of Quaker Dress', 58; Gummere, *The Quaker: A Study in Costume*, 19; William Beck and T. Frederick Ball, *The London Friends' Meetings* (1869), 77, 17, 227. See also Ed Bronner's comparison of William Penn's public statements and the conduct of his life in the introduction to Penn, *Writings*, p. xxviii.

[88] Richard Bauman points to the change from an incantatory to a catechistical style among Quaker ministers which reflected the profound organizational change in the movement. See his *Let Your Words Be Few*, 146–53. EUL, COLTW 1, 32, 34. Isaac Potter was reported to his meeting in 1672 by another Friend for removing his hat before public officials at the moot hall in Colchester and using worldly language in their presence.

[89] Immanuel Bourne, *A Defence of the Scriptures* (1656), 33; Hallywell, *An Account of Familism*, 20, 21; J.C., *A Skirmish Made Upon Quakerism* (1676), 7; Brown, *Quakerism: The Path-way to Paganisme*, 533, 539; Benjamin Keach, *The Grand Impostor Discovered* (1675); and id., *War with the Devil* (1676).

PLATE 5. From Benjamin Keach, *War with the Devil* (1676), frontispiece

Speech, dress, and body language were all sensitive to social distance in the seventeenth century, and when Quakers refused to countenance normal practice they not only appeared discourteous but seemed to challenge in a profound manner the social basis of authority. Quaker body language struck fear into the heart of the elite because it represented a different set of social values, frighteningly different from that which then prevailed. And dislike of Quaker practice was not limited to the gentlemanly and clerical class. Friends' brazen and public dismissal of what passed for good manners made them seem subversive and offensive to a wide range of people.

4

Levelling Quakers?

They hold that all things ought to be common, and teach the Doctrine of Levelling privately to their Disciples . . . Several of them have affirmed that there ought to be no distinction of Estates but an universal parity . . .

Francis Higginson, *A Brief Relation of the Irreligion of the Northern Quakers* (1653), 20.

Let all those Fines that belong to Lords of Mannors, be given to poor people, for Lords have enough . . . Let all the poor people, blinde and lame and creeples be provided for in the Nation, that there might not be a begger in *England* . . .

George Fox, *To the Parliament of the Commonwealth of England* (1659), 8.

Much has been made of the radicalism of early Quakers. Some commentators suggest that Friends and other Interregnum sectaries expounded beliefs which anticipated modern egalitarian values and democratic ideals.[1] If true, this would have constituted a major reason for opposition to the sect, since the notion of hierarchy was the cornerstone of social and political life in the seventeenth century.[2] There is no doubt that a strong vein of egalitarianism informed the views of early Friends. The Quaker refusal of hat honour and the 'theeing' and 'thouing' of rich and poor alike are surely proof of the sect's radicalism. There is also evidence that during the 1650s prominent political radicals joined the Quaker ranks. For instance, John Lilburne, a leading figure among the Levellers, and Gerard Winstanley, the spokesman and founder of the Digger community,

---

[1] G. P. Gooch, *English Democratic Ideas in the Seventeenth Century*, 2nd edn. (1927), chap. 2; David W. Petegorsky, *Left-Wing Democracy in the English Civil War: Gerrard Winstanley and the Digger Movement* (repr. Stroud, 1995); Eduard Bernstein, *Cromwell and Communism: Socialism and Democracy in the Great English Revolution*, tr. H. J. Stenning (1963), *passim*; Tony Benn (ed.), *Writings on the Wall: A Radical and Socialist Anthology, 1215–1984* (1984), 13–15; W. D. Morris, *The Christian Origins of Social Revolt* (1949). See also William M. Lamont's thoughtful comments in 'The Left and its Past: Revisiting the 1650s', *History Workshop Journal*, 23 (1987), 151–2. Useful for a broader perspective is John W. De Gruchy, *Christianity and Democracy* (Cambridge, 1995).

[2] A useful exploration of this theme is E. M. W. Tillyard, *The Elizabethan World Picture* (Harmondsworth, 1972).

became followers.[3] In 1659 Edward Billing, one of the most radical of the early Quaker pamphleteers, issued a manifesto, many of the demands of which, it is suggested, would not have been out of place in the Levellers' own political programme.[4] However, it has been emphasized that the Quakers' political stance changed dramatically after 1660, when the movement was transformed in both its ideology and its organization and moved sharply away from the radicalism characteristic of the sect's early years.[5]

Quakerism was widely rated by contemporaries in the 1650s and after as a subversive movement. The dismissal of social conventions and the supposition that Quakers disapproved of the ownership of property or the payment of rents and the fact that some former Levellers joined the sect[6] were taken as proof that the Quaker creed was a 'Levelling' one.[7] Surveying the early years of Quakerism from the decade of the 1670s, Thomas Comber, a critic, commented that Friends favoured the community of goods:

that several Levellers settled into Quakers, incline to take them for *Winstanleys* Disciples and a *branch* of the *Levellers . . . levelling men's estates . . . that none should have more ground that he was able to Till and Husband by his own labour.*[8]

Others unjustly attributed to Friends the belief that with the coming of Christ the right to property became void.[9] These views were interpreted as inimical to the stability of the established order, and it is not surprising that few could resist concluding that, if left to itself, Quakerism would result in a social and political cataclysm. Indeed, we saw earlier how opponents feared that a consequence of the new faith would be religious and social anarchy similar to that which raged in the German town of Münster in the early sixteenth century.[10]

However, identifying the extent to which the principles of equality and social justice underpinned Quaker thought is no easy matter.[11] Critics of

---

[3] Aylmer (ed.), *The Levellers in The English Revolution*, 15; James Alsop, 'Gerrard Winstanley's Later Life', *Past and Present*, 82 (1979), 73–81.

[4] H. N. Brailsford, *The Levellers and the English Revolution* (repr. Nottingham, 1976), 639–40.

[5] Christopher Hill, *The Experience of Defeat: Milton and some Contemporaries* (1984), 164–9; Reay, *The Quakers and the English Revolution*, 104–5.

[6] [Anon.], *The Quacking Mountebanck* (1655), 20; Mad Tom, *Twenty Quaking Queries* (1659), 5; Say and Sele, *Folly and Madness*, 3, 17–18.

[7] See the citations at the head of this Chapter.

[8] Comber, *Christianity No Enthusiasm*, 6–7.

[9] For example, Higginson, *A Brief Relation*, 10.

[10] Fowler and Ford, *A Sober Answer*, 41; Say and Sele, *Folly and Madness*, 19.

[11] Christopher Hill has recently drawn attention to the work of the Russian scholar Tatania Pavlova, who argues for a radical egalitarianism in the writings of James Parnel. See his *The English Bible and the Seventeenth Century Revolution* (1993), 242 n. 275.

the movement, on whom we often rely for evidence of the Quakers' political canon, deliberately attributed to members beliefs that were extreme in order to discredit them. These authors feared that allegiance to the Quaker inner light would result in the total destruction of the social order and the values it supported. Quaker behaviour and attitudes which they witnessed merely confirmed that their prognosis was correct. They often confused, sometimes deliberately, what they felt were the implications of Quakerism with what Quakers actually believed.

So where should the emphasis be placed when assessing the nature of Quaker radicalism? Christopher Hill and Barry Reay have pointed in particular to the social and economic objections of Friends to the political order as reasons for hostility towards the sect.[12] While these were important, it is the contention here that they should be considered in the context of Quaker religious doctrines which were central to the ideals the Society espoused. Indeed, it was the spiritual awakening of conversion and new biblical insight which were the driving force of Quakerism. For example, the ruling class was overtaken with near apoplexy at the thought of Quakers refusing 'hat-honour' and their 'theeing' and 'thouing' of inferiors and superiors alike, but these practices stemmed from the sect's desire to show equal respect to all because they believed that all men were as one before God. If we consider that at bottom the reason why Friends refused to distinguish between individuals was that human pride should not be glorified, and that in any case it was the Lord God alone who deserved human reverence, the emphasis is somewhat changed. It was not a general notion of human equality which was derived from the Quaker doctrine of the light but the demand that equality before the Lord should be given due reverence. It is apparent that religion was central to the Quaker notion of equality and the social implications that flowed from it were subversive enough in their time.

Even so, it is not acceptable to view early Quakers merely as the pious and introspective precursors of their later quietist brethren. Quakerism did not formulate its new ideas in a vacuum or on a tabula rasa. The religion was part of a milieu in which progressive ideas flourished and many no doubt joined the sect with strongly held radical convictions which they were not to forsake. None the less, Quaker leaders certainly repudiated the notion that they were Levellers or that they supported the abolition of property rights.[13] Friends were prepared to campaign for changes in the

---

[12] Hill, *The World Turned Upside Down*, chap. 10; Reay, *The Quakers and the English Revolution*, parts 1–3.

[13] Cole, 'The Quakers and the English Revolution', in Trevor Aston (ed.), *Crisis in Europe* (1965), 347; Barbour, *The Quakers in Puritan England*, 163, 193.

laws which would allow them freedom of worship, and demanded exemption from particular legal obligations such as oath-swearing in order that they could go about their daily lives and business unhindered. But they appear not to have taken the revolutionary step of calling for the abolition of the existing political order itself. Indeed, there is some evidence that during the 1650s Friends adopted what might be considered a conventional posture in this respect. James Nayler, for instance, advised: 'give to Caesar his due and honour to whom it belongs, but all glory and worship to God alone'.[14]

The sect's political ideals also need to be considered in the context of the Quaker belief in the second coming of Christ. We saw earlier how the movement argued that conversion to the new religion was contingent upon a personal transformation, which was itself informed by a new understanding of the scriptures. But the implications of the Quaker millennium were not only that man should develop a deep personal relation with God, unhindered by the trappings and hierarchies of conventional religion, but that social and economic conditions should prevail on earth which would be consistent with Christ's arrival. In the 1650s, for instance, Friends called for the abolition of tithes, the dissolution of the Church and universities, religious toleration, and reform of the law, demands which were testimony to the fiery radicalism of the early movement and most unwelcome to the ruling elite.[15] The Society also expressed a passionate concern for the welfare of the poor. The fury with which early Quakers denounced social injustice is remarkable. Whosoever was judged guilty of exploiting his fellow creatures or needlessly seeking personal gain at the expense of others was denounced. Quakers drew inspiration from the Old Testament prophets who showed scant respect for nobles, the wealthy, clergy, and landlords who failed to respect their fellow citizens. It is not possible to read James Parnel's diatribe against the rich and be in doubt about the horror with which some Quaker preachers were greeted. Parnel warned the wealthy and powerful: 'high and lofty ones, Howl and Mourn in Sackcloth and Ashes: for the Lord is coming to burn you up as stubble before him.'[16] The radical social values which the early movement fostered were apparent in his writings.

---

[14] James Nayler, *Behold You Rulers* (1658), 398, quoted by William G. Bittle in *James Nayler 1618–1660: The Quaker Indicted by Parliament* (York, 1986), 43.

[15] Reay, *The Quakers and the English Revolution*, 82; Geoffrey F. Nuttall, 'Overcoming The World: The Early Quaker Programme', in Derek Baker (ed.), *Sanctity and Secularity: The Church and the World, Studies in Church History*, 10 (Cambridge, 1973), 153–4; Hugh Barbour and J. William Frost, *The Quakers* (Richmond, Ind., 1994), 69–70.

[16] Parnel, *Collection*, 34.

All your Gay Clothing and Rich Attire was Pride and not for Decency, and that many of your Fellow-Creatures wanted that for to cover their Nakedness, which you spent upon your Lusts: then you shall be rewarded for grinding the Faces of the Poor, for your Oppressions and for Rackings and Taxings, and your heavy Burdens, wherewith you oppressed your Fellow-Creatures.[17]

Yet Quaker criticism of the rich was more complex than it at first seems. Indeed, Quaker attitudes towards the creation and consumption of wealth are instructive in that they reveal how closely religious and social ideas were enmeshed when Friends drew up their particular credo. Wealth was not disapproved of in itself or looked upon as an inherent evil. After all, it is unlikely that the prosperous Edward Grant, a Colchester merchant who joined the movement in the 1650s, or the former Alderman and Mayor of the town, John Furly, and his wealthy merchant son, would have been attracted to a movement which believed the possession of wealth was of itself unacceptable. Yet, the Society did recognize the Pauline warning that riches were apt to corrupt.[18] Friends' anxiety stemmed particularly from what they considered to be the dangers of covetousness. They feared that an obsession with attaining riches diverted men and women from their true purpose on earth, the glorifying of the Lord, towards the favour of transitory things. It was easy for attention to be misdirected from praise of God to worship of worldly success, and Friends emphasized that it was an error to assume oneself 'rich' on account of material wealth.[19] Whatever one's worldly success, men and women could still be poor and naked in spirit. Another danger associated with the accumulation of riches was the temptation to display the fruits of it conspicuously, thus dishonouring God by satisfying human pride.[20]

The other side of the coin was the Quaker attitude to poverty. Since the poor and lowly in society were part of God's creation, Quakers believed not only that others had a duty to care for them but that the poor had a legitimate interest in how the social and economic system was organized. In 1666 Stephen Crisp called upon the rich landowners who exploited the labouring classes excessively and drove them into poverty to behave in a way that was guided by 'righteousness' and 'equity'. He also expressed disapproval of property owners who sought to halt customary practices which traditionally assisted the less well-off; he cited

---

[17] Parnel, *Collection*, 36.
[18] William Penn, *No Cross, No Crown*, 2nd edn. (1682, repr. York, 1981), 201.
[19] Crisp, *Works*, 43.
[20] William Tomlinson, *Seven Particulars* (1657), 4–5; Parnel, *A Shield of The Truth*, 23; Penn, *No Cross, No Crown*, 201; Crisp, *Works*, p. xiii (my pagination).

landowners who overrode parishioners' rights to collect gleanings at harvest time.[21] Friends also feared that if mankind was left to its own devices,
the predisposition to accumulate and display, a consequence of human
weakness derived from mankind's fallen state, might lead to the avoidable
poverty of others.[22] Even so, while Quakers attacked the feckless rich and
unscrupulous landlords openly, they promoted no programme of open rebel-
lion on the part of the poor themselves. Change would materialize only
when the conscience of corrupt humanity was sufficiently enlightened to
lead them to desist from their evil practices. The outspoken rhetoric of
the 1650s quickly faded after the Restoration as Friends became much cooler
in their criticisms of the social order. But, even in the sect's earliest years,
it is unlikely that the Quakers had ever intended the complete end of hierarchy and division in society, whatever had been the objections of their
critics.

The context in which attitudes to poverty and wealth should be viewed
is a religious one. There was a profound, spiritual reason for Quakers to
argue against social injustice. The Society was fearful that need might drive
the poor to dishonour God by stealing. Even worse, in the struggle for
personal or familial survival the will to nourish spiritual growth might go
by the board. Quakers recognized poverty could limit man's spiritual potential. This viewpoint held significant implications. The first was that moderation in personal riches was considered to be desirable. The argument
was one that applied as much to the poor as the better-off, for excess in
either poverty or wealth was liable to distract mankind from achieving its
spiritual goal. Secondly, wealthy Friends were considered to be blessed
with riches at God's behest and they were reminded that riches were a
possession they held on earth only as God's stewards. They were enjoined
to use it with due prudence.[23] The arguments in favour of supporting
the poor were varied. But, above all, Friends believed that individuals,
poor or otherwise, should have the opportunity to achieve a new spiritual
awakening.

The issue of tithes is one where the argument whether Quakers were
influenced more by religious or social motives in their campaigns has recently crystallized.[24] Friends sometimes argued that payments should be

---

[21] Crisp, *Works*, 152, 148–9.

[22] James Parnel, *Goliah's Head* (1655), 28–9; Tomlinson, *Seven Particulars*, 4.

[23] EUL, Supplementary Papers (1697), 7; Davies, 'The Quakers in Essex', 129–31; Parnel, *Collection*, 36; and see also his *The Trumpet of the Lord Blown* (1655), 4.

[24] Bitterman, 'The Early Quaker Literature of Defence', 211–14; Barry Reay, 'Quaker Opposition to Tithes, 1652–1660', *passim*; Hill, *The World Turned Upside Down*, 244–5. An important discussion of the Quaker case against tithe payment, which takes issue with the

withheld since the tax threatened the livelihood of the poor. However, the sect also argued that their property rights were being violated when tithes were collected.[25] Indeed, this proposition led some opponents to infer that Quaker resistance to tithes was the first step in a campaign for the complete abolition of rents and other property rights. But it was rather the sanctity of private property, in this case their own land, which often influenced the decision of Quakers to refuse payment.[26] Moreover, Friends claimed that tithes constituted a tax which served as a disincentive to hard work.[27] The corollary was that the clergy should be obliged to maintain themselves, a view which would have appealed to those members of the middling ranks in society who made up a substantial proportion of the sect's followers.[28]

The Quakers' views were sometimes radical in the sense that they reflected a robust individualism. To argue, as Friends did, that tithes were iniquitous because they exploited the poor, and at the same time that refusal to pay could be justified on the grounds of individual property rights, or that they infringed Quaker religious doctrines, was not inconsistent. Friends used whatever arguments were available and were consistent with their faith to justify resistance to tithes. Moreover, the Quaker ranks included newly prosperous craftsmen and farmers with an already existing prejudice against tithe payments. Indeed, one critic noted that many joined the movement because of the Society's campaign against tithes.[29]

With the defeat of the Commonwealth's 'Good Old Cause' at the Restoration, Quakers began to moderate the way in which they presented themselves to the world. They began to desist from aggressive proselytizing, and from disturbing church services, performing signs and wonders, or claiming miracle cures. They became less outspoken in their criticism of the rich and appear to have relinquished some of the political demands which characterized their earliest years. Order and hierarchy were openly stated by Friends to be consistent with the natural order.[30]

---

arguments of Reay and Hill, can be found in Nicholas Morgan, *Lancashire Quakers and the Establishment*, chap. 5. What evidence there is of rank-and-file hostility to tithes in Essex is couched in religious terms. See FHL, Great Book of Sufferings, i. 399 (1656); PRO, E112/398/277 (1673); PRO, E112/391/223 (1665); EUL, COLMM 34 (Letter from George Fox).

[25] Cole, 'The Quakers and the English Revolution', 347; Crisp, *Works*, 68–9.

[26] Morgan, *Lancashire Quakers and the Establishment*, 179–80.

[27] EUL, EQ 27, Letter from George Fox (*c.*1670); Parnel, *Goliah's Head*, 24–5.

[28] Crisp, *Works*, 69; Parnel, *Goliah's Head*, 24–5, 30–1, 36, 51, 57. PRO, E112/397/144, Joshua Litle of Little Clacton complained in 1669 that Quaker tithe refusal would mean that he would be expected to labour with his own hands; Fowler, *A Sober Answer*, 34.

[29] Samuel Hammond, *The Quakers' House Built Upon Sand* (1658), 3–4.

[30] Joseph Pike, *Some Account of the Life of Joseph Pike* (1837), 92.

The comments of Robert Barclay in 1678 are revealing in reaffirming the belief in the social system:

I would not have any think, that thereby we intend to destroy the mutual relation that exists betwixt prince and people, master and servants, parents and children; nay, not at all: we shall have evidence, that our principle in these things has no such tendency . . . Let not any judge that from our opinion in these things, any necessity of levelling will follow . . .[31]

Some historians have argued that by the late 1680s 'towards the poor the reversal of Quaker moral concern was much more complete than towards luxury'.[32] But perhaps too sharp a dividing line is sometimes drawn between the Quakers of the 1650s and their post-Restoration brethren. Quaker radicalism was not to disappear altogether after 1660, for the Society still held fast to the social testimonies regarding dress and speech, and members also continued to absent themselves from church and to refuse payment of tithes and church dues. These were still radical and provocative beliefs which were backed up by action. The dangers which wealth posed to spiritual health and the need to care for the poor were also laboured by Friends. Indeed, it is possible to see where the seeds of future and more celebrated Quaker concern for the poor were sown.[33]

None the less, it is true that post-Restoration Quakers did become more introspective and concerned to weather the storm of persecution which was to break around their ears and to do so in a spirit of meekness and resolve.[34] The sect was also very careful to dissociate itself from any sort of plot or upheaval which threatened the body politic. And, of course, the degree of hostility towards Friends moderated as people became more accustomed to Quakerism. But one must also be sceptical about the argument that the sect's struggle for survival after the Restoration resulted in Quaker withdrawal from politics.[35] It was rather that Quakers altered their strategy as the political circumstances around them changed. From the mid-1670s, for instance, they organized themselves into an effective lobbying group to influence the central and local organs of government in their favour.[36] This stance is not by and large suggestive of a movement which

[31] Robert Barclay, *Apology for the True Christian Divinity* (1678; repr. Glasgow, 1886), 371.

[32] Barbour, *The Quakers in Puritan England*, 250.

[33] For instance, Ian Campbell Bradley, *Enlightened Entrepreneurs* (1987), chaps. 4 and 7.

[34] Geoffrey F. Nuttall, 'Record and Testimony: Quaker Persecution Literature, 1650–1700' (unpub. typescript), 21, 26. Xerox copy available in FHL, Box L/32, 17.

[35] Reay, *The Quakers and the English Revolution*, 104–5.

[36] N. C. Hunt, *Two Early Political Associations: The Quakers and the Dissenting Deputies in the Age of Sir Robert Walpole* (repr. Westport, Connecticut, 1979), Section 1. See also Chapter 13 below.

had spurned political action, though its concerns and strategy were different from those which animated members in the 1650s.

Yet, though the movement abandoned its militant proselytizing shortly after the Restoration, its opposition to Church and anti-communal values meant that Friends were still perceived as subversives. The political reforms called for by Friends and their belief in social justice should be placed alongside their attack on clerical authority, church doctrine, and the social disruption they caused in the parish as reasons for antagonism towards them. All can be seen to have derived from the new understanding of man's relation to God brought about by the spiritual awakening of Christ's inward coming.

PART II

A Peculiar People

5

A Community of Worship

The favour of the world and friendship thereof is enmity to God, man may soon be stained with it. Oh! love the stranger, and be as strangers in the world, and wonders to the world . . . and condemned by the world.

George Fox, *A Collection of Many Select and Christian Epistles* (*c.*1650; repr. Philadelphia, 1831), 1, 17.

Thou art a holy People unto the LORD thy God, and the LORD have chosen thee to be a peculiar people unto himself, above all the nations that are upon the earth.

Deuteronomy 14: 2.

The purpose of the present chapter is to understand the effects of membership upon individual followers of the Quaker faith. The issue is tackled in two ways. First, the informal social and economic relations which developed among ordinary Friends as a result of membership are examined, for conversion to the Quaker faith had important social repercussions in everyday life. Indeed, conversion led Friends voluntarily to seek greater association with one another and the sect became the main focus of social identity so far as adherents were concerned. Second, Quakers gradually developed an alternative administrative structure which was as much concerned with order as the church and secular courts it displaced. By 1670 Quaker institutions, in the form of quarterly, monthly and particular meetings, exercised significant control over the daily lives of followers. Considered free by Friends from the taint of worldly pollution, these meetings sought to relieve the poor, locate masters for Quaker youths, lend money to meet debts, and settle internal disputes between members. They were also used by the Society to discipline or even disown those who fell short of the approved standards of Quaker behaviour. It was to the meetings that erring Friends submitted themselves when they failed to implement Quaker social testimonies regarding, for example, 'hat honour', sexual standards, swearing oaths, and paying tithes. Studies of sectarianism indicate that over the generations religious groups like the Quakers increasingly limit the freedom allowed to members. An attempt will be made to assess how far Quakerism conformed to this pattern of sectarian development.

SACRED SPACES: THE CHURCH AND MEETING HOUSE

the true Church is the Body of *Christ* made of tried stones, elect and precious,
washed and cleansed by his blood and spirit . . . but this is not a house of Lime
and dead stones, nor the people that meets in it; for all manner of unrighteous
people meet there which is the synagogue of Satan.

James Parnel, *A Shield of the Truth* (1655), 35.

John Isaac of Halstead for bearing a paper at ye steeplehouse at Halstead agst the
Idoll's temple was committed to prison & after fined 20 nobles by Judge Hill . . .

Great Book of Sufferings, Part One (1657), 408.

It is essential to note the steps by which the Quaker sect became a separated worshipping people and came to constitute an alternative community. A contention of this study is that the role of ordinary Quakers in promoting the success of the movement has been insufficiently recognized and this chapter will attempt to redress the balance in that respect. Indeed, the steps taken by rank-and-file Friends to provide meeting places and burial grounds for the Society helped to secure its future in the early years of Quaker evangelism. Also, the marriages of Friends were solemnized in ordinary Quaker households. Because the sect considered that the church buildings and the worship that took place within them were riddled with 'superstition', Friends steadfastly ignored calls to present themselves for worship or any other ritual at the parish church, even though attendance was compulsory by law after the Restoration. According to the Quakers the notion that a physical building might constitute a church was dubious and deserved only dismissive contempt.

In keeping with apostolic example, Friends worshipped when and where the spirit moved them.[1] The frequent citations in the ecclesiastical and secular courts suggest it was often at the homes of ordinary Friends that followers congregated, probably for reasons of convenience. In the 1650s the wealthy Colchester merchant John Furly gave over some of his ground and a room to be used for worship. The house of Robert Beard, a husbandman of Theydon Garnon, Essex was another venue for Quaker worship. He was reported at a Quarter Session in 1666 to have held a meeting attended by forty parishioners with one of their number, contrary to the law, 'laying the scriptures open to them, as if he had been preaching to them'.[2] In 1670, at St Osyth, Giles Cook, a Quaker mariner, invited a

---

[1] James Parnel, *The Watcher* (1656), 1–9, 12.
[2] *FPT*, 96; ERO, Q/SR 408/19 (1666).

handful of sympathetic villagers into his house, while in the same year another Friend, Thomas Bennet, from Waltham Abbey, regularly entertained over fifty parishioners for worship at his home.[3] The records of prosecution are testimony to the commitment of ordinary Quakers who often undertook great personal risks in the name of the faith.

Descriptions of early meetings for worship are rare, though one is provided by the notable Quaker opponent Francis Higginson, the Cumberland cleric. His description written in 1653 is revealing:

The places of their Meetings are for the most part, such private houses as are most solitary and remote from Neighbours . . . their Speakers . . . standing . . . with his hat on, his countenance severe, his face downward, his eyes fixed mostly towards the earth, his hands & fingers expanded, continually striking gently on his breast . . . If . . . their cheife Speaker be . . . absent, any of them speak that will pretend a revelation; sometimes girles are vocal . . . Sometimes . . . there is not a whisper among them for an houre or two together.[4]

Meeting in a follower's home enabled Friends to escape the despised rituals of the Church and more generally made it a focal point for the community. For instance, because the 'steeple house' was unacceptable as a place of congregation, the Quaker marriage ceremony was performed in the homes of Friends, attended not only by the couple intending marriage, but also by others who would be expected to act as witnesses. The marriage of Thomas Cornell and Mary Reynolds in 1662, for instance, was celebrated at the home of John Cockerill, a Fordham Quaker. Quaker marriage registers regularly record such events. There are also numerous protests by churchwardens in the Archdeaconry Courts against Friends' 'marrying clandestinely' and neglecting the Church's authority in this regard.[5] It is clear that the role of ordinary members in supporting the early movement should not be underestimated. When Mary Smith, a Quaker widow from Rayne, volunteered in 1682 to open up her premises for worship as often as Friends required, the offer was eagerly accepted.[6] Indeed, the local meetings were aware of the importance of such selfless acts, for the death of a Friend and the consequent loss of a convenient meeting place sometimes coincided with the decline of the movement in a parish.[7]

---

[3] ERO, Assize File 35/112/9 No. 25; 35/112/2 No. 12.

[4] Higginson, *A Brief Relation*, 12–14. A larger extract from Higginson can be found in Barbour and Roberts (eds.), *Early Quaker Writings*, 64–78.

[5] PRO, RG6 1395, 5; ERO, D/AMV 2, fo. 12ᵛ (22 Feb. 1664), Zach Child of Felsted; fo. 62ʳ (23 July 1664), Walter Cutt of Saling Magna; D/ABV2, fo. 141ʳ (25 July 1684), Thomas Smith of Braintree.   [6] PRO, RG6 1262, 2.

[7] EUL, COLMM 1, 26 (1675).

As the number of Friends in a parish or town increased, a new meeting house might be erected. In 1664 the growing and prosperous Quaker community in Colchester built a large meeting place for the expanding Quaker population in the town.[8] The churchwardens of Felsted and Stebbing reported in 1678 that the Friends in these parishes had 'a Quaking meeting house'.[9] The erection of a meeting house was considered by some Friends a crucial step in establishing the movement in a parish, and there is no doubt that the contributions of ordinary Friends were vital. Bequests made in Quaker wills towards erecting or maintaining Quaker meeting places are indicative of rank-and-file commitment. A Coggeshall Quaker directed in 1672 that the sum he bestowed on his local meeting in the town was to purchase a venue hired by Friends for worship; he knew they needed a place for the 'worship and service of God'.[10] Henry Haslum, a Southminster Friend, had already built a meeting place in his own ground, the ownership of which he pledged would be transferred on his death to the Quaker community in the parish.[11] Daniel Vandewall, a wealthy Harwich merchant, also bequeathed to his meeting a house in his keeping in Great Oakley.[12]

Rich and humble alike made contributions in their wills towards the upkeep of meeting houses. William Swan, a wealthy Halstead Quaker, left ten pounds in 1695,[13] while the less-well-off Ann Shonk, a widow from Barking, arranged in 1682 for the meeting house to be kept in good repair by placing twenty shillings in the hands of Thomas Townsend, the local Quaker bricklayer.[14] The symbolic importance of establishing a meeting place for the Quaker community was not lost on the authorities, who sometimes, as in Colchester in the early 1660s and Thaxted in the 1680s, removed the benches and boarded up the meeting house doors in order to deny Quakers access. Ralph Josselin was alarmed when he discovered in 1674 that John Garrad, whom he termed 'the head' Quaker in Earls Colne, was intending to build a meeting house in the parish.[15]

Friends thought that a meeting place was essential to nourish a vibrant worshipping community. Though, as the movement grew in strength, many

---

[8] *FPT*, 94–5.   [9] ERO, D/AMV 6 (May 1678).

[10] PRO, Prob 11/342/47, John Guyon of Great Coggeshall.

[11] ERO, D/NF/1/1 (12 May 1701).   [12] ERO, D/ABR 17/178 (1716).

[13] ERO, D/ABR 13/321.

[14] ERO, D/AEW 27/20. See also the will of Thomas Debbett of Barking, who left five pounds for the repair of the meeting house in 1679, D/AER 23/319.

[15] Besse, *Sufferings*, i. 208; *FPT* 95; [Anon.], *A True and Faithful Relation of the Proceedings of the Magistrates from the People of God (called Quakers) in Colchester* (1664), 6; Josselin, *Diary*, 581.

meetings gradually adopted a formal venue for worship, such buildings were deliberately not decorated or erected in the manner of parish churches, but were built in such a way as to be in keeping with the Quaker principles of modesty and simplicity. Moreover, besides servicing Quaker worship, the buildings might also find use of a practical nature as lodging houses for the Quaker poor.[16] Of course, not all meetings possessed established venues; in some rural areas the Society remained dependent on the goodwill of individual Friends to volunteer their property and homes as meeting premises.[17]

THE LIVING AND THE DEAD: BURIAL GROUNDS

several received the Truth in the love of it, in and about the Town, so they could not for Conscience sake pay for the repairing of the *Steeple house* any longer; and therefore had not freedom to Bury their dead in the ground belonging thereunto; but they joined together and bought a parcel of ground to bury their dead (*as did Abraham, the Father of the Faithful*).

George Fox, the younger, *A True Relation of the Unlawful and Unreasonable Proceedings of the Magistrates of Harwich in Essex* (n.p., 1660), 1.

Even after death, Friends maintained their separation from other Christians. Early in the sect's history local meetings were urged to acquire separate burial grounds so that members might not be interred in 'polluted' church ground and subjected to superstitious ceremonies.[18] Disputes arose between local Quakers and the non-Quaker kin of deceased Friends as to how the corpse should be disposed of. Conforming kin sometimes wanted relatives who had converted to Quakerism to be interred in the parish yard, an outcome which was anathema to local Friends.[19] These quarrels sometimes culminated in disruption of burials or ugly squabbles in the parish yard. The Quaker John Rolfe interrupted a service at Tollesbury, Essex in 1661; and in Boxted Quakers and dissenters were involved in several fracas at the graveside. In 1664 at the burial of Ann Dymon scuffles broke out; parishioners disrupted the service and attempted to inter the corpse without the office of burial, and kicked the Prayer Book into the grave, one proclaiming in justification that 'she used

---

[16] Hubert Lidbetter, *The Friends Meeting House*, 2nd edn. (York, 1979), 4–5; EUL, COLTW 1, 193 (1693). [17] ERO, Q/SO3, 207, 218, 229, 230 (1705).
[18] *Somersetshire Quarterly Meeting of the Society of Friends, 1668–1699*, 20; Braithwaite, *Beginnings*, 308; FHL, MYM, iv. 81; George Fox, *Epistles*, i. 181 (1659).
[19] Davies, *An Account of the Convincement*, 44 (*c*.1662).

not to go to church when she was alive, and she should not be carried into the church when she was dead'. Another remarked that the minister was a 'shame to the kingdom for doing such actions'. When Edward Warner from the same parish was buried, Nathaniel Plumsted, a Friend, was reported at the Quarter Session to have:

layd violent hands upon the minister Mr. Edward Hickeringill, taking him by the arm and turning him about, and calling him several times 'Hireling' and bidding people beware of that dealer and beware of that priest, having a great crew about him who with shouts and cries did abet and condone what he said and did.[20]

Many Friends directed in their wills that they were to have a 'decent' burial, the implication being that the rituals of the established Church should be avoided at all costs. A few were explicit about the location and instructed that interment should be 'among Friends called Quakers' or in the 'place of Quakers'.[21] Clearest of all on this count was Edmund Blatt, a Barking Friend, who in 1665 requested interment among Quakers, believing it was the only means to ensure a 'true Christian burial'.[22]

Harwich Quakers collected funds to purchase a Quaker graveyard in the borough soon after the movement became established there in 1656.[23] The acquisition of independent grounds normally followed quickly upon the establishment of the sect in a town or parish. The quickest method of procuring a burial yard was to purchase land from a Friend, though, when this was not possible, the Society might take over any plot which members were prepared to lease or loan.[24] The goodwill of ordinary brethren was a crucial factor in enabling the Society to acquire burial grounds. Drawing up his testament in 1663, William Simpson of Pebmarsh, for example, reserved a portion of his freehold land so that Friends could be assured a burial 'free of any molestation'.[25] That such a view was shared more widely by the Quaker community is evident from the contributions made towards the purchase and upkeep of burial grounds. William Sewell bequeathed ten shillings to the Society in 1678 to keep the burial yard in good order.[26] Thomas Bayles from Colchester, John Claydon from

---

[20] Besse, *Sufferings*, ii. 198; EUL, Crisp MS fo. 303ᵛ; ERO, Q/SR 400, 133, 134, 135.

[21] For example, ERO, D/AER 24/49, Stephen Dennis of Barking (1681); D/ABR 17/233, Thomas Rochford of Woodham Water (1715); D/AEW 30/232, Nicholas Oakman of Hornchurch (1708); D/AEW 29/145, Ann Bailey of Barking (1685); D/AEW 29/144, Thomas Townsend of Barking (1695); D/DRa/126 No. 9, Robert Barwell of Witham (1704).

[22] ERO, D/AER 21/133.   [23] George Fox, the younger, *A True Relation*, 1.

[24] EUL, EQ 29 (1660). See also Crisp MS, fo. 185; EQ 29, 54; COG MM 27 (24 June 1708).   [25] ERO, D/AMW 6/281.

[26] ERO, D/AMR 1/7.

Halstead, Robert Grassingham from Harwich, and Matthew Day from Newport all made private land available[27] which was subsequently handed over to the Society as a gift in perpetuity.

That there was widespread use of independent burial grounds is evident from the considerable number of church court presentments listing Quakers for this offence. John and Joseph Pollard, two Quaker brothers from Steeple whose names appear regularly for failure to attend church, were reported to the Archdeacon's Court in 1663 for not 'burying their dead in church or churchyard'.[28] Against the name of John Dawson, a Shalford Quaker, the officer of the court recorded that neither the whereabouts nor the time of his or his children's burial was known.[29] Some Friends looked upon the prospect of burial in the parish graveyards with such repugnance that they chose to inter parents, children, and local members in their own gardens. The Quakers' own burial registers and the visitation books of the ecclesiastical courts confirm this as a widespread practice.[30] John Pettit, for instance, was reprimanded in 1664 by the churchwardens in Wimbish parish for burying a child in his garden without a Christian burial, an offence for which his sister was likewise presented the following year.[31]

The process whereby sectarian communities emerged and evolved is often explained by referring to the actions and statements of the movement's leaders, while the importance of rank-and-file Friends is overlooked. Given that Quakerism was the quintessential expression of a lay religion, this lack of attention is surprising. Judging from the experience of the Quaker community in Essex, the role of ordinary members ought to receive far greater recognition, for it was their wishes and efforts which in large measure determined the success of the movement locally. Indeed, without the opportunity for worship, marriage, and burial free of church influence which members provided, the Society would have found it difficult to survive as a separated religious community.

---

[27] EUL, Crisp MS, fo. 185 (1659); EQ 29, 64–5 (1668 and 1675), and 82 (1676).
[28] ERO, D/AEA 43, fo. 16ʳ.   [29] ERO, D/AMV 1, fos. 113ʳ, 115ʳ (Nov. 1663).
[30] PRO, RG6 1382, 217–18 (1674); 1262, 179 (1667); 1394, 256 (1662).
[31] ERO, D/AMV 1, fo. 117ʳ, D/AMV 2, fo. 5ʳ. See also the comment on garden burials in Keith Thomas, *Man and the Natural World: Changing Attitudes in England, 1500–1800* (Harmondsworth, 1983), 237–8.

6

The Brotherhood

RELIEF OF THE POOR

This People increasing daily both in Town and Country, an Holy Care fell upon some of the Elders among them, for the Benefit and Service of the Church. And the first Business in their View, after the example of the Primitive Saints, was the exercise of *Charity*; to supply the necessities of the Poor, and answer the like Occasions.

William Penn, *A Brief Account of the Rise and Progress of the People Call'd Quakers* (1694), 69.

And above all things have fervent charity among yourselves: for charity shall cover the multitude of sins.

1 Peter 4: 8.

Alongside the network of meeting places and burial grounds of the early Friends there developed an elaborate system for dispensing relief to poor brethren. This is one of the clearest indications of how the Society functioned early on as an alternative community and provides another clear example of the social consequences of religious belief. Records extant from the late 1650s suggest that care of the poor was a priority. But the Society also prohibited recourse by members to the parish authorities for assistance, even though members still paid the parish poor rate. This prohibition perhaps reflected a fear that an alternative route for relief might place too great a temptation before members.[1] The response of the Society to the needs of its own poor must be examined in an ideological context. Some of the arguments have already been outlined but they are worth considering more generally. The understanding of the sect was that personal prosperity was dependent upon God's will, and better-off Quakers possessed riches on earth merely as 'God's stewards'. The expectation was that these should be dispersed to the poor, widows, and orphans.[2] But another

---

[1] EUL, Supplementary Papers, 13 (1699): COLMM 35, 101 (1658); COLTW 1, 74 (1691); M. R. Watts, *The Dissenters*, i. *From the Reformation to the French Revolution* (Oxford, 1978), 336.

[2] Crisp, *Works*, 437 (1690). This idea was not peculiar to Friends; see R. B. Schlatter, *The Social Ideas of Religious Leaders* (repr. New York, 1971), Part I, chaps. 3 and 4.

reason for relieving the indigent among the Quaker flock was the conviction that rich and poor alike were members of the Quaker family. The same spirit that guided Friends into one Christian fellowship also directed that they should relieve poor brethren, since this was thought a natural expression of Christian love.[3]

The charitable impulse was also given a fillip by a consideration other than the opportunity to fulfil Christian duty or the need for the rich to disperse their God-given wealth.[4] There was another moral imperative which underlay Quaker alms-giving, namely: concern for the spiritual well-being of the poor. Friends feared that poverty might force individuals to dishonour God. For example, a poor man's necessity might lead him to steal. But more important was the fear that the poor might be so over-come by the difficulty of earning a livelihood that the nurturing of their own spiritual growth went by the board. For this reason poverty had to be relieved since failure to do so might lead to the 'seed' within being choked.[5]

The care exercised on behalf of the poor was extensive. Shoes, stock-ings, scarves, coats, shirts, linen, sheets, and many other items were provided by the local meeting. Sometimes a weekly income was paid for rents and for the indenture of Quaker pauper apprentices.[6] At death the cost of the coffin, the burial suit, the laying out of a corpse, the digging of the grave, and even the cost of food and wine for those who gathered to pay witness might be borne by the local meeting.[7] The surviving Quaker wills for the county of Essex reveal that 18 per cent of the testators made some bequest to the poor, a striking figure given that these were in addition to contribu-tions already made to local meetings and monies compulsorily raised from members through the parish poor rate. This is surely positive evidence

---

[3] EUL, EQ 27 (June 1718); EQ 27 (1686); FHL, MYM, iii. 219.

[4] EUL, COLMM 34, 163 (1692); FHL, MYM, v. 338-9 (June 1718); MYM, ii. 145-6 (1696).

[5] EUL, Supplementary Papers, 7, the date is June 1697. Brian Pullan has argued that the conviction that poverty should be relieved because it imperilled the well-being of the soul was one factor which differentiated Catholic from Protestant attitudes to poor relief. See his 'Catholics and the Poor in Early Modern Europe', *Transactions of the Royal Historical Society*, 5th ser., 26 (1976), 26, 28-34, *passim*. Quakers, however, appear to have shared the Cath-olic conviction. Further research may reveal whether Friends were unusual or whether other Protestant groups held similar views. See Keith Thomas, 'The Utopian Impulse in Seventeenth-Century England', *Dutch Quarterly Review of Anglo American Letters*, 15 (1985), 177-8.

[6] EUL, Loose Leaf Disbursements for the Poor (28 May 1706 to 27 Oct. 1710).

[7] Ibid. (28 May 1706); FHL, Waltham Abbey Monthly Meeting Minutes (15 Feb. 1674); EUL, COLTW 2, 139 (1714).

of the genuine sentiments Quakers harboured about the welfare of their poorer members.

Personal charity, however, was not the main source of relief for indigent Friends, since most relied for subsistence upon the rate levied by their local Quaker meetings. The system of relief developed by the Friends was an important method of control of poorer members by the meeting. This dispersion of monies was at the discretion of the local meeting and this enabled the society to exercise considerable influence over the daily behaviour of the poor. This was especially so when Friends were in danger of backsliding or were reluctant to heed the advice of a local meeting on matters of discipline. In 1674, for instance, Susan Roberts was threatened by the meeting with the removal of her subsistence if she persisted in living apart from her husband.[8] When members were recalcitrant assistance ceased and they were directed to seek alms from the parish. Though there is no evidence that Essex Quakers were more or less generous than the parish authorities to their own poor, the positive attitude harboured by the Society towards the indigent must have been a reason for attracting converts from the lower ranks in society.

RELIGION AND SOCIAL IDENTITY

His dear People, and who are as to one, as my Mother, my Brother, my Sister, yea even my own Children, finding a natural love in my heart to all my Father's Children, and a true love to all the Brotherhood.

Crisp, *Works*, 51.

they do not seem much to regard any man with any true love or honour as to real worth unless they be of their *fraternity* . . .

John Gauden, *A Discourse Concerning Publick Oaths* (1662), 5.

Crisp described the sect as a 'brotherhood' and one could well say that it functioned as a surrogate family. Friends helped one another informally as did kin or neighbours, whether it was by visiting the sick, or assisting at confinement or at time of bereavement.[9] Indeed, the movement fostered informal contacts between members which cut across normal kin and neighbourly relations. It needs to be stressed that these developments occurred independently of the direction of the local meeting. Because business and social contacts among Quakers were often voluntary and thus free of

---

[8] EUL, COLTW 1, 43, 7.　　　[9] EUL, COLMM 1, 53 (1682).

influence from meetings, their existence is rarely recorded. However, it is possible to discover more about these informal relations from local records.

An important insight into Quaker social networks and how they operated is evident from the process of will-making among members. When drawing up testaments, Friends often sought scribes from their religious community rather than the wider parochial society. Quakers such as Stephen Crisp, Thomas Kendall, and Solomon Freemantle in Colchester and John Saxby in Barking all performed the task for Friends during the seventeenth century.[10] Common belief was that the parish scribe was a figure of some importance and was expected to undertake the task with considerable discretion. Friends who chose a will-maker from within their own religious community were defying the norm. One of these was Quaker Edmund Rigg, who around 1670, wishing to dispose of his estate in a manner which he anticipated would cause concern to his children, chose Stephen Crisp as the scribe in order to ensure confidentiality regarding his intentions.[11]

There were also economic advantages to be derived from membership. For example, increased opportunities for employment might arise as a consequence of fellowship with Quakers. When Thomas Story arrived in London in 1696 and was seeking employment, his name and trade were read out at a meeting and then passed among Friends.[12] Unemployed Friends in Colchester were directed to Quaker clothiers in the town in the hope that they might gain work. Poor Quakers might find an income through sweeping the meeting house or working yarn bought for them by the local meeting in order that they could pursue trade.[13] Sectarianism certainly had tangible social and economic benefits for members. Contemporaries remarked upon Quakers' preference for doing business with one another which, it was implied, was a well-recognized benefit of membership. A pamphlet written in 1681 on *The Trade of England Revived* observed the business practice of Friends:

And of Quakers, great numbers of late years are become shopkeepers; for that if a man hath been very meanly bred, and was never worth much beyond a groat in all his life, do but turn Quaker, he is presently set up in one shopkeeping trade or other, and then many of them will compass sea and land to get this new Quaking shopkeeper a trade. And if he be of a trade that no other shopkeeper is of in the town or village, then he will take all their money which they have to lay out and

---

[10] This information is derived from an examination of Quaker manuscript wills.

[11] EUL, Crisp MS, fos. 9ᵛ–10ʳ.

[12] *Journal of the Life of Thomas Story*, i. 138 (c.1696).

[13] EUL, COLTW 2, 236 (1718); 150 (1715); COLMM 51 (23 May 1702).

expend in his way, their custom being to sell to all the world, but they will buy only of their own tribe.[14]

This is by no means an isolated comment. Other contemporaries were quick to remark that Friends would 'favour one another in all things, particularly in trade'.[15] Local meetings gave loans to Friends, sometimes on favourable terms, but independent ventures and business dealings between individual members were far greater in number than those sanctioned officially by the group through the local business meetings.[16] Sometimes disputes between followers over trade and business ventures were laid before Quaker business meetings for adjudication, and meetings were also urged to intervene and order the payment of debts which were outstanding.[17] Quaker wills contain evidence of joint economic activity among Friends, and the Exchequer records reveal a striking instance in 1686, when a vessel owned by Quaker John Abraham from Colchester was under the command of the Wivenhoe mariner Edward Feedum, and carried the goods of Josiah Taylor, John Furly, Abraham Case, and Stephen Crisp, all Friends.[18] Quakers may have preferred to trade with one another because of a common religious allegiance. They may also have felt sure of reliability and honesty in business dealings. It is clear that with membership came an informal network for trade and other economic relationships which stretched beyond the local meeting and was country-wide.[19]

Quaker inheritance customs also enable us to discover whether the attitudes and behaviour of ordinary Friends in the local community were different from those of others. Several hundred wills of the community in the county of Essex have survived which make it possible to consider this question. It appears that, when making wills, Friends' intentions were little different from those of their contemporaries as regards the recognition of wives, children, and wider kin. Similarly, the appointment of executors was conventional, with 90 per cent of those chosen being from the deceased's family, most of them spouses.[20] However, a closer study reveals that certain testamentary duties normally undertaken by near kin or the most trusted of village acquaintances were instead exercised by members of the religious group.

---

[14] Joan Thirsk and J. P. Cooper (eds.), *Seventeenth-Century Economic Documents* (Oxford, 1972), 394.   [15] Quoted in *Journal of the Life of Thomas Story*, i. 105.

[16] EUL, COLMM 27, 1; COLTW 2, 145, 148, 163, 165; Supplementary Papers, 31 (1702); FHL, BARMM 1 (16 Dec. 1712).

[17] FHL, Six Weeks Meeting, 3, 128; EUL, COLTW 2, 56–7; COGMM 27 (5 Dec. 1706); ERO, DNF/1/1/2 (4 Feb. 1707).   [18] PRO, E190/610/3 (1686).

[19] *The Autobiography of William Stout*, ed. J. D. Marshall (Manchester, 1967), 13.

[20] Two hundred and thirty eight wills from the period 1655 to 1725 were examined.

Over 80 per cent of the supervisors of Quaker wills were the co-religionists of testators.[21] This striking figure implies Friends gave first consideration to sect members when dealing with matters of a private or sensitive nature. The role of supervisors was various: easing the grief of the bereaved, ensuring a trouble-free probate, discharging outstanding debts, and acting as referees when a will was disputed.[22] Supervisors were sometimes also given the responsibility of ensuring the welfare of a child on a parent's decease. Near to his death in 1664, the Quaker Humprey Smith, for instance, placed his son under the guidance of the two Essex Friends George Weatherley and Robert Ludgater, with the instruction that they should arrange his apprenticeship and be responsible for his spiritual education and well-being.[23] One supervisor was required to ensure that a child's education was adequately funded, another was given the authority to examine a family's account books to ensure that a child's inheritance was properly invested.[24] So much trust did the Quaker Christopher Inman from Thorrington place in a fellow member in 1695 that he gave him authority to take custody of his daughter if her inheritance was interfered with or not properly invested.[25] It is significant that most Friends chose fellow members when making the appointment of supervisors. Quakerism encouraged links and associations between members which cut across normal kin and neighbourly relations with the result that influence normally exercised by kin and neighbours within local society was diminished. Ignoring customary practice in this regard was yet another way in which Friends drew apart from the host community.

THE DEATH BED AND MOURNING

If Thou art Wise Thou wilt remember Thy latter End, before it be too late; for if the Harvest be over, and the Summer be ended, and Thou not gathered to the

---

[21] Just over 80 per cent, that is 76 of the 94 supervisors of Quaker wills were co-religionists. For the duties of supervisors and overseers see Keith Wrightson and David Levine, *Poverty and Piety in an English Village: Terling, 1525–1700* (1979), 100; Richard T. Vann, 'Wills and the Family in an English Town: Banbury, 1550–1800', *Journal of Family History*, 4 (1979), 365–6.

[22] For example, PRO, PROB 11/351/404, Thomas Shortland of Colchester (1676); PROB 11/383/96, Phillip Fuller of Colchester (1682). ERO, D/ABR 15/50, Josiah Parker of Great Burstead (1703).

[23] EUL, COLMM 46, Copy of a letter of Humphrey Smith to his son (23 Feb. 1664).

[24] PRO, PROB 11/342/42, John Guyon of Great Coggeshall (1672); PROB 11/387/126, Rebecca Everitt of Colchester (1687), ERO, DAMV 7/249, John Crosier of Felsted (1671).

[25] ERO, D/ABR 13/316.

LORD, the woful Night of Darkness when no Man can work will overtake Thee, out of which there will be no Redemption.

Thomas Bayles, *The Serious Reading and Comfort of Holy Scriptures* (1714), 5.

it is appointed unto men once to die, but after this the judgment.

Hebrews 9: 27.

There is a final aspect of Quaker social behaviour which illustrates the nature of sect cohesion. The evidence is less clear, but it appears that members of the sect took over many of the roles normally performed by other members of local society when a member died. For example, the deathbed scene was a significant event for Puritans and Quakers alike in seventeenth century society; the nature of the death was all important since it signalled the character of a person's life, and those who were present gave support to the dying in the last hours and themselves learned about the importance of religious commitment.[26] However, at the point of a Quaker's expiry it was sect members and not the family or neighbours who were most often the main focus. This can be inferred from the recollections of the deathbed scenes of Friends, many of which were published. The final words of the Earls Colne Quaker William Allen, who died in 1680, were reported:

I am glad to see my friends about me. I go to my God and your God, my Father and your Father. My bosom is full of love, to all my Father's children: and he then said 'Now, Lord Jesus, how acceptable it is to leave all the world, and be gathered up to thee:'[27]

Such gatherings enabled Friends to affirm their faith, sure in the knowledge that eternity awaited. The death-bed provided the sect with an opportunity to emphasize Quaker values and to remind followers that salvation came through obedience to the Quaker faith alone. John Matern, a Quaker schoolmaster at Waltham Abbey, summoned his pupils to his deathbed in 1678 and warned them to be faithful to the Lord.[28] Priscilla Cotton from Colchester told Friends in 1664 to spurn the world's ways in speech and manners. The expiring Friend warned those present to live up to Quaker expectations regarding personal conduct, and to beware of backsliding, since death could strike at any time.[29] Anna Turner, of Coggeshall, told an acquaintance that she, like Anna, would 'come before

---

[26] Ralph Houlbrooke, 'The Puritan Death-bed, *c*.1560–*c*.1660', in Christopher Durston and Jacqueline Eales (eds.), *The Culture of English Puritanism, 1560–1700* (1996), 122–3.

[27] John Tomkins, *Piety Promoted in a Collection of the Dying Sayings of Many of the People Called Quakers*, ed. William Evans and Thomas Evans (Philadelphia, 1854), i. 213.

[28] Ibid., 82.   [29] Ibid., 239.

the bar of the great God . . . and can no way shun it'.[30] For the unfaithful there lay in wait, according to the young Elizabeth Furly, only 'torment forever, where the fire never goes out'.[31] The deathbed enabled Friends to impress upon the minds of followers the essential truth that salvation came by being loyal to Quaker values. What better place to remind Friends of the benefit of their faith than at the point of death itself?

Most of these published accounts relate to Friends who were certain that eternity awaited them. Stephen Crisp proclaimed to Friends around him that he had 'full assurance of his peace with God in Jesus Christ'.[32] Thomas Upsher in 1704 announced his joyful surprise that the Lord had poured down his love and mercy upon him.[33] Such words served as incentives to those gathered and other Friends to follow the examples set by the lives of good men. Of course, eternity was never guaranteed. The Society took the opportunity to remind followers of the character of deceased Friends at public meetings and entries were sometimes made in burial registers reflecting these judgements. Solomon Freemantle was described in 1676 as a 'faithful man' and Mary Pettit in 1711 as a 'person of known integrity'.[34] But for Thomas Buck of Ashdon there was a reprimand; the register noted in 1693 that he had been 'too much short of his duty of collecting for the relief of the poor'.[35]

Non-Quakers were not excluded from the final days nor from Quaker burials, but their participation appears to have been peripheral. Ralph Josselin visited a Quaker parishioner during an illness in 1678 in the vain hope that he might persuade him to 'pray together and join in God's public worship'.[36] We know that Quaker women often nursed infirm Friends and laid out their corpses once deceased. Moreover, it was the local meeting which had oversight and control regarding the choice of burial plot and, if the Friend had been poor, the provision of the coffin.[37] Friends also disliked mourning customs, for they seemed to exalt the individual and contradicted Friends' desire for simplicity. Some form of celebration was not ruled out. Food and drink were consumed after a Quaker burial, and the cost met by the meeting if the Friend had been poor.[38] Ann Morrill

---

[30] Ibid., 304.

[31] [Anon.], *The Substance of a Letter sent to the Magistrates of Colchester*, 2nd edn. (1670), 23. [32] Tomkins, *Piety Promoted*, i. 112.

[33] Ibid., 307. [34] PRO, RG6 999, 144. [35] PRO, RG6 1382, 235.

[36] Josselin, *Diary*, 613. See also Keith Wrightson, 'Love, Marriage and Death', in Lesley M. Smith (ed.), *The Making of Britain: The Age of Expansion* (1986), 111.

[37] ERO, T/A 261/1/1 (25 Aug. 1712); EUL, COLTW 2, 133 (1714); Loose Leaf Poor Relief Accounts, 1711–1790, see 18 May 1710, 22 Sept. 1710.

[38] EUL, Loose Leaf Poor Relief Accounts, 1711–1790.

from Littlebury instructed that no more than four pounds should be spent at her funeral in 1704, and Ann Shonk from Barking expressed the wish in 1682 that forty shillings were to cover the cost of her coffin, a burying flannel, and a glass of wine for each Friend present.[39] Mourning clothes and gravestones were altogether discouraged. Robert Barwell, a wealthy Witham clothier, gave instructions in his will of 1702 that no black clothes or any clothes which could be described as 'mourning garments' were to be worn at his funeral.[40] Occasionally Friends erected gravestones without the Society's permission but these were removed.[41]

It is clear that as worshipping people Friends rejected the rituals and doctrines of the Anglican Church and this led them to establish alternatives for prayer, marriage, and burial. As a result of the cohesion that developed among sect members, kin and neighbourhood ties in the local community could be fractured. The cohesion which developed among members constituted a major challenge to existing social arrangements and had disruptive consequences for the wider community.

[39] ERO, D/ARC 12/8; D/AEW 27/20. [40] ERO, D/DRa/126. No. 9.
[41] EUL, COLTW 2, 200, 202 (1700).

7
Love and Marriage

But in marriage do thou be wise; prefer the person before money, virtue before beauty; the mind before the body: then thou hast a wife, a friend, a companion, a second self; one that bears an equal share with thee, in all thy toils and troubles.

William Penn, *Some Fruits of Solitude* (1693), No. 92, repr. in Penn, *Writings*, 34.

Children, obey your parents in the Lord: for this is right . . . And, ye fathers, provoke not your children to wrath: but bring them up in the nurture and admonition of the Lord.

Ephesians 6: 1 and 4.

A prominent feature of sectarian communities is the expectation that personal inclinations should be disregarded when they conflict with the behaviour approved by the religious group. How far does the experience of ordinary Quakers conform to the general sectarian pattern of behaviour? To answer this question, courtship and marriage among Friends have been examined, for here the conflicts between the group and the individual are at their most acute. An assessment of these particular issues reveals much about the evolution of the early sect and also provides an extraordinary insight into the emotions and personal convictions which operated when Friends sought a suitable marriage partner.

COURTSHIP, SPIRITUAL COMPATIBILITY, AND PARENTAL CONTROL

others mixed themselves with ye world and have been married by ye priests which is contrary to ye command of God under ye first covenant and practice and advice of ye Apostles under ye second, also contrary to ye testimony of truth in our days . . .

Note of Advice to Young Friends (4 March 1695), EUL, Colchester Monthly Meeting Records, 34, p. 146.

We now know from the work of modern historians of the family that a multiplicity of factors determined the choice of partner in early modern society: among them parental consent, a degree of mutual affection, and parity in wealth and age.[1] But how far did these criteria apply to the Friends when a partner was being decided upon?

In one significant respect Quakers were different: their mode of courtship appears to have diverged markedly from the practice which was common in local society. An immediate consequence of the Quaker preference for endogamy, allied to their social exclusivity, was an alteration in the circumstances under which the opportunity for courtship might occur. Normal venues for matchmaking activities such as local dances were of little attraction to young Friends. Instead, partners were probably sought out at meetings for worship, which were among the few occasions when male and female Quaker young persons mixed socially in any degree or numbers. In time, the Society developed its own equivalent to the 'Season', with the Yearly Meeting in London enabling new marital alliances to be forged.[2] However, even in the seventeenth century the conventional courtship procedure was undermined.

Quakers shared the views of contemporary moralists who advised that seeking the guidance of the Spirit was the primary requirement when deciding upon a partner.[3] They also warned that those who were distracted too much by the tug of personal attraction or the pursuit of worldly interest put in jeopardy the happy outcome to a union.[4] Spiritual equality or compatibility between partners was also thought necessary before a match could proceed. In 1681, for example, Friends from Great Dunmow initially withheld permission for the coupling of John Vent and Mary Christenwheat on the grounds that they were 'spiritually unequal'.[5]

The exercise of parental influence in the choice of partner was given great prominence by contemporary moralists. Friends concurred, arguing that parental authority was derived from natural and divine law.[6] Parents

---

[1] Keith Wrightson, *English Society, 1500–1680* (1982), 70–2; Ralph Houlbrooke, *The English Family 1450–1700* (1984), chap. 4; Jacques Tual, 'Sexual Equality and Conjugal Harmony: The Way to Celestial Bliss. A View of Early Quaker Matrimony', *JFHS* 55 (1988), 161–73. An interesting overview of Quaker attitudes to marriage from the earliest years of the sect can be found in Alison MacKinnon, ' "My Dearest Friend": Courtship and Conjugality in some Mid and Late Nineteenth-Century Quaker Families', JFHS 58 (1997), 44–58.

[2] Davies, *An Account of the Convincement*, 26–7; Houlbrooke, *The English Family*, 71; Michael Mitterauer, *A History of Youth* (Oxford, 1992), 158–63; Leonora Davidoff, *The Best Circles* (1986), 75; John Gillis, *For Better, For Worse: British Marriages, 1660 to the Present* (Oxford, 1985), 27, 30.   [3] FHL, MYM, ii. 107 (1695); Pike, *Some Account of the Life*, 8.

[4] For example, Thomas Ellwood, *The History of the Life*, 210–12.

[5] EUL, COLTW 1, 85–6. See also Benjamin Holme, *A Collection of the Epistles and Works* (1753), 143; Moses West, *A Treatise Concerning Marriage* (1707), 16.

[6] Pike, *Some Account of the Life, 12.*

(often, in effect, fathers) were required to express an opinion on a pro-posed match either in person or at a local meeting or alternatively to dis-patch a certificate expressing consent or disapproval. So vital was this endorsement, that the absence of a certificate, a lack of clarity in its com-position, or a failure to add a signature might delay the progress of a marriage.[7]

However, what was in theory an overwhelming authority on the part of parents seems not to have been exercised in practice. A striking feature of Quaker disciplinary records is how few incidents there are of disagree-ment over the choice of marriage partner. This apparent harmony sug-gests that there was a considerable amount of 'give and take' between parents and children when potential candidates were being discussed. Asked to comment on his daughter's plans to marry in 1687, the father of Lydia Warner answered that he was 'passive', implying that she had a consid-erable degree of freedom in the matter.[8] Thomas Gwin revealed that his non-Quaker father held the opinion that he should 'marry no one in contradiction to his judgement, yet he would not impose on me against my judgement'.[9]

Where disputes over marriage proposals appear in the disciplinary records the reason was normally a child's failure to inform parents of a courtship. For example, the mother of Elizabeth Marriage complained in 1711 that the young Samuel Maskith captured her daughter's affections without first seeking maternal approval.[10] Weighty Friends at the meeting agreed that children should first inform their parents when entering into a period of courtship. An important caveat was added, which was that parental veto was limited by and large to ensuring partners came from within the Society, and that objections to a match might be overruled if the basis of the com-plaint was insufficiently grave. The extent of parental influence approved of by the Society was less than at first appears. Parental say seems to have been employed in the main to screen out unsuitable partners.

Parental authority was exercised most fiercely when children sought part-ners from outside the sect. Friends strongly disapproved of this, fearing that the upshot of an 'unequal yoking' would be slackening of commit-ment and a confusion as to the faith in which the issue of such a union was to be raised. Disapproval of exogamous unions had been expressed throughout the sect's history. In 1672, for example, the father of Martha

[7] EUL, COLMM 1, 63 (1684); COLTW 1, 194 (1693); PRO, RG 6, 1396, 91.
[8] EUL, COLMM 1, 76–7 (1687).
[9] FHL, MS vol. 77, The Journal of Thomas Gwin of Falmouth (*c.*1680).
[10] EUL, EQ 1, 3.

Potter approached his local meeting for assistance when his daughter spurned his advice and proposed to take a suitor from the world.[11] Concern over out-marrying reached a peak in the early 1690s and coincided with the first real decline in Quaker numbers. The Society urged parents to be vigilant in the face of this threat. The meeting in Colchester, for example, warned parents in 1694 to do all in their power to impede the progress of children to unacceptable unions.[12] However, the campaign was hampered by the sentiments of some parents who considered the personal wishes of children to be paramount, no matter what the religious inclination of the intended spouse. In the event, the Society sometimes disciplined parents who seemed ineffectual or indifferent to the Society's endeavours and appealed directly to their offspring.[13]

The parental role was complex. To be sure, parents exercised considerable influence over the process of marriage and attempts to defy them outright were unlikely to be successful. Yet Friends were unable to coerce children into a match they did not accept; the expectation was that parents should exercise a veto only on undesirable candidates.[14] The parental role then appears to have been largely a negative one, though a few parents were prepared to permit a larger degree of freedom to children. The attitudes of Quaker parents were not dissimilar to those of others in society who allowed children a considerable latitude when matchmaking.

LOVE AND THE CHOICE OF PARTNER

Dear Wife, who art dear and near to me, beyond what I can write, or in words express, and I hope ever shall be, whilst I am thy dear and loving husband.

John Banks, letter to his wife, 27 July 1668, reprinted in *A Journal of the Life, Labours, Travels and Sufferings (In and for the Gospel) of that Ancient Servant to and Faithful Minister of Jesus Christ, John Banks* (1798), 67.

Love was rarely mentioned in Quaker tracts which proffered advice on the selection of a mate. Indeed, the first impression is that 'love' as understood by Friends was a 'Godly Love' devoid of emotion and any notion

---

[11] ERO, COLTW 1, 27.

[12] EUL, COLTW 1, 201. Friends were advised to use every lawful means to achieve this goal.

[13] EUL, COLMM 34, 144–6 (1695); Crisp MS, fo. 215 (1694); *Journal of the Life of Thomas Storey*, ii. 10–11 (c.1708/9).

[14] PRO, RG6 359, 80. This conclusion is also evident from an examination of matrimonial cases in Quaker minute books.

of romance.[15] But despite the absence of the term in the pamphlets giving advice on matchmaking, love was recognized at an official level as an important feature of marriage. During the Quaker matrimonial ceremony, for instance, the couple made a mutual declaration to be 'loving and faithful to one another'. William Allen told his wife that he would be 'loving and tender', while John Baker in 1681 promised to be a 'faithful and tender husband'.[16] And the appearance of terms such as 'loving wife' in wills and the desire of spouses to be buried next to one another suggest that couples looked upon one another with a marked degree of affection.[17]

That personal attraction was the chief factor which determined the choice of partner among some Quakers is implied by the behaviour of those members who spurned religious considerations and followed the tug of their heartstrings by choosing partners from outside the Society. Ruth Woodward, a Witham Friend, informed her local meeting in 1698 that her affection for another led her to marry out.[18] Another female Friend from Earls Colne expressed the opinion to members in 1700 that, though she well understood the reason for the prohibition against out-marriage, her choice of mate was a personal matter over which the Society had no legitimate concern.[19] The strength of personal affection for partners sometimes outweighed loyalty to the movement.

But what of those who remained loyal and sought a match from among Friends? We can get a fair idea of the attitudes of ordinary Quakers from the Society's books of discipline, which contain accounts of disagreements over marriage proposals. The importance of personal attraction and affection was apparent in the case of John Chandler and Mary Brand in 1672. Having refused Mary permission to marry because John's membership had ceased, the meeting relented on hearing Mary's plea that the decision be reversed, giving as one reason the fact that the couple's 'affection for each other was great'.[20] On another occasion in 1675 Richard Prittlove and Elizabeth Blower requested of the Epping meeting that their proposal of matrimony be withdrawn, 'there not being a true and real love and affection between them'.[21] There is more evidence of this kind. In 1680 Elizabeth Everitt told the meeting in Colchester that she could not marry

[15] Frost, *The Quaker Family in Colonial America*, 162–3.
[16] PRO, RG6 1379, 13; RG6 1391, 42, 47.
[17] ERO, DAEW 30/232, the will of Nicholas Oakman of Hornchurch (1708); PRO, RG6 1262, 179 (1669), RG6 1384, 213 (1669), the burial of John and Grace Day together.
[18] PRO, RG6 1335, 114.   [19] EUL, COGMM 27 (15 Sept. 1700).
[20] ERO, COLTW 1, 37 (1673).
[21] FHL, Waltham Abbey Monthly Meeting Minute (5 July 1675).

Richard Webb, as they had both proposed, since 'she had not love for him, so as to make him her husband'.[22] The previously mentioned John Vent and Mary Christenwheat reveal feelings perhaps nearest to our notion of affection. Though permission to marry had been withheld by the meeting, the couple declared they 'could not find it in their hearts to leave each other'.[23] Often the sympathetic approach of meetings to marriage proposals with which they were not wholly satisfied was determined by the fear that a hard line might drive a couple to seek marriage by a priest.

Of course, the reasons for choosing a mate were various and love might not have figured as largely in the marital calculations of all. Widowed Friends were sometimes motivated as much by practical needs, such as help of a wife to raise children, or simply the desire for companionship.[24] Even so, the Society's willingness to sanction the withdrawal of marriage proposals indicated that love was recognized as an important factor in marriage.

MARRIAGE AND THE LOCAL MEETING

Persons who desire to be married in accordance with the usages of Society are to apply to the clerks of their respective Monthly Meeting for advice as to procedure and for the necessary forms.

Christian Discipline of the Religious Society of Friends in Ireland
(Dublin, 1971), 50.

The Society's oversight upon those who married within the Quaker faith has long been a feature of Quaker discipline. Indeed, in the seventeenth century the tight control exercised by the Quaker business meeting over the steps to matrimony was a factor which sharply distinguished Friends' marriage procedure from that of others. A couple proposing marriage had first to attend their local business meeting, where two Friends were appointed to scrutinize their public and private conduct by directing inquiries to other Quakers and neighbours. Once the good character of the couple was established, and their freedom from any prior engagement confirmed, a certificate granting permission to proceed was issued.[25] This served as an affirmation of the meeting's consent to marriage and was signed by business meeting members. Without this document the initial steps to

---

[22] EUL, COLMM 1, 42 (1680).   [23] EUL, COLTW 1, 85–6.
[24] Edmundson, *Journal*, 161.
[25] EUL, COLTW 1, 103 (1683); ERO, DNF 1/1/1 (11 Oct. 1708); PRO, RG6 978, 19 (1662).

matrimony could not be followed. The process was in several respects similar to the Anglican custom of publishing the banns, since it provided an opportunity for objections to be lodged. However, the stringency with which personal lives of Quakers were examined and the extent to which the decision over marriage lay effectively under the control of the meeting sharply distinguished Quakers from their Anglican counterparts.

Conduct which seemed disreputable to the local meeting, such as swearing oaths, associating with 'separate spirits', indebtedness, or failing to speak in the manner approved of by the Society, was sufficient to postpone or cancel a marriage proposal. Another reason was suspicion of infidelity. The proposal of Jeptha Selly and the widow Mary Sayer, for example, was barred in 1668 on the grounds of their living together in supposed adultery before her husband's decease.[26] For Richard Potter it was the discovery of a church wedding in a previous marriage which he was called upon to explain in 1672.[27] Of course, if a couple were able to prove that the cause of delay was ill-founded or if they displayed sufficient contrition concerning a previous misdemeanour, then permission to solemnize marriage might be forthcoming. However, personal attraction or parental intervention were insignificant compared with the power the Society might exercise over marriage. The meeting was at all times prepared to override a proposal if this was considered to be in the best interests of the Society or indeed of the couple.

During the Sect's earliest years, the obstacles to be negotiated by couples proposing marriage were few.[28] But because the procedure for the oversight of marriage proposals by the meeting was deficient it was sometimes abused. For instance, it was noted that Friends sometimes turned up at meetings and announced that they proposed to take husbands or wives without any prior consultation or investigation by the meeting. The creation of a monthly and quarterly meeting system in the late 1660s, which reflected a greater concern with discipline, put a stop to such behaviour. Evidence of change can be found in Quaker marriage certificates in the county of Essex. During the 1650s and 1660s they indicated little more than a couple's identity and place of marriage and were presumably written to serve as proof of marital status. After 1670 the tone and content of the marriage certificates altered dramatically, corresponding to the increased power vested in the Quaker meeting. The later certificates informed the reader that the couple had attended various meetings when making their proposal, had

[26] EUL, COLTW 1, 16.   [27] Ibid., 33.
[28] Arnold Lloyd, *Quaker Social History* (1950), 54.

sought and obtained the permission of the relevant Friends and kin. However, though the meeting was the crucial determining influence in the marriage procedure, the wishes of Friends proposing marriage were to be considered sympathetically.

SOCIAL STATUS, MOBILITY, AND AGE AT MARRIAGE

Just as the demography of the Quakers cannot be understood without a know-ledge of their history, Quakerism cannot be fully understood without a knowledge of their marrying, giving birth and dying.

Richard T. Vann and David Eversley, *Friends in Life and Death:*
The British and Irish Quakers in the Demographic Transition, 1650–1900
(Cambridge, 1992), 10.

There are other areas where social behaviour and religious belief among the Friends are closely linked but where that relation is not so readily vis-ible to the historian. Friends left no literary accounts of the mobility of members nor of their age at first marriage, though it is possible to get an understanding of Quaker practice indirectly by analysing Quaker records. Unlike contemporary moralists, Friends did not counsel that differences in wealth constituted a serious obstacle to a couple's proposal of marriage. Indeed, the strong sense of community ethos among members and the prac-tice of endogamy may have encouraged marriage across social boundaries. We know from evidence compiled on the social profile of Friends that the sect contained on the one hand weavers and labourers so poor they were unable to contribute to the nationally levied Hearth Tax and on the other hand merchants and clothiers who were more than comfortably placed. Did the Quakers, in contrast to common practice, sanction or perhaps unconsciously promote marriage across social boundaries?

There is no doubt that some Friends were motivated by the concerns of wealth and social position when deciding on a partner. This is implied by the actions of a Quaker meeting in reproving some parents who showed more interest in the size of a marriage portion than the well-being of their children.[29] And to judge from the details of Quaker marriage con-tracts and the care with which they were drawn up, the material gains to be derived from a union were certainly not considered insignificant.[30] Phillip

---

[29] EUL, EQ 27, 14 and 18 May 1722.
[30] CBR, Roll 237 fos. 10–11 (May 1716); ERO, D/ABR 16/46 (1708), Arthur Cotton of Colchester.

Richmond of Roxwell, a wealthy Quaker yeoman, expressed clearly the importance of marrying within the correct social grouping when drawing up his will in 1698. He declared that his wife's inheritance was to be reduced if she took after his death a husband who was worth less than one hundred pounds.[31]

It is difficult to decide whether these are merely individual examples or representative of a wider sentiment among Friends. It is difficult in a local study such as this to measure up to the wide canvas and methodological rigour of Vann and Eversley. However, an analysis of partners' or their families' social groupings based on the Hearth Tax assessments of 1662 and 1671 for one Essex town indicates that a significant number, nearly 40 per cent, married across social status boundaries.[32] In Great Coggeshall 28 per cent of Quakers married across the groupings 'comfortable' and 'prosperous', and a further 11 per cent were joined from the categories of the 'poor' and 'prosperous'. If it is accepted that these figures are representative of Quaker behaviour at large, they indicate that comparability in wealth or social status was not an overriding factor in determining the choice of partner. Quaker insistence on endogamy and the sect's acutely developed self-consciousness probably account for this. The breach of status barriers in Quaker unions would have seemed odd to non-Quaker contemporaries, for it challenged one method by which the social boundaries within society were reinforced.[33]

There were other factors which made Quaker unions seem strange in the seventeenth century. Two demographic features distinguish marriage among Quakers from that among the host community. The first of these is that Friends were extremely mobile in pursuit of partners. In the county of Essex, during the first decade of the movement, between 1655 and 1664, a third of Quaker unions joined Friends from different parishes, but subsequent decades witnessed between a half and three quarters of marriages solemnized with partners from different parishes.[34] Since the Society demanded that marriage be restricted to Quaker partners alone, a high degree of mobility was to be expected. Figures, though of a less reliable nature, suggest that the average age at first marriage among Essex Friends

---

[31] PRO, PROB 11/448/254.

[32] It is possible to trace the partners or families of origin of eighteen couples. Seven couples married across social-status boundaries; two couples involved partners who were from the categories of both the prosperous and the poor. The Hearth Taxes consulted were ERO, Q/RTh1 (1662), Q/RTh5 (1671); PRO, E179/242/22 (1674).

[33] Ingram, *Church Courts, Sex and Marriage*, 136, 141.

[34] The subject is considered in greater detail in Davies, 'The Quakers in Essex', 44–5.

was lower than that in the rest of local society.[35] For Quaker males the average age was 25.3 and for women 24.4. These statistics, intriguing though they are, need to be treated with caution since they are derived from a relatively small sample. Nevertheless, it is tempting to speculate that the Society's prohibition on fornication accounts for these figures which indicate low age at marriage.

[35] The sample is limited and therefore the figures of age at marriage for Essex Quakers must be read with a degree of caution. The definitive study of Quaker demography is Richard T. Vann and David Eversley, *Friends in Life and Death: The British and Irish Quakers in the Demographic Transition, 1650–1900* (Cambridge, 1992), esp. 86–103.

8

Gospel Order

For as they that truly believe receive Christ in all His tenders to the soul, so as true it is that those who receive Him thus, with Him receive power to become the Sons of God; that is, an inward force and ability to do whatsoever He requires; strength to mortify their lusts, control their affections, resist evil motions, deny themselves, and overcome the world when in its most enticing appearances.

William Penn, *No Cross, No Crown*, 2nd edn. (1682), 19.

Be ye therefore perfect, even as your Father which is in heaven is perfect.

Matthew 5: 48.

DISCIPLINE AND MEMBERSHIP

The expectation of the Society was that followers should be able to avoid many of the failings of human nature by strictly adhering to the Quaker inner light. As a movement that had so often condemned the world and its values the sect presumed that Quakers should live a life of purity and righteousness and thus set an example to others. But individual followers sometimes failed to live up to the required standards. The Society developed its own administrative structure to deal with the problem of erring Friends and other matters. This also policed the marriage procedure and serviced the more general needs of members such as care of the poor and supervision of apprenticeships.

According to Friends their 'institutions' for governing and disciplining were not affected by the 'worldly' pollution which vitiated state and ecclesiastical bodies. It was ironic, however, that as the Quaker faith prospered, an increasing concern was shown by the sect's business meetings to regulate the behaviour of members in a manner similar to that of the secular and church courts which they had displaced. The local meeting always kept a close eye upon and sought to redirect those who strayed from the path of righteousness. But the discipline meted out by the local meeting also enabled the Society to distance itself from the actions of members which were considered to have undermined the reputation of the movement in local society.

The steps the movement took to erect a disciplinary framework by which it could exert greater control over the social lives of its members are familiar to historians of Quakerism.[1] The emphasis on individual expression and spiritual fulfilment, initially the principal reason for the religion's success, was to a degree discarded within a generation or so. For spontaneity and personal satisfaction, a demand for uniformity and submission to corporate power is substituted. This development was given a boost after the Restoration by the onset of persecution. However, the growth of Quaker discipline in Essex does not fit the conventional model of sectarian development, for here the movement's approach towards disciplining members was distinctive.

Some notion of a disciplinary process or 'Gospel Order' had existed since the movement's early years but it was not extensive nor organized to any great degree. The crucial step in enabling the Society to police the behaviour of members more effectively was the intervention of George Fox, who, partly in reaction to the John Perrot controversy, urged the creation of a network of particular, monthly, and quarterly meetings in the late 1660s. Perrot had led a significant separatist group within Quakerism, which peaked in 1663, when Perrot openly and vociferously disagreed with Fox as to whether the hat should be worn during prayer. The dispute foreshadowed arguments about the direction the movement should take and led to the establishment of stricter control.[2]

The consensus among historians is that the primary aim of Quaker discipline was to maintain the reputation of the Society; and some have gone so far as to imply that this was the sole purpose of the disciplinary process. This view is consistent with what some modern historians have termed the concept of 'invisible membership'.[3] Backsliders or wrongdoers, it is argued, were looked upon only as 'reputed' or 'esteemed' Quakers; that is the Society in retrospect judged that they were persons in whom the truth had not taken proper root, so that they were not proper Quakers.[4] However, evidence on the Quakers' disciplinary procedure in Essex is remarkably different from this picture.

Meeting records document the behaviour considered disreputable by the Society and the action which was appropriate. Though the allegations by

---

[1] Braithwaite, *Second Period*, chaps. 9 and 12; Bryan Wilson (ed.), *Religious Sects* (1976), 235–6;

[2] Kenneth Carroll, 'John Perrot: Early Quaker Schismatic', Supplement 33, *JFHS* (1971), 83–94.

[3] Vann, *Social Development*, 137–8; Charles F. Carter, 'Unsettled Friends: Church Government and the Origins of Membership', *JFHS* 51 (1967) joins Vann on this.

[4] Vann, *Social Development*, 132.

critics of widespread sexual deviance in Quaker ranks were untrue, there were none the less instances of fornication, cohabitation, illegitimacy, prenuptial pregnancy, adultery, and bigamy which were investigated by business meetings.[5] Of course, a desire to ensure that the reputation of the Society was upheld was one motive for investigating the conduct of Friends, especially when the Society was fearful of the prospect of persecution at the hands of the authorities. None the less, Friends were as much concerned about the spiritual implications of backsliding by their members. The purpose of the disciplinary process was, where possible, to return members to the path of Quaker righteousness.

DENIALS AND DISOWNMENT

When a minor offence occurred, a private visit and reprimand may have been sufficient to satisfy the meeting. Usually two respected Friends were dispatched to visit the culprit first to persuade him or her to recognize the seriousness of the offence. If the meeting decided to pursue the disciplinary process further, a written statement was required from a wrongdoer admitting misconduct. In such cases the home visit was generally a prelude to a request to appear at a business meeting.[6] One such gathering was convened in 1697 at John Ludgater's house in Great Coggeshall, where Mary Tibball was quizzed to discover whether she showed any signs of 'God's judgement' upon her.[7]

The reclamation of the offender was a significant part of the disciplinary procedure. Isaac Anthony, a Friend from Great Coggeshall, was first investigated by his local meeting in 1705 for fornication and was visited repeatedly for two years despite his refusal to acknowledge visiting Friends.[8] A display of contrition was expected of the erring Friends; and this is reflected in the papers of self-condemnation they wrote. If the local meeting thought fit, the statements were retained by the Society for fear of further backsliding. In such an event the testimony was used to demonstrate that the culprit had been out of unity with the Friends. However, wrongdoing was not always an impediment to the Friend's reclamation or return

[5] For example, EUL, COLTW 1, 117 (1684), 73 (1679); ERO, Witham Monthly Meeting Minutes (9 May 1722). EUL, GOGMM 27 (12 Mar. 1705); FHL, BARMM 1 (7 Feb. 1697).

[6] EUL, COGMM 27 (23 Apr. 1710, 7 Mar. 1711). The case of Daniel Wallis.

[7] EUL, COGMM 27 (18 July 1697).

[8] EUL, COGGMM 27 (21 Mar. 1704/5, 21 Nov. 1706).

to the Quaker fold. Indeed, when after a time a backslider's behaviour seemed consistent with the principles of the Society and the prospect of further error seemed unlikely, the written testimonies were excised from the meeting's files.[9] This is a remarkable instance of liberality on the part of Essex Friends towards backsliders. The disciplinary procedure of the sect elsewhere was certainly harsher and the general temper of Friends much less forgiving.

However, outright refusal to acknowledge 'outrunning' led to the meeting issuing a statement of disownment against erring members. The document was first read or sent to the backslider and then dispatched to as many meetings as the Society judged fit. The purpose of the disownment was to dispel any idea that the behaviour was sanctioned by the Society and further to prevent unacceptable actions from damaging the good name of Quakerism. The readiness of some backsliders to submit to the disciplinary procedure depended perhaps less upon the efforts of visiting Friends appointed by the meeting than the realization that social ostracism was the lot of erring members. Friends were told not to meet or communicate with backsliders personally. The renegade Friend John Toldervy recalled in 1656 that he was referred to as 'Judas' in the street by his former co-religionists. Reclaimed Friends admitted that the period of isolation was traumatic, since the community they relied upon for worship and the bulk of their social relationships was no longer welcoming.[10]

SALVATION

A prime motive for the meeting's taking disciplinary measures was the fear that by their actions backsliders had jeopardized their prospect of eternal salvation. Phrases such as the 'condemnation' or 'hurting' of the soul, the 'ruin of my own soul', and 'burden upon my soul' are familiar expressions in the confessions of those who had wandered from the Gospel path.[11] Moreover, the Society feared that the misconduct would be a stumbling block to others, especially to the newly convinced among Friends. The disciplinary procedure and the testimonies which followed served as a warning to others not to repeat the same error. The Quaker Thomas Sloman,

---

[9] EUL, COLTW 1, 272 (1702); EQ 1, 31 (1715); COLTW 1, 2 (1681).

[10] Toldervy, *The Foot out of the Snare*, 42; see also COGMM 27 (26 June 1712; 14 Mar. 1698); COLMM 34, 146 (1691); COLTW 1, 333 (in reverse).

[11] PRO RG6 558, 124 (1692); EUL, COLTW 2 (15 Apr. 1706 (in reverse)); COGMM 27 (2 June 1720).

who fornicated with a maidservant, wrote in his confession that others should not be as 'unwatchful'; and John and Elizabeth Danks went to the extraordinary lengths of circulating and printing their confession among Colchester Friends in 1680 at the price of three farthings a copy.[12]

Disowned and disciplined Friends were reckoned to be out of unity with the Society. They were considered to have detached themselves from membership rather than to have been expelled. 'Out of Truth' or 'not in fellowship' were the terms used to describe them in Quaker records. Elizabeth Hickford, a fornicator, described herself in 1695 as having 'broken myself off from the unity of his [God's] people'.[13] Two Witham Friends, John Rutledge and Sarah Goodson, who contravened Quaker convention by marrying in the parish church, were depicted as having 'no claim' to truth and 'having denied Truth by going from it themselves'.[14] While the testimonies confirm that Friends had detached themselves from unity, this did not amount to their never having been looked upon as members. This position is exemplified by the case of two Saffron Walden Friends, Francis Emmerson and Sarah Pettit, who were described by the meeting in 1714: 'Whilst they walked orderly were counted persons of unity with us, the people called Quakers . . . but now . . . they are none of us'.[15]

Disowned or backsliding Friends were not considered to have forfeited membership in perpetuity. A display of remorse and genuine repentance was sufficient to justify renewed membership. Ann Blaykling, who had wavered in her loyalty to Quakerism, wrote in a personal testimony that she was sure the Lord would preserve her.[16] Elizabeth Hickford professed that she had felt the Lord's righteous judgement and knew implicitly that redemption was not to be denied her.[17] The conduct of the meeting towards Jane Freeman of Sampford epitomizes the position of Friends in this regard. Though she was disowned in 1707 for ill-treatment of an aged father and associating with men of questionable character, the meeting still judged her to be capable of returning to unity so long as she displayed 'proof' of a 'chaste life and conversation'.[18]

The Society believed that all members had the potential for spiritual growth. If they could follow the light according to their potential, they would follow the Quaker 'truth'. Individuals could grow in an understanding of the truth or fall away from it. When Richard Claridge, a senior Friend,

[12] EUL, COLTW 1, 327–8 (in reverse) (*c.*1685); COLTW 2, 77, 80.
[13] PRO, RG6 1335, 122.   [14] ERO, D/NF 1/1/2 (12 May 1707).
[15] ERO, T/A 261/1/1 (29 Dec. 1714).
[16] EUL, COLTW 1 (in reverse), 339 (1674).   [17] PRO, RG6 1335, 122.
[18] ERO, T/A 261/1/11, Thaxted Women's Meeting.

was resident at Barking in the early eighteenth century he wrote in the back of the meeting book an account of the Quaker ideal of the church.

The Church in Christ Jesus is a Spiritual Body or Society and hath many members, and these of severall growths for several services. But the diversity of growth and Services are all from the same Spiritual Head. Even Christ himself, who assigns every one his Place and Service and disposeth to everyone as he pleaseth for his Glory the good . . . So that there will be no Schism in the body, but the Members will have the same one, one of another, whether they be Eyes, Hands, Head or Feet; yea, those very Members what seem to be least honourable and moste feeble will be thought necessary.[19]

The Society recognized that it contained a variety of individuals in different states of spiritual growth. Those who fell from the Gospel path could be welcomed back into the Quaker fold if the light within was rekindled. That members possessed different understanding of the truth was not tantamount to saying that they had never been members, though the Society could distinguish between those in membership and those without. Absence from the established church and refusal to pay church dues were essential indicators. Maturity in the truth was also symbolized by adherence to the sect's social testimonies regarding clothes, speech, and deportment. Failure to heed the Quakers' moral injunctions also indicated the extent to which an individual had been unsuccessful in pursuit of righteousness.

Much of the evidence on the development of the Society in Essex confirms the validity of established theories on sectarian evolution. For example, as the movement became settled, the freedom of individual action was eroded. Even so, there are significant divergences from what one might have expected from these theories and from general studies of the evolution of Quakerism. By comparison with their co-religionists elsewhere, Essex Friends appear to have shown an extraordinary tolerance towards their fallen brethren.[20] Not only did they accept the voluntary return of erring members so long as a deeply-felt contrition was evident; they also held out the prospect that disowned Friends might again join the Quaker fold. The meetings also showed an unexpected understanding of the wishes of those for whom love was the chief motive in marriage, though this was a factor not necessarily sufficient on its own to enable marriage among Friends to proceed. Some historians of Quakerism have pointed to the system of discipline as a chief cause of the movement's failure to halt decline.[21] While

---

[19] FHL, BARMM 1 (6 May 1701).   [20] Vann, *Social Development*, 129, 137–8.
[21] J. S. Rowntree, *Quakerism: Past and Present* (1859), 62–5, 94; Braithwaite, *Second Period*, 633–4.

denial or disownment could be the final outcome of backsliding, the sect seems to have shown a remarkable tenderness towards erring members. Indeed, it is more likely that the system of discipline was responsible for maintaining the good health of Quakerism than its decline. In Essex the Quaker movement continued to expand alongside the growth of Quaker discipline. The chief causes of Quaker decline must be sought elsewhere.[22] In this sense the experience of the sect in Essex diverges from theories that explain the source of sectarian decline by emphasizing the process of institutionalization.[23]

The study of Essex sources suggests previous explanations for sectarian development have been insufficiently sensitive to local factors in different regions; perhaps we should accept that the movement might have exhibited different patterns of development in different regions because of a variety of local and other circumstances.

---

[22] See Chap. 12 below and Conclusion.

[23] T. F. O'Dea and Janet O'Dea Aviad, *The Sociology of Religion*, 2nd edn. (Englewood Cliffs, NJ, 1983), 5, 7.

9

Spreading Forth the Truth

PAMPHLET WARS

at the sign of the *Black-spread Eagle* near *Pauls* . . . you may be furnished by such writings, books and pamphlets that shall deny God, Christ, Spirit, Word, Ordinance, Resurrection, Heaven Hell, what not? Brethren, I shall give you a sad view of some of those wares, though I do not advise the buying of any of them but beseech you to abhor and detest them . . . take heed what you hear so also what you read.

William Grigge, *The Quakers' Jesus* (1658), 57.

Here is a great want of books that might be serviceable in spreading forth the Truth. Now I leave it to thee, my dear sister, whatever way thou may seest best, that some books be sent to this land, with my dear love. I desire my salutation to all the Children of Light, &.

Edward Burrough to Margaret Fell, 5th ll m 1655 Waterford, FHL, Swarthmoor MS 3/16.

Friends took advantage of the freedom to preach and publish which followed the breakdown of censorship after the Civil War and the sect was unusual among the separatist congregations of the time in that it placed an extraordinary premium upon the printing and dissemination of its own literature. Testimony to this is provided by the remarkable number of Quaker books and pamphlets, almost four thousand in number, which poured from the press before the end of the seventeenth century.[1] Indeed some contemporaries argued that the apparent ease with which the new movement won converts could be explained by Friends' constant proselytizing in print. John Gaskin, an irascible and inveterate opponent of Friends, suggested in 1660 that it was Quaker diligence in 'writing and printing so many books' that accounted for the sect's popularity.[2]

---

[1] Friends had published 3,750 titles by 1700. See Barbour and Roberts, *Early Quaker Writings*, 5. For an analysis of the types of Quaker writings published between 1650 and 1699 see the 'Appendix' compiled by David Runyon, ibid., 567–76. See also Margaret Spufford, 'First steps in Literacy: The Reading and Writing Experiences of the Humblest Seventeenth-Century Spiritual Autobiographers', *Social History*, 4 (1979), 407 n. 2.

[2] John Gaskin, *A Just Defence and Vindication of Gospel Ministers* (1660), To The Reader.

In the following pages it will be suggested that the Society's desire to avoid the worldly contamination of members influenced the determination of Quakers to publish so many books and pamphlets, and the levels of education and literacy among male and female Friends. Quaker books and pamphlets allowed Friends to evangelize, but also, by reading and contemplation, to fortify themselves with the truth. Quaker schools and teachers acted as barriers between the children of Friends and outsiders. And Quaker literacy rates reflected in large part Quaker separatism, since an incentive to improve literacy in the sect was provided by the need to inculcate members with the values of the faith, which were acquired by reading the scriptures and Quaker books.

The circulation of Quaker literature certainly vexed the Church and parish clergy. In this respect John Gaskin's treatise, though no doubt tainted by exaggeration, is indicative of official alarm. 'There is a thousand of their printed books published every week', he noted, 'and most of them given away . . . to delude ignorant people'.[3] The civil authorities were as much frightened as their religious counterparts by the pamphlet campaigns waged by Friends. When the evangelist James Parnel and John Isaac, a local Friend from Halstead parish, were arrested in 1655, the indictment against them at the Essex Assize Court noted anxiously that in addition to interrupting worship there, both carried certain 'false and scandalous papers, writings and pamphlets'. Justices were also worried about the nature of the books and pamphlets that were dispersed by the sect at their meetings for worship.[4]

To judge from the surviving evidence, it appears that Quaker works were distributed to parishioners and enquirers in large numbers. That the dissemination of Quaker literature was considered a priority by the sect is evident from those occasions when meetings organized collections to fund distribution free of charge. There was also some discussion as to the most appropriate location for the sale of Quaker books and pamphlets, presumably with the aim of selling as many as possible.[5] Moreover, entries in Journals and other accounts confirm that an acquaintance with Quaker literature was often a cause of conversion to Quakerism or a spur to further interest

[3] Ibid.
[4] PRO, Assi 35/96/2, No. 5 (11 Aug. 1655); Fox, *Journal*, 213; Christopher Wade, *Quakerism Slain Irrecoverably* (1657), Postscript.
[5] EUL, COLTW I, 241 (1699), 12–13 (1667); COLMM 34 (29 May 1678); FHL, MMS, i. 165 (1680); Portfolio MS 4/72; Crouch, *Posthuma Christiana*, 91; William Penn, *An Account of William Penn's Travels in Holland and Germany* (1694), 45–6; William Dundas, *A Few Words of Truth from the Spirit of the Truth* (1673), 3, 9–10, 11.

in the movement.[6] Friends were acutely aware of the power of the printed word; for instance, the newly convinced Thomas Story, prohibited by his father from seeking the company of Friends, was sent a small parcel of Quaker books to sustain him in isolation.[7]

That the Quakers were successful in propagating their particular doctrines via pamphlet campaigns is also evident from the reaction of their direct competitors. William Thomas, the rector of Ubley in Somerset, was much troubled in 1656 by the dissemination of Quaker books, which he thought assisted the spread of the new religion. He denounced the Quakers' 'Corrupt and corrupting books, Satan's Library; which yet are not chained and fixed, but flying Books; purposely made little, that they may be made nimble, and pass with more speed, and at an easy rate to infect the Nation'.[8] John Faldo, a leading Congregationalist, argued that a way had to be found of countering the Quaker strategy. He was wary, as were many others, of the snares which Quakers set for supposedly simple-minded parishioners. He wrote in 1673:

By this course have the Quakers more increased in the country, than by all others; for when you shall find one sheet against them, you may find a hundred of their pamphlets which are generally put into their hands if a Quakers at the cheap rate of accepting: High poyson taken into the body, and delusions into the soul, are ever dear and costly . . .[9]

At times the secular and ecclesiastical powers acted in unison to check the spread of Quaker propaganda. According to the Colchester Friend Stephen Crisp, the clergy in Essex petitioned magistrates to suppress what they termed the spread of 'heretical books', and in 1656 at the Quarter Sessions in Essex the justices received orders to check the 'damnable opinions' of the sect both as they were preached and as they were published.[10] So alarmed were some local clergy by the appetite of parishioners for the sect's literature that they took the initiative and challenged Quaker propagandists head on by publishing their own pamphlets attacking Quaker theology and practice, which they hoped might serve as an antidote to the Quaker infection. Hundreds of pamphlets against Friends were issued and

---

[6] Henry Lampe, *An Apothecary Turned Quaker* (1895), 47–8; Henry Borke, *A Few Words* (1659), 9; Haworth, *The Quaker Converted to Christianity*, 37.

[7] *Journal of the Life of Thomas Story*, i. 88–9.

[8] William Thomas, *Rayling Rebuked* (1656), Epistle.

[9] Faldo, *A Vindication of Quakerism No Christianity*, Preface; EUL, COLMM 34, 29–30 (1678), Crisp MS, fo. 268ʳ; Supplementary Papers, 134 (1711); Thomas P. O'Malley, 'The Press and Quakerism, 1653–1689', *JFHS* 54 (1979), 174.

[10] EUL, Crisp MS, fo. 260; Allen, *Essex Quarter Sessions Order Book*, 88.

many of their authors called upon parishioners to shun Quaker literature or at the very least to give the teachings of the mainstream religion a fair hearing.[11] The efforts of these disgruntled clerics must have met with some success. The recollections of Josiah Langdale reveal that he was convinced that Quaker pamphlets held some kind of malevolent spell that made those who read them powerless to resist. In the long run Langdale was unable to avoid succumbing to the lure of Quakerism, but he thought prior to his conversion in 1693 that:

any time I had met with a Book I had thought was of a Quaker writing, immediately I would shut it, and lay it by lest I should be deluded or drawn to the Belief of Quakers . . .[12]

It is evident that pamphlets were an important tool in the propaganda war waged by both sides. Friends in particular deployed this literary form with a great deal of finesse not only to win new members but also to defend the reputation of the Society in the local society. For instance, when a hostile cleric published a work against Friends, or, as on one occasion, when a town's library contained literature which was critical of the Society, the Friends moved quickly to counter the threat that was posed by circulating Quaker literature in defence.[13] Friends also used books to bolster the morale of their own members. A meeting which felt that members were backsliding, for example, in respect of the Quaker testimony regarding tithe payments or over marrying out, would acquire Quaker works deprecating the practice and pass them among followers so as to bolster wavering convictions.[14]

The great volume of literature penned by Friends and the speed with which Quaker detractors responded suggest that a battle was being fought for the minds and souls of a vulnerable and largely literate audience. Given this, widespread evidence of book and pamphlet ownership among ordinary Quakers might be expected, but surprisingly this is not borne out by much of the primary evidence. An examination of the substantial number

[11] William Haworth, *An Antidote Against the Poysonous and Fundamental Error of the Quakers* (1676), fo. A2ʳ⁻ᵛ; John Bewick, *An Answer to a Quakers Seventeen Heads of Queries* (1660), Dedication; Gaskin, *A Just Defence*, To The Reader; Thomas Welde, *A Further Discovery* (Gateside, 1654), 90; Jeremiah Ives, *Innocence Above Impudency* (1656), To the Reader; Keith Wrightson and David Levine, *Poverty and Piety in an English Village: Terling, 1525–1700*, 153.   [12] FHL, MS Box 10 (10).
[13] EUL, EQ 1, 2 (1711); COLTW 2, 7 (1706), 26 (1711), 117 (1713); Supplementary Papers, 134 (1711); FHL, MMS, v. 30 (1687), xiii. 162 (1699).
[14] FHL, BARMM 1 (6 Oct. 1698); ERO, TA 261/1/1 (26 Dec. 1704); EUL, Supplementary Papers, 64 (1704).

of Quaker wills and lesser number of inventories which survive from the sect in the county of Essex suggest that few Friends possessed a substantial number of books and pamphlets. Arthur Cotton, a Colchester merchant, bequeathed in 1708 a Great Bible to his wife and a library for distribution among Friends. The inventory of the erstwhile Colchester Friend Benjamin Furly recorded a collection of over two thousand works.[15] Elsewhere, there are sporadic references to the Bible, a few other titles, and one mention of Foxe's *Book of Martyrs*.[16] This evidence does not confirm the expectation that followers were eager consumers of Quaker literature. However, it would be mistaken to conclude that the absence of books and pamphlets indicated a high level of illiteracy or of rank-and-file indifference to Quaker literature. The paucity of Quaker works mentioned in these sources can probably be accounted for by their being too cheap to be noted or by lack of inclination on the part of an appraiser to record them.[17] It was probably the exceptional number of books owned by Cotton and Furly which was the reason for the attention drawn to the content of their libraries.

The literary evidence describing the wide circulation of Quaker and anti-Quaker polemics cannot be disregarded. Indeed, accounts of the delivery of significant quantities of books and pamphlets to local meetings in Essex suggest that Quaker literature was available and sought after by Friends. We know that twenty-five books were dispatched to the county from London in 1672, thirty-seven in 1673, the same number in 1677, and a further twenty in 1678.[18] The Quarterly Meeting for the county also took delivery of over one hundred copies of Robert Barclay's *Apology* in 1700.[19] Earlier, in 1667, the meeting in Colchester town emphasized the need to purchase all James Parnel's publications with the intention of making them available to followers in the town.[20] Though local Friends or parishioners sometimes purchased books from shopkeepers, most of the sect's publications remained in the possession of the local meeting.[21] It was

[15] ERO, D/ABR 16/46; Charles R. Simpson, 'Benjamin Furly and his Library', *JFHS* 11 (1914), 70–4.

[16] PRO, Prob 11/382/233, the will of John Furly (1684); ERO, D/AMR 7/1, the will of William Sewell of Pebmarsh (1678).

[17] For a discussion of this point see D. G. Vaisey, 'Probate Inventories and Provincial Retailers in the Sixteenth Century', in Philip Riden (ed.), *Probate Records in the Local Community* (Gloucester, 1985), 101; Jonathan Barry, 'Popular Culture in Seventeenth-Century Bristol', in Barry Reay (ed.), *Popular Culture in Seventeenth-Century England* (1985), 66–8.

[18] FHL, MYM, i. 4, 62; EUL, COLMM 34, 32–3, COLMM 1, 2.

[19] EUL, Supplementary Papers, 15 (1700).   [20] EUL, COLTW 1, 14.

[21] For example, see EUL, COGMM 27 (17 July 1709); Supplementary Papers, 13 (12 Oct. 1710); PRO, DNF 1/1/1 (13 Oct. 1707).

probably through borrowing that most Friends in the later seventeenth century became familiar with Quaker works; these were held by the organization locally in order to furnish a network of meeting libraries.

Evidence of the quantity and type of literature borrowed by Friends survives from the early eighteenth century. The best measurement of book-lending is to be found in the archives of the Particular Meeting at Maldon from 1707 to 1711. It is clear that the printed works loaned by this meeting's library were varied in subject matter, with authors pondering such weighty questions as the legitimacy of tithe payments, mixed marriages, and the best method of raising children in the Quaker faith. Also borrowed by Friends were a significant number of Quaker autobiographies, an attack on the Quaker apostate George Keith, and some works by non-Quaker authors. An idea of the level of borrowing can be gathered by comparing membership of the local meeting with the names of those who were entered as having borrowed books from the meeting library. It appears that at one time or another all Friends in the Maldon meeting had books from the Quaker repository, while many Friends had in their possession several copies at once.[22] The existence of Quaker libraries and lists of borrowers in meeting records suggest that ordinary Friends were keen to be acquainted with the Society's literature.

To Friends, books served a dual role: they were a means whereby new converts were won to the faith, and they were also used for the internal purpose of reinforcing the values of the group, through either inculcating Quaker values or defending the reputation of the faith against the attacks of critics. However, the question remains why it was that Friends in particular placed such emphasis on the publication and circulation of their written works. It is evident that Quaker pamphlet campaigns were successful in winning new converts; and this may have fed off itself, as success encouraged Friends to push ever further with this strategy. But the key to Quaker perseverance with their pamphlet campaigns lay elsewhere. Friends judged the power of the written word as set down in their own works to have an efficacy as great as that of hearing Quaker ministers preach or of reading the Bible itself (see Plate 6). The spirit was at work in the

[22] PRO, RG6 1335, 57–9. In February 1707 twelve Friends were noted as borrowers by the meeting: John Pearce was lent four books and his wife Joan one; John Baker borrowed six, and Thomas King and Michael Corder two each. The rest possessed one book each. In the same month for 1709 the meeting lent books to eleven Friends: seven had one book and the remainder between two and three books each. Finally, in October 1711 the records show that sixteen Friends borrowed books: the majority had just one with five Friends borrowing five apiece. From what is known of the membership of Maldon Meeting, it seems that most Friends were in possession of books at one time or another.

PLATE 6. From Benjamin Keach, *The Grand Impostor Discovered* (1675), facing
p. 193

writings of Friends. One early critic of Quakers remarked that '*they equal
their books and pamphlets* (though commonly stuft with non-sense and railings, even with wicked errors) *to the Holy Scriptures*'.[23]

One should not forget the significance of oral transmission when assessing the reasons for the success of the new faith. The recollections of the
'first publishers of truth' indicate that preaching was more important in
winning new converts.[24] None the less, the Society placed greater emphasis
on propagating the message in print than did other dissenting congregations, and Quaker publications were recognized as important and integral
to the sect's missionary campaigns.

QUAKER LITERACY

We frequently recommend that Friends should be diligent in providing schools
for the Education of their Youth: not only in useful and necessary learning but
also to bring them up in the fear of God, and in a sense of his holy life upon their
spirits, and in frequent reading the Holy Scriptures and other good Books.

June 1718: Epistle to Friends from Yearly Meeting.

[23] Clapham, *A Full Discovery and Confutation*, 8; Comber, *Christianity No Enthusiasm*, 142.
[24] *FPT*, 96.

The impetus given to Bible-reading by the emergence and spread of Protestantism was once considered the primary factor which promoted the acquisition of literacy. The substance of the argument was that reforming divines counselled congregations to read the Scriptures so that they could develop a direct and personal relationship with God, the result being a significant growth in literacy rates across the board.[25] However, the significance of religion in fostering reading and writing ability has been re-examined of late, with critics countering that the drive for literacy was as much, if not more, dependent on a person's gender or social status.[26] The data on Quaker literacy will be examined within the context of the debate concerning the growth of literacy in early modern society. Quakerism certainly generated a far higher level of literacy among its members than was the norm in English society, and what emerges about the factors which encouraged Quaker literacy throws valuable new light on the general debate.

However, on the basis of the Essex evidence it is not possible to calculate the literacy rates of the earliest converts. The sources which allow detailed statistical analysis survive only for the late seventeenth and early eighteenth centuries. And we cannot as yet claim with any statistical certainty that the propaganda efforts of Quakers and their critics were indicative of a widespread reading public. We shall have to await a full-scale statistical analysis of literacy rates among the earliest Friends before we can decide the matter one way or the other. The present section is limited to assessing the literacy rates among followers from the end of the seventeenth century and in particular the role of Quakerism in determining them.

What exactly do we mean when we talk of literacy? Before we examine the evidence we need to be clear what is being discussed in the pages that follow. The capability to affix one's name to a document has been recognized by historians of literacy in the early modern period as an indicator of reading ability. The reasoning for this is that since the skill of reading was taught separately from that of writing, a signature probably indicated that an individual who could subscribe his or her name to a document had at least achieved a competent degree of reading ability. This is admittedly

---

[25] Lawrence Stone, 'Literacy and Education in England, 1640–1900', *Past and Present*, 42 (1969), 76–7; R. A. Houston, *Literacy in Early Modern Europe: Culture and Education, 1500–1800* (1988), 35–7.

[26] For a discussion of this see Houston, *Literacy in Early Modern Europe*, chap. 7, 120–9 and David Cressy, *Literacy and the Social Order: Reading and Writing in Tudor and Stuart England* (Cambridge, 1980), chaps. 6. and 7.

TABLE 1. *Literacy Rates of Male Quakers in Colchester, 1696*

	Percentage	Total
Male literacy	81.8	125

Source: Association Roll

a crude measurement, for it may mask a whole range of reading skills. None the less, it provides a valuable and so far the only plausible statistical method of calculating literacy rates in the early modern age.[27] It is with the ability to read that this section of the chapter is primarily concerned, and it is this skill which in the main is referred to when literacy is discussed.

Two main sources from the county of Essex provide evidence about literacy of this sort among Friends. The first of these is the 'Affirmations' of loyalty to which Friends subscribed at various times. Second, and more important, are the records kept by monthly business meetings which contain the signatures of Friends proposing marriage; these latter documents are particularly useful, since they contain the signatures of women as well as men and are not obviously skewed toward any one social group. However, they have their limitations: they survive only for certain areas within the county, and some Friends failed to subscribe their names or had them written in by the hand of the meeting clerk. It has thus been possible only to measure a percentage range of literacy for certain meetings. It has been calculated that by the middle of the seventeenth century 30 per cent of Englishmen were literate. For the county of Essex an analysis of literacy among menfolk suggests that the number able to sign their names rose from 37 per cent in the 1640s to 46 per cent in the 1690s.[28] However, this latter figure is still low when compared to what is known of the levels of Quaker literacy in the county.

The Association Roll of 1696[29] provides a snapshot of literacy among male Friends at Colchester, with slightly over 80 per cent of the community, 125 strong in all, able to subscribe their names (Table 1). In a similar affirmation drawn up by Friends in Colchester in 1723 only one out

---

[27] Cressy, *Literacy and the Social Order*, chap. 3, 53–4; R. S. Schofield, 'The Measurement of Literacy in Pre-Industrial England', in Jack Goody (ed.), *Literacy in Traditional Societies* (Cambridge, 1975), 319. For criticisms of this approach see Patrick Collinson, 'The Significance of Signatures', *Times Literary Supplement* (9 Jan. 1981), 31 and Keith Thomas, 'The Meaning of Literacy', in Gerd Baumann (ed.), *The Written Word: Literacy in Transition* (Oxford, 1986), 101–3.

[28] Cressy, *Literacy and The Social Order*, 99–100.   [29] PRO, C/213/264/3, 17.

TABLE 2. *Literacy Rates of Male and Female Quakers in Colchester, 1723*

	Percentage	Total
Male literacy	96.3	27
Female literacy	69.0	22

Source: Affirmation of Loyalty

TABLE 3. *Literacy Rates of Male Quakers from the Monthly and Two Weeks Meetings in Essex, 1697–1730*

Meeting	Percentage male literacy	Total sample	Date
Saffron Walden	66–86	75	1700–1730
Witham	81	43	1697–1702
Coggeshall two weeks meetings	89	38	1711–1725
Coggeshall monthly meetings	78–88	50	1699–1709

of twenty-seven Quaker males affixed a mark instead of signing (Table 2). This was Thomas Pewter, a baymaker, who also failed to sign the earlier 1696 roll.[30] To judge from these two pieces of evidence there seems to have been a progressive advance in male literacy among Quakers in the town.

Male literacy rates can also be calculated for the Monthly Meetings at Saffron Walden and Witham, and the Two Weeks and Monthly Meetings at Coggeshall.[31] These are more representative than the 'Affirmations' because they range over a longer time-span, include the signing ability of both genders, and derive from a wider geographical area.

The years during which the intentions of marriage were recorded by the various meetings do not correspond exactly, but they are sufficiently close to be of value (Table 3). As with the 'Affirmations', they suggest a comparatively high level of literacy. The degree of literacy among male Friends at Walden Meeting was between 66 and 86 per cent, at Witham 81 per cent, for the Two Weeks Meeting at Coggeshall 89 per cent, and for the Monthly Meeting in the same town between 78 and 88 per cent.

[30] CBR, Order Book, 320–3 (23 Sept. 1723, 19 Dec. 1723).
[31] These meetings contain a good cross section of Friends from urban and rural areas. For an analysis of literacy according to geographical area see R. A. Houston, 'The Development of Literacy in Northern England, 1640–1750', *Economic History Review*, 2nd ser., 35 (1982), 211, Table 8.

On the face of it there seems to be a correlation between Quakerism and high levels of literacy among male Friends. But is it correct to assume that Quakerism was of itself a force which promoted the acquisition of literacy? Perhaps the high literacy level among Quakers was the result of other factors. Could the prevalence of reading skills among Friends be better explained by their position in the social hierarchy rather than by their religious inclination? Studies have shown that literacy was greatest among the gentry and members of the professional classes who constituted the top of the social order, while it was least prevalent amongst those at the bottom of the scale like labourers and the poor.[32] Since many Friends were drawn from the middling ranks, where literacy skills were relatively prevalent, there was a good chance that members of the sect would be able to read. Economic factors certainly need to be recognized as important when assessing the reasons for literacy among Friends and in society at large. For instance, poverty was without doubt a serious impediment to the acquisition of literacy by Friends even though the Society sought to compensate for this. Some poor families were reluctant to allow their children a Quaker education even when the cost was to be borne by the local meeting, for they feared that the loss of potential earnings to the family economy would be too great.[33]

However, when searching for the cause of the particularly high literacy rates among Friends, it would be mistaken to conclude that the influence of Quakerism was slight or of a lesser significance than other factors. The Society put an extraordinary effort into educating poorer Friends, and this was to benefit members considerably. Moreover, social status alone cannot account for the consistently high reading ability of Quaker members. It is the contention here that Quakerism raised literacy levels independently of other social factors. There was a culture of Quakerism which encouraged high levels of reading and possibly writing ability among followers. Positive evidence for this argument is to be found when assessing the influence of Quakerism on the literacy rates of female members.

Quaker Women and Literacy

Research indicates that most women in the seventeenth century were illiterate, that is, unable to sign their names. David Cressy, who has written an influential study of literacy, has calculated that only 11 per cent of women

---

[32] Houston, *Literacy in Early Modern Europe*, 130–4.
[33] ERO, Supplementary Papers, 99 (1707); COLTW 2, 355 (1723).

TABLE 4. *Literacy Rates of Female Quakers from the Monthly and Two Weeks Meetings in Essex, 1697–1730*

Meeting	Percentage female literacy	Total sample	Date
Saffron Walden	57–81	75	1700–1730
Witham	43–66	32	1697–1702
Coggeshall monthly meetings	67	38	1711–1725
Coggeshall two weeks meetings	58–68	50	1699–1709

were able to sign their names in the diocese of Norwich during the period from 1580 to 1700. Another valuable piece of evidence on female literacy is provided by Keith Wrightson and David Levine in their local study of the Essex parish of Terling. They discovered that all the women who lived there between 1600 and 1660 were illiterate. They found that between 1660 and 1690 there was some improvement, though only around 30 per cent of women were able to sign their names.[34] It is widely accepted that gender was a crucial factor in determining access to education and this in the main explains the poor literacy rates among females in general.

However, by contrast with women in English society at large, the literacy rates among female Quakers were extremely high. Even at Witham Monthly Meeting, where the figure for the literacy level of Quaker women was the lowest, a significant number, between 43 and 66 per cent, were able to sign their names. At Walden Meeting female literacy was between 57 and 81 per cent, at Coggeshall Two Weeks Meeting 56 to 68 per cent, and at Coggeshall Monthly Meeting the figure was 67 per cent. Literacy among female Quakers compared favourably with that of English males in general and is not so much at odds with the figures calculated for Quaker men (Table 4). The percentage of Colchester women who signed the Affirmation of Loyalty in 1723 confirms the impression of high literacy among female friends (Table 2). The most plausible explanation is that the influence of Quakerism produced high literacy rates among these women compared with others.

That so many female Friends were able to write is not surprising. Quakers disregarded to a degree the conventional gender role assigned to females, because of the heightened status accorded to women by the faith. As

[34] Cressy, *Literacy and the Social Order*, 119, 120–1; Wrightson and Levine, *Terling*, 148.

preachers, women were given a status equal to that of men, for the Holy Spirit recognized no gender barrier.[35] They also often nurtured Quakerism by fulfilling the important duty of passing on reading and writing skills from one generation to the next and socializing Quaker children into the values of the faith. Several Quaker women were cited to the church courts for teaching without a licence. One of these, Elizabeth Wiseman from Pebmarsh, Essex was reported in 1676 and again in 1678 to be teaching with 'Quaking books'.[36] Another, Thomazin Hockley, a Quaker widow, refused in 1684 to send her pupils to be catechized.[37] Husbands too entrusted wives with the responsibility of educating children. In his will of 1664 Arthur Condor, a baker, directed his wife to act as 'tutor' to their son.[38] Later, in 1683, George Guyon, a well-off clothier from Great Coggeshall, required his wife to undertake the 'tuition' of their daughter until she attained the age of fourteen.[39]

The experience of Quaker women seems to have contrasted markedly with that of their peers in seventeenth-century society and sits uneasily with what we know to have been the restricting effects of gender on women across a whole range of social situations. However, there is some evidence in Quaker records that their gender might have limited the type of literacy which Quaker women were to acquire. For example, the indenture of one female apprentice who was funded by the local Quaker meeting revealed that she was to be taught to sew and read English but not to write.[40] The education of Quaker women might then have conformed somewhat to the gender stereotype. There is also a suggestion that after the Restoration the demands of the Society for uniformity somewhat restricted the freedom allowed Quaker women.[41]

But we ought to be cautious about accepting the proposition that after 1660 Quaker women satisfied only conventional gender roles. The Society was confident enough after 1660 to encourage women to debate with ministers in other dissenting churches without the support of male

---

[35] Opponents were quick to remark upon the elevated status of women in the movement. On this see, for instance, Miller, *Antichrist in Man*, 27; Hallywell, *An Account of Familism*, 122–3; Fowler, *A Sober Answer*, 30. See also P. Collinson, *The Birthpangs of Protestant England: Religious and Cultural Change in the Sixteenth and Seventeenth Centuries* (1988), 75.

[36] ERO, D/AMV 5 (Sept. 1676, June 1678).   [37] ERO, D/AEV 13 fo. 16ᵛ.

[38] ERO, D/ACW 17/175.   [39] PRO, Prob 11/374/295.

[40] EUL, COLMM 1, 17 (1674). On the educational prospects of women in general see Rosemary O'Day, *Education and Society 1500–1800: The Social Foundations of Education in Early Modern Britain*, (1982), chap. 6; Christine Trevitt, *Women and Quakerism in the Seventeenth Century* (York, 1991), 115–30; Sarah Heller Mendelson, *The Mental World of Stuart Women: Three Studies* (Brighton, 1987), 187.

[41] Elaine Hobby, *Virtue of Necessity: English Women's Writing 1649–88* (1988), 26.

colleagues.[42] To judge from their literacy rates alone, Quaker women were far from conforming to the stereotypical role attributed to their sex. Quaker records also indicate that on several occasions it was wives alone, not husbands, who possessed the skill of reading within the family.[43] Elsewhere there are indications that the desire to spread the skills of 'reading, writing and casting accounts' was not limited to the male gender.[44] Moreover, unusually for this time, many female Friends, most notably Margaret Fell, the wife of George Fox, as well as several other women, published pamphlets and journals expounding the Quaker faith or recalling their travails endured on behalf of the new movement.[45] However, while the status of women in the movement may account for the removal of barriers to female literacy, it does not explain what was so unusual about the culture of Quakerism itself as to produce such high signing ability among both male and female Friends.

There were several reasons for wanting to be literate in the seventeenth century. In a society where the market-place assumed an ever greater prominence, reading and writing abilities were an obvious advantage. For instance, when one was buying and selling property or disposing of wealth it was better to oversee business arrangements and documents personally than to rely on the word of another. Friends were as susceptible to these arguments as others. The Society was also aware that literacy skills heightened considerably the chance of gaining employment and a worthwhile trade, which is one reason why Friends were eager that poor members should acquire such skills.[46] It would be mistaken to play down economic factors in explaining the spread of literacy in general. Indeed, it is likely that many of those who joined the ranks of Friends would in any case have acquired literacy skills whether they were Quakers or not. None the less, there are several reasons for supposing that it was the influence of the Quaker faith which was decisive in producing such a remarkably high level of reading ability among sect followers.

---

[42] Allen, Ludgater, *et al.*, *The Glory of Christ's Light Within*, 11. See Jean E. Mortimer, 'Quaker Women in the Eighteenth Century: Opportunities and Constraints', *JFHS* 57 (1996), 228–59 and Mack, *Visionary Women*, esp. 286–93, which challenges the standard assumptions about the limited role of Quaker women after the Restoration.

[43] This was particularly evident from the intentions of marriage records of the Coggeshall Monthly and Two Weeks Meetings.

[44] EUL, Supplementary Papers, 23 (1700). On the long-term significance of female sectarianism see Patricia Crawford, 'The Challenges to Patriarchalism: How did the Revolution Affect Women?', in John Morrill (ed.), *The Revolution and Restoration: England in the 1650s*, (1992), 124–8.   [45] On this see Trevitt, *Women and Quakerism*, chap. 2.

[46] ERO, D/ACR 10/189 (1685). This will of Cyprian Cornwall of Terling is evidence of this emphasis.

To begin with, the large number of books and pamphlets published by the movement suggests that Quakerism fostered an expectation of reading ability. The movement was also important in promoting literacy skills in other respects. For example, it was the hope of George Fox, one of the chief Quakers, that the written words of suffering Friends would inspire future generations to follow the example of fortitude displayed by their ancestors. For this reason he urged those who could read and write to pass these skills on to those who could not, so that their valuable experiences could be committed to paper.[47] Fox's injunction must have been a powerful incentive to the acquisition of literacy by members.

However, to the present author it seems that the remarkably high level of signing ability among Friends can be accounted for above all else by the Quaker desire to escape worldly contagion. Early on in its history, the movement recognized the danger which social contamination posed to the purity of the faith. One response was to insulate members from such danger by full or partial withdrawal from the world. Another means of combating the danger of social infection was to strengthen the faith of members by ensuring a greater communion with the sect's moral and religious values. The route to attaining this was by encouraging Quaker children to receive a 'Godly education' in which they became familiar with the central values of the Quaker faith, and this was itself achieved in part by reading the Bible and other approved literature. The attainment of reading and possibly writing skills became part of the process whereby young Quakers were socialized into the culture of their sect. In striving to avoid the dangers of worldly contagion the Society raised literacy rates among members to a higher level than would otherwise have been the case. However, the influence exerted by the religion was complex and seems to have been due to more than the conventional desire to reach a personal relationship with God through reading the scriptures.

'FAITHFUL FRIENDS AND WELL QUALIFIED'

Take care for the good education and order of Friends' children in God's holy feare in the way of truth out of the snares of the Enemy and curruptions of the world and also to see that schools and schoolmasters, who are faithful to Friends and, well qualified, be placed and encouraged . . . where there may be need . . .

1696: Yearly Meeting Minute.

---

[47] EUL, COLMM 34, 18 (*c*.1669). On the significance of religious factors in promoting reading skills in later life see T. C. Smout, 'Born Again at Cambuslang: New Evidence on Popular Religion and Literacy in Eighteenth-Century Scotland', *Past and Present*, 97 (1982), 125–7.

The True knowledge of the Doctrine of Christ is not given to humane Learning, but to obedience to the will of God . . . John 7, 17.

William Tomlinson, *A Word of Reproof*, 2nd edn. (1656), 35.

They deny it to be needfull to bring up children in any Learning and some of them have taken their children from the school . . .

Francis Higginson, *A Brief Relation of the Irreligion of the Northern Quakers* (1653), 27.

Friends were not deterred from educating members or promoting literature because of the primacy attached by the Society to the doctrine of the indwelling light. The diminution of biblical authority and mistrust of formal, humane education—'brain knowledge' as Friends referred to it—which were characteristic of early Quakerism did not lead Friends to disavow learning together. However, the Society was eager that members should not become familiar with works which were considered to be out of keeping with the Quaker ethos: books of a frivolous or romantic nature, for instance, and those which were unsympathetic to Quakerism were regarded as a wasteful distraction, injurious to spiritual health.[48] Of course, once reading skills had been acquired there was no guarantee that ordinary Quakers would heed the instructions of the meeting. The genie had been let out of the bottle. Indeed, that a number of followers were known to have read the works of adversaries and to have on occasion been convinced by them was a matter of grave concern to local meetings, who must have feared the damaging effect that this might have on other followers.[49]

Quaker schools and schoolteachers made a significant contribution to the heightened literacy levels of Friends and acted as buffers isolating children and young Friends from the outside world. More attention was given to educating the children of Friends by the central administration of Quakerism from the 1690s, when there were clear signs that the number of Quakers was in decline, though locally the sect had shown concern for educating children in the faith from an early stage. Within Essex several educational institutions are known to have existed. A school at Waltham Abbey, founded by George Fox in 1668, was the first Quaker school to be formally established in England.[50] The children of Isaac and Mary Penington and the granddaughter of Margaret Fell attended, and

---

[48] Robert Barclay, *Apology*, 8; FHL, MYM, v. 469 (1720); EUL, EQ 27 (3 and 8 June 1723).

[49] For example, EUL, COLTW 1, 222 (1697); ERO, TA 261/1/1 (27 Nov. 1711).

[50] Arnold Lloyd, *Quaker Social History* (1950), 168.

the teachers were Friends of some distinction.[51] There are records indicating the earlier presence of Quaker masters and mistresses. Thurston Read, a Colchester Friend, was prosecuted for teaching children to read and write while unlicensed in 1663 and 1664.[52] Another teacher, John Saxby from Barking, was cited to the Archdeacon's court in 1684 for teaching at a school without licence from the Bishop, and in 1681 had been noted for possessing an unlawful primer 'contrary to the Church Government and Scripture itself'.[53] The names of Quakers who acted as unlicensed schoolteachers are often mentioned in the records of the church courts. They are to be found at Pebmarsh (1676 and 1678), Henham (1682), West Ham (1684), Stebbing (1697 and 1707), Great Coggeshall (1691 and 1707), Epping (1698), and Little Easton (1684).[54]

Besides imparting basic reading and writing skills, Quaker masters inculcated into pupils the rudiments of Quaker theology and the social practices approved by the faith. Alternative manuals for the education of children were produced by Friends which enabled them to satisfy this need. Indeed, there is plenty of evidence that Quaker masters spurned the conventional 'primers' and substituted the sect's guidebooks.[55] Moreover, Quaker children, it appears, were quite different from their peers; their speech and dress seemed unusual because of their plainness and simplicity. Children too rejected what Quakers understood to be pagan terminology for days of the weeks and months of the year and were expected to behave with a degree of gravity and sobriety unusual among youngsters.[56] In his Journal Thomas Chalkley recalled his daily journey to the home of the Quaker schoolmaster Richard Scoryer:

Many and various were the exercises I went through, my beatings and stonings along the street, being distinguished to the people by the badge of plainness which my parents put upon me . . .[57]

The purpose of Quaker schools was to fortify young Friends against the contamination of the world. For this reason parents were urged not to allow

[51] L. M. Wright, *The Literary Life of Early Friends 1658–1725* (New York, 1932), 84–5.
[52] Besse, *Sufferings*, i. 202.
[53] ERO, D/AEV 11, fo. 39ᵛ (1681); D/AEV 13, fo. 16ʳ, 47ʳ (1684).
[54] ERO, D/AMV 5 (Sept. 1676, June 1678), Pebmarsh; D/AEV 13, fo. 16ᵛ (May 1684, July 1685), West Ham. D/AMV 7 fo. 329ʳ (June 1684), Little Easton; D/ACV 8 fo. 109ʳ (Feb. 1682), Henham; D/AMV 10, fo. 14ᵛ (June 1707), Stebbing; MYM, i. 269 (1691); PRO, RG6 1177, 60, Epping.
[55] ERO, D/AEV 13, fo. 16ʳ (May 1684), 47ʳ (July 1684); D/AEV 11, fo. 39ᵛ. See also the manuscript copy of John Stubbs, 'A Primer for Children to Read', in the Bodleian Library, Oxford.   [56] EUL, EQ 26, 46 (1696), 44–5 (1690).
[57] Quoted in Christine Trevitt, *Women and Quakerism*, 107.

children to be schooled at the hands of non-Quaker masters and mistresses, though it is known this advice was not always heeded.[58] Quaker teachers were encouraged to exchange views on what they considered the most effective method for keeping children loyal and how best to overcome the various difficulties that confronted them as Quaker masters.[59]

Not all children, of course, attended an established Quaker school. The steps towards acquiring literacy skills were for most less formal. For example, we know that the main trade of Quaker Joseph Besse was that of a tailor, though he taught Friends' children at Great Burstead and later at Colchester.[60] A return to Yearly Meeting for 1709 noted that children in Essex received a 'Godly education', though it is known that in some areas of the county there were no established Quaker schools or masters.[61] That parents were as keen as the Society that children should be provided with an appropriate education is evident from those Quaker wills where provision was made for the instruction of children and grandchildren. In 1688 Joseph Smith expressed a general sentiment when he asked that his offspring be brought up 'well in learning to read and write', realizing that literacy increased the chances of acquiring a trade or employment.[62] More important was the desire that through learning children would be assured a 'Godly education'. In 1687 Rebecca Everitt, a Colchester Friend, remarked that after her death she wanted her four offspring raised in the fear of God and instructed her executor to choose a teacher suitable for that purpose.[63] Earlier in 1659 Samuel Burton also made explicit the connection between the acquisition of literacy and the well-being of the faith, when he asked his wife to ensure that their children were well educated and taught the 'fear of God'.[64]

Poor children were not disregarded by Friends. Indeed, educational provision for them was considered essential, since it was believed that without it the opportunities for obtaining a trade or apprenticeship would be greatly diminished.[65] The Society feared that idle Friends might become dependent on the local meeting or that their indolence might encourage wanton and depraved behaviour out of keeping with the Quaker

---

[58] Parnel, *Collection*, 231–2; FHL MYM, ii. 144 (1696).
[59] EUL, EQ 27 (May 1695); FHL, BARMM 1 (7 Sept. 1703); MYM, iv. 206 (May 1711); MYM, ii. 95–6 (1695).
[60] ERO, D/AEV 16 (22 June 1697); D/AEV 18 (Nov. 1707); GL, MS 9583, Bundle 2 (July 1706).
[61] FHL, MYM, iv. 23 (1709); EUL, EQ 26, 52 (1714); FHL, MYM, ii. 338 (1707).
[62] ERO, D/ABR 12/243.   [63] PRO, Prob 11/387/126.
[64] ERO, D/ACW 16/185.
[65] EUL, EQ 27 (June 1718); Vann, *Social Development*, 179.

light.[66] There is evidence from extant account books that the cost of educating poor children was borne by local meetings. In 1675, for example, women from the Quaker meeting of Barking and Plaistow paid for the education of George Hickman's children.[67] The sum of one hundred pounds was bequeathed in 1691 to the Six Weeks Meeting at London for the purpose of teaching orphaned children to read and write.[68] Children placed at the workhouse in London were given a copy of Barclay's *Apology* for their instruction.[69] In Essex concern about the education of Quaker children reached a peak in the early eighteenth century. In 1711 every meeting in the county appointed a Friend to discover whether poverty deterred parents from educating their offspring. Where this was found to be the case, local meetings took action to ensure that the children of the poor were not neglected.[70]

Considerable efforts were made to ensure that Quaker children, poor or otherwise, were given opportunities to acquire reading and, where appropriate, writing skills. This is surely one reason why such high literacy levels were discovered among Essex Quakers. However, education was not concerned primarily with acquiring an ability to read and write. The Society was as much concerned that children should be familiar with the spiritual and moral values of Quakerism and be socialized into the culture of Quakerism; the acquisition of literacy skills was a means to that end.

---

[66] EUL, Supplementary Papers, 63 (1702); FHL, MYM, iii. 81 (June 1709).

[67] FHL, Plaistow and Barking Women's Meeting, 29 July 1675; Six Weeks Meeting, i. 19 (1674); EUL, Supplementary Papers, 99 (1707).

[68] FHL, Six Weeks Meeting, iii. 56–7 (1691).

[69] FHL, London and Middlesex Quarterly Meeting, ii. 98.

[70] EUL, EQ 27 (1709); COLMM 1, 176 (1712); Supplementary Papers, 99 (1707); COLTW 2, 357–8; COLMM 35 (Collections and Disbursements for the Poor), 22.

PART III

Origins and Development

10

From Lollards to Quakers

THE LINEAGE OF QUAKERISM

I passed into Essex and came to Coggeshall . . . And there were about two thousand people at a meeting (as it was judged) and Amor Stoddart and Richard Hubberthorne were with me, and a glorious meeting there was, and the word of life freely declared, and people were turned to the Lord Jesus Christ their teacher and saviour, their way, their truth and their life.

Fox, Journal, 213 (1655).

The eagerness with which the Quaker message was received raises an important question. To what extent were itinerant ministers like Parnel responsible for the movement's early growth? The journals of Fox and other Quaker evangelists often recount the harvesting of souls which accompanied their missionary campaigns. But should we attribute the success of the early movement to the heroic labours of early Quaker evangelists alone? The influence of these itinerant preachers should be acknowledged, but it is possible that the explosion of interest which greeted the new faith owed much to its ministers tapping a pre-existing vein of dissatisfied lay opinion. It may be that the likes of Fox and Parnel articulated and brought into the open ideas which had been half formed and rarely expressed. The theme has been much debated by historians of popular religion, some of whom, including Margaret Spufford and before her Christopher Hill, have raised the possibility of a continuity in radical ideas, a subterranean tradition stretching possibly from the Lollards across the generations up to the Levellers, Baptists, and Quakers of the Interregnum.[1] The question is important and a convincing answer would help us to understand how radical ideas are disseminated and passed on over time.

A group of scholars, under the oversight of Dr Spufford, has examined in detail the nature of rural dissent in the early modern period and has

---

[1] For example, Christopher Hill, 'From Lollards To Levellers', in Maurice Cornforth (ed.), *Rebels And Their Causes: Essays in Honour of A. L. Morton* (1978), 49–64; Margaret Spufford, 'The Quest for the Heretical Laity in the Visitation Records of Ely in the late Sixteenth and early Seventeenth Centuries', in G. J. Cumming and Derek Baker (eds.), *Schism, Heresy and Religious Protest, Studies in Church History*, 9 (Cambridge, 1972), 223.

taken a significant step towards identifying a definite connection between the Lollards of the 1520s and the Quakers and Baptists of the 1660s.[2] The particular research carried out by Dr Nesta Evans showed that 81 per cent of Lollard surnames in the Chiltern Hundreds recurred among the sects.[3] The team argued that 'dissent descended in families, and concluded that this was not only true but that such families were the least mobile population group so far examined in early modern England'.[4] The analysis has met with a note of caution, most notably from Patrick Collinson, who added a rider to the collection of essays which included this research. His chief concern was that there was little evidence of the religious inclination of the intervening generations between the Lollards and the later sects to prove the case conclusively.[5] The new research is sure to set off a lively and stimulating debate, though it has not as yet been possible to establish with absolute conviction a continuous hereditary link between some Restoration radicals and earlier dissenters.

The present enterprise is more modest than that of Dr. Spufford's team, though the objective here is to look again at the debate and to try to discover whether it is possible by means of local study of one radical group to identify a connection. The contention is that historians who have proposed such a connection were correct to do so, for there was indeed a radical tradition of sorts in Essex stretching from the Lollards to the Quakers, but it is also argued that the rise and spread of Quakerism was not for that reason assured or inevitable. It is clear that the areas in which earlier forms of dissent flourished were later susceptible to the Quaker message, for a pattern of geographic continuity is evident. Moreoover, an examination of records relating to the township of Great Coggeshall was revealing in that it allowed a better understanding of the nature of the tradition and the factors which underlay its transmission locally. There follows a discussion of continuity in the symbols of dissent; and finally an attempt is made to link Quakers and pre-Quaker dissenters directly over a thirty- to forty-year period.

Literary evidence certainly supports the idea of continuity: contemporary authors suggested a link between Quakerism and earlier forms of

---

[2] Margaret Spufford, 'The Importance of religion', *The World of Rural Dissenters*, 6.

[3] Nesta Evans, 'The Descent of Dissenters in the Chiltern Hundreds', ibid., 288–308 and Appendix A (pp. 397–400).   [4] Abstract, ibid.

[5] Patrick Collinson, 'Critical Conclusion', ibid., 394. Prof. Collinson also raises the significance of another alternative radical tradition which deserves consideration: that of the East Anglian Brownists of the 1580s and the Barrowists and Dutch radicals of the 1590s, leading to the separatist and quasi-separatist movements of the early seventeenth century in England, Holland, and America (p. 395).

dissent. Some critics stated that the Quaker religion was descended from an older tradition of dissent. James Parnel's views on 'Perfection', 'Sin', and the 'Last Days' were proof, according to the Colchester minister Henry Glisson in 1656, that he was a 'disciple' of Henry Nicholas, the Familist.[6] More important was the contemporary pamphleteer who in 1661 traced the spiritual pedigree of Quakers and other sectaries back to the Lollards and cited many examples drawn from Essex.[7] One commentator declared that the new movement was but 'several old Errours, now revampt', while another remarked that Quakerism was but a concoction of all the 'errours and abominable opinions formerly scattered up and down the Christian world'.[8] These works suggesting a continuity of dissent are plausible, for the county of Essex in particular was prominent in the history of reforming movements; John Ball had preached at Colchester, and the Lollards flourished in the county during the late fifteenth and early sixteenth centuries.[9]

Quakerism was strongest in those parishes in Essex where Lollardy had previously taken hold; that is, in the area above a line drawn from Colchester to Thaxted, and in the textile villages and townships in the centre and north-east of the county such as Coggeshall and Witham.[10] The first missionary campaigns of James Parnel were launched in the north of the county and it is clear these areas were susceptible to the Quaker message.[11] It would be misleading to suggest that Quakerism took hold in these areas alone, for the movement registered a measure of success elsewhere. Nevertheless, that Quakerism took such deep root in that region of Essex where Lollardy had a substantial following suggests a continuity. Indeed, almost half of the Quakers were domiciled in the textile areas where Lollardy was known to be strong.[12] Among the laity there was evidence of radical religious opinion in Essex throughout the sixteenth century and up to the outbreak of the Civil War.[13]

---

[6] Henry Glisson, *A True and Lamentable Relation* (1656), 4.

[7] [Anon.], *Semper Idem: or a Parallel Betwixt the Ancient and Modern Phanaticks* (1661), 3, 4–7.

[8] [Anon.], *The Papist's Younger Brother*, 1; Brown, *Quakerisme, The Path-way to Paganisme*, 534.

[9] William Hunt, *The Puritan Moment: The Coming of the Revolution in an English County* (Cambridge, Mass., 1983), 87; Harold Smith, *The Ecclesiastical History of Essex under the Long Parliament and Commonwealth* (Colchester, n.d.), 6–15; Hill, 'From Lollards to Levellers', 52–3.

[10] For Lollardy see J. F. Davis, *Heresy and Reformation in the South-East of England, 1520–1559* (1983), 2–3.

[11] The distribution of Quakerism in the county is discussed in Chap. 12 below.

[12] See Map outlining Quaker distribution, p. 4.

[13] Smith, *Ecclesiastical History*, chaps. 4–5; Hunt, *The Puritan Moment*, Pt. III.

The township of Great Coggeshall reveals a continuity in dissenting opinion and dissatisfaction with orthodox belief from the early sixteenth century up to the arrival of the Quakers. The township harboured in 1523 a certain Quyntyne, a butcher, who subscribed to Lollard doctrines on such issues as the eucharist, fasting, and images;[14] another parishioner was noted as railing against the eucharist as a form of Popery in 1541; and just over a decade later the image of a crucifix was found abandoned in the street.[15] The records of the relevant Act and Visitation Books of the Archdeacon's court which had jurisdiction over Coggeshall indicate a considerable degree of independent thinking and action among the town's inhabitants. During the 1570s and 1580s several parishioners regularly absented themselves from church and refused to receive the communion. Female parishioners also frequently repudiated the ceremony of churching as set out in the rubric in the Book of Common Prayer.[16]

In the early seventeenth century there was the first sign of a separatist movement in the parish. The births of children to Brownists are noted by the parson in the baptismal register in 1615, and later, in 1633, sect members are recorded as holding illicit conventicles.[17] In keeping with the township's radical tradition, the Puritan John Owen, who became minister in the 1640s, argued against using civil penalties to punish those who did not hold strictly orthodox opinions.[18] A little over a decade later, the Quakers appeared in the town. Like that of Great Coggeshall, the economy of north and central Essex was dominated by clothiers and middlemen who were often free from harassment by Church and State because of the economic power they wielded. Furthermore, those employed in the textile trades such as weavers and clothiers were also likely to be literate and thus possibly showed a greater receptiveness to unorthodox ideas. As an important weaving centre, Coggeshall would also have been close to important communications networks which often served to transmit heretical ideas.[19]

---

[14] Davis, *Heresy and the Reformation*, 64.

[15] Bryan Dale, *The Annals of Coggeshall* (n.p., 1863), 124–5, 127. A broader view of popular dissent in Essex is provided by Patrick Collinson, 'The Godly: Aspects of Popular Protestantism', in id., *Godly People: Essays on English Protestantism and Puritanism* (1983), chap. 1.

[16] See, for example, the records of the Church Courts. ERO, D/ACA 4, fo. 50ʳ (1570); D/ACA 8, fo. 99ᵛ (1578); D/ACA 13 fo. 153ᵛ (1585), fo. 167ᵛ (1581); D/ACA 18, fo. 114ᵛ (Jan. 1589), fo. 201ᵛ–203ᵛ (Oct. 1590), fo. 267ᵛ (1589).

[17] Dale, *Annals*, 154; ERO, D/ACA 49, fo. 65ᵛ (1633); D.ACA 50, fo. 193 (1635).

[18] Dale, *Annals*, 166.

[19] On this see, for example, Capp, *The Fifth Monarchy Men*, 78 and Michael Frearson, 'Communications and the Continuity of Dissent in the Chiltern Hundreds during the Sixteenth and Seventeenth Centuries', in Spufford, *The World of Rural Dissenters*, 275–7.

A number of factors facilitated the transmission of religious radicalism. But surprisingly there is no evidence of familial links between Coggeshall Quakers and much earlier dissidents mentioned in the church records as might have been anticipated. The surnames of Great Coggeshall dissenters who appear in the Archdeacon's Act Books for failing to conform in the sixteenth century are not to be found in the nominal index of Quakers. It may be that the subsequent generations of these people found other sects more congenial, or they may not have been prosecuted and therefore were not noted in the court's documents. The study by Dr Evans mentioned earlier on the Chiltern hundreds also traced dissent in some parishes on the Essex border and similarly failed to uncover conclusive evidence of a family tradition.[20] Nevertheless, the existence of dissenting thought and behaviour among peoples in the same area across several generations and the experience in one Essex township of a significant radical tradition over many years points certainly to the importance of the environment in nourishing dissenting thought and more than hints at a continuous tradition stretching back a century before the arrival of Friends.

THE HAT AS A SYMBOL OF DISSENT

John Davage . . . for coming into church . . . with his hat on his head where he so continued all the time of singing and prayer and after sermon ended said unto Mr. Sams and the people with a loud voice in the back of the church that Mr. Sams was a hireling, a teacher of lies and deceiver of the people.

ERO, Q/SR 370/100, Michaelmas 1656.

That some areas seem to have shown a greater receptiveness to unorthodox ideas gives credibility to the notion of a radical tradition. There is also evidence of a more tangible nature linking Quakers and earlier radicals. The act of keeping one's head covered as a gesture of defiance is normally associated with Friends; it signified a refusal to recognize one person's superiority over another, and was also used, for example, in church to indicate disapproval of the minister's authority and unacceptable 'popish' ceremonies.[21]

However, the practice of hat-wearing long pre-dates Friends and here once more there is evidence of a continuous radical tradition. Lollards kept their heads covered as a symbol of protest, and there are instances of

---

[20] Spufford, 'The Quest for the Heretical Laity', 228–9; Hill, 'From Lollards to Levellers', 49–50; and Nesta Evans in Spufford, *The World of Rural Dissenters*, 397–9.
[21] ERO, D/AMV 2, fo. 42ʳ (May 1664).

similar conduct by individuals in Essex churches during the 1580s.[22] A surprising number of incidents involving the hat over the twenty or so years before the arrival of the Quaker sect in the county have come to light. In 1650 Ralph Josselin noted, five years before the mission of Parnel in Essex, that the 'unrreverent carriage of divers sitting with their hats on when the psalm is singing is a strange to mee'.[23] Earlier, in 1642, John Traps, a tailor from Radwinter, entered the parish church after the service had begun. With his head covered he provocatively addressed the curate with the words, 'Are you at Mass again?'[24] To judge from the citations in the records of the church courts it is apparent that the hat was on occasions worn by one or more parishioners during parts of the service which were disapproved of, for example, on the reading of the lesson in 1635, the baptism of a child and bowing at the name of Jesus in 1637, and the reading of psalms in 1638.[25]

While some parishioners may have considered church attendance an obligation, they nevertheless wished to dissent from certain church ceremonies. The legal requirement of church attendance posed a dilemma for nonconformists and remaining covered was to some an acceptable compromise. When Brownists grudgingly attended their local church in Chelmsford in the 1640s, they kept on their hats for fear of bringing the accusation of idolatry upon themselves. An amusing spectacle followed, for while the Brownists 'would very stubbornly clap on their hats . . . some of the congregation would in violent zeal pluck them off again'.[26] Attempts to uncover parishioners by persuasion or force rarely succeeded. Of course, hat-wearing may in some cases have indicated merely ignorance of correct behaviour or laziness.[27] But the outraged response of ministers, churchwardens, and congregations suggests that more often than not the gesture was intended as a protest.

There are also examples of parishioners remaining covered in church some twenty years before they joined the Friends. In 1637 Simon Josselin of Felsted wore his hat in church, stood at the creed, and refused to answer

---

[22] 'From Lollards To Levellers', 56; ERO, D/ACA 13 fo. 174ᵛ (Apr. 1586).

[23] Josselin, *Diary*, 208.   [24] Quoted in Smith, *Ecclesiastical History*, 181.

[25] ERO, D/ACA 50, fo. 103ʳ (Apr. 1635), Colchester; D/AEA 42, fo. 18ᵛ (Aug. 1638), Bradwell-juxta-mare; D/ALV 2, fo. 218ʳ (Dec. 1637), Mayland. At Great Bursted Church a parishioner sat with his head covered and suggested that Common Prayer was a 'Bumbasted Prayer' and accused the minister of 'preaching Popery'. ERO, D/ACA 39, fo. 240ᵛ.

[26] Smith, *Ecclesiastical History*, 179, the date is unclear from the context. See also ERO, D/ACA 48, fo. 232ᵛ (Oct. 1632), East Donyland.

[27] A Chelmsford parishioner, for instance, told Church officials that he kept his hat on in church 'not out of any contempt'. ERO, D/ALV 2, fo. 10ᵛ (1634). See also D/ACA 53, fo. 112ᵛ, Elsenham (Nov. 1638).

public prayer.[28] Thomas Tirrell also remained covered, declaring in 1639 that only if he was first drawn apart by 'wild horses' would his hat be removed. In a similar display of defiance he was also reported to have said that there was 'no difference between the church and other places'.[29]

The wearing of the hat was but one of several gestures which symbolized disapproval. At St Peter's Church, Colchester in 1640 several parishioners remained covered while the minister delivered the sermon, stood at the creed, and refused to kneel during prayer.[30] At Little Bromley in 1635 John Goodale kept his head covered and turned his back to the minister. It was taken as a further snub that, despite frequent warnings, Goodale slept during the service and sermon.[31] Such behaviour caused considerable distress to ministers. One feared that parishioners in general might be encouraged to imitate these disruptive actions,[32] and there seem to have been occasions when a whole congregation donned their hats in church, as at Easthorpe in 1631, while at Langley in 1638 and Witham in the same year a significant portion of the congregation did so.[33]

The Quaker practice of keeping the head covered as a gesture of protest and disapproval was not, then, as novel as it at first seems. Parishioners remained covered when they wished to show their distaste for certain church ceremonies or dislike of a particular minister. This discovery is significant since it establishes a link between Quakers and the dissenters who preceded them, and suggests that there was a core of dissatisfied opinion in the county on which Quakers might draw for support.

FROM DISSENTER TO QUAKER

In the 1640s, when the censorship broke down and church courts ceased to function, a whole host of radical ideas popped up and were freely expressed. The question I want to ask is how far these ideas had an underground existence before 1640, so that the novelty is only in the freedom to express them: or were the novel ideas the product of novel circumstances?

Christopher Hill, 'From Lollards to Levellers', in Maurice Cornforth (ed.), *Rebels and their Causes: Essays in Honour of A. L. Morton* (1978), 49.

---

[28] ERO, D/ABD 7, fo. 147ʳ (18 Mar. 1637).

[29] ERO, D/ACA 53, fo. 164ʳ (Mar. 1639); D/ACA 54 fo. 10ᵛ (Oct. 1639).

[30] ERO, D/ACA 54, fo. 75ʳ (Mar. 1640).

[31] ERO, D/ACA 50, fo. 179ᵛ (Aug. 1635).

[32] ERO, D/ALV 2 fo. 218ᵛ (Dec. 1637), Mayland.

[33] GLRO, D/LC (Bishop of London's Consistory Court, Miscellaneous Series), 324 fo. 151ᵛ (Dec. 1631), now housed at the London Metropolitan Archive; ERO, D/ACA 53, fo. 59ᵛ (Sept. 1638); fo. 74ᵛ (Oct. 1638); fo. 99ᵛ (Dec. 1638).

The next step in establishing whether Friends were part of a dissenting tradition must be to locate them more directly within it. The recollections of Friends encourage the view that the Society was heir to a dissenting lineage. George Fox wrote that many former Baptists were drawn into the movement, and Stephen Crisp, a prominent Colchester Friend who was himself a Baptist before conversion, recalled in his writings a personal pilgrimage in which he examined the doctrines of several sectarian groups before settling on Friends.[34] We know too that Quakers sometimes took over the congregations of separatist meetings already in existence.[35] Contemporaries were aware of the fluid nature of sect membership.[36] The comments of Quakers and others add substance to the argument that Quakerism may have been able to exploit a pre-existing tradition of dissent.

Of course, accounts in Quaker journals may not represent the experiences of the more humble brethren in the movement. One method of checking whether literary recollections match up to the experiences of rank-and-file Friends is to search through the records of the church courts, for indications of the behaviour of Quakers prior to conversion. If one assumes that a recurring name and place of residence refer to the same person, there is convincing evidence that those who were to become Friends had become disenchanted with the Church some considerable time before converting to the movement. The name of Edward Grant, for example, one of the first to witness the preaching of James Parnel, appears in the church court records in 1638 and 1639 for absenting himself from church, not receiving communion, and being an unrepentant excommunicant.[37] Stephen Crisp, a Quaker convert in the 1650s, was cited with his wife for not accepting communion in 1639. After repeated warnings both were excommunicated.[38] Upset at the Laudian innovations of the 1630s, these parishioners had already begun to distance themselves from the established religion.

Dislike of church ceremony found a variety of expressions. The future Quaker Arthur Condor refused in 1636 to pay a rate towards the cost of the rails for the communion table. Richard Allen, another who was later to find solace in Quakerism, bluntly declared his opposition to the placing

---

[34] Fox, *Journal*, 18–9, 25–6, 207–10; Craig Horle, 'Quakers and Baptists', *Baptist Quarterly*, 26 (1976), 218–38; Crisp, *Works*, 12; Vann, *Social Development*, 23–7.

[35] *FPT*, 73.

[36] William Prynne, *A New Discovery of Some Romish Emmissaries* (1656), 2; Harris, *An Answer to Some Queries*, 23.

[37] ERO, D/ACA 54, fo. 204ʳ (May 1639); D/ACA 53, fo. 11ʳ (June 1638).

[38] ERO, D/ACA 54, fo. 96ʳ (May 1639); see also D/ACA 53 fo. 42ᵛ (June 1638).

of the communion table within the rails.[39] John Furly, a leader of Friends in Colchester, was summoned to the court with his wife in 1638 where both were charged with ignoring summonses to attend church and communion. Both had previously refused to kneel at prayer and confession, claiming that conscience would not permit them.[40] There are several other instances of future Colchester and Essex Quakers being summoned to the courts during the 1630s for absenting themselves from church, not accepting communion, standing at the creed, and a variety of other offences.[41]

Even such episodes as these were to be surpassed when in 1637 William Allen of Earls Colne was presented for 'pissing in the clock chambers so that it ran down amongst the church', an offence which offended 'the parishioners' noses'. Allen, who was to become a leading supporter of the Quaker movement, also refused to pay tithes in the early 1650s a few years before he found fellowship with Friends.[42]

Not only were certain areas of Essex predisposed to be sympathetic to radical and dissenting opinion; it was also possible to establish a more direct link between Friends and pre-Civil War dissent over a period of twenty or thirty years. The coincidence of Quaker names with those presented in the records of the church courts for the 1630s, coupled with the other literary material mentioned earlier, is convincing evidence that some parishioners had been dissatisfied with the doctrines of the Church some time prior to their becoming Quakers. When James Parnel and his fellow evangelists preached in the county there was already a seam of dissatisfied opinion which they could profitably exploit.

The spiritual pedigree of ordinary Friends may often be traced through the records of the church courts, but is it reasonable to conclude on this evidence that the emergence and success of the Quaker movement were somehow preordained? Was the rise of Quakerism merely an inevitable development of a radical strain in the Reformation? And were Quaker evangelists giving coherence to views which were already formed in embryo? The behaviour of Tirrell and Allen referred to above suggests that they may have been proto-Quakers awaiting the arrival of Parnel before

---

[39] ERO, D/ACA 51, fo. 149ᵛ (July 1636), Arthur Condor. For Richard Allen, D/ACA 51, fo. 233ʳ (Feb. 1636).

[40] ERO, D/ACA 53 fo. 12ᵛ (June 1638), fo. 24ᵛ, 25ʳ (July 1638); fo. 239ʳ (June 1639).

[41] See, for example, ERO, D/ALV 2, fo. 100ᵛ (Jan. 1635). Robert Beard of Theydon Garnon, fo. 227ᵛ (Dec. 1637), Samuel Warner of Great Horkesley; D/ABA 8, fo. 322ᵛ, William and Mary Hall of Great Burstead (June 1638).

[42] ERO, D/ACA 52 fo. 8ᵛ (Apr. 1637), fo. 32ʳ (May 1637), fo. 78ʳ (June 1637), fo. 141ᵛ (Oct. 1637); Assize File 35/93/2, No. 24 (1652).

realizing their true kinship with Quakerism. There is also evidence from the 1630s and earlier of parishioners who had abandoned public worship altogether. In the court records one can find groups and individuals listed variously as 'Brownists', 'Schismatics', and 'Heretics'. Others were reported as holding and attending conventicles.[43]

None the less, caution is necessary when interpreting this evidence. The behaviour of many of the future Quakers described above may be explained as a reaction to the demands of the Laudian Church, rather than as evidence that they were sectarians or advanced separatists. Much hostility was directed at Laudian Arminianism expressed in a renewed emphasis on the Book of Common Prayer and the sacraments.[44] It is also striking how little evidence there is in the church records of total separation from the established church. Most conventiclers also attended public worship; they were in effect semi-separatists.[45] Not until the 1640s did a more virulent form of separatism emerge in Essex that coincided with the suspension of the church courts and the effective lapse in censorship. Ralph Josselin recorded in his Diary in 1642 that 'I began to be a little to be troubled with some in matter of separation'.[46] By 1645 the clergy in the county petitioned the court of Quarter Sessions to halt the growth in church absenteeism and the spread of 'Antinomian, Anabaptist and other errors'.[47] Complaints of this nature continued through the decade.

[43] According to the records of the ecclesiastical courts there were several Brownist congregations in the county. See ERO, D/ACA 49, fo. 65ᵛ, Great Coggeshall (May 1633). Also at Chingford, D/AEA 41, fo. 177ᵛ (June 1637). At or around Colchester Brownists were to be found at St Leonard's in March 1637, D/ACA 51, fo. 253ᵛ, at St Nicholas's in Dec. 1637, GLRO, X/19/77, fo. 57ᵛ, and at Greenstead in December 1637; ERO, D/ALV 2, fo. 232ʳ. Parishioners described as 'Schismatics' were to be found at St Mary Magdalen, Colchester ERO, D/ACA 47, fo. 97ᵛ (May 1630); Broxbourne, D/ABA 4, fo. 50ᵛ (May 1629). For a 'heretic' see D/ACA 49, fo. 35ᵛ (Feb. 1632); GLRO, D/LC 326, fo. 44ᵛ, Wigborough Parva. A note of caution needs to be sounded: one cannot be sure how accurate are the descriptions of 'Brownists', etc. given by church officials when assessing the religious allegiance of parishioners. On this see Hill, 'From Lollards to Levellers', 55.

[44] Nicholas Tyacke, 'Puritanism, Arminianism and Counter Revolution', in Conrad Russell (ed.), *The Origins of the English Civil War* (1973), 129–30, 133. See also Dr Tyacke's later work, *Anti-Calvinists: The Rise of English Arminianism, c.1590–1640* (Oxford, 1987).

[45] For example, see ERO, D/ACA 53, fo. 271ʳ⁻ᵛ (Aug. 1639), Kelvedon. After evening prayer the parishioners went to a conventicle. For a discussion of semi-separatism and the relative absence of complete separatism before the 1640s and 1650s see Patrick Collinson, *The Religion of Protestants: The Church in English Society, 1559–1625* (Oxford, 1982), 274. John Morrill contends that 'it seems probable that at no point in the critical period 1634–54 did more than five percent attend religious assemblies other than those associated with their parish churches.' See his 'The Church in England, 1642–1649', in John Morrill (ed.), *Reactions to the English Civil War* (1982), 90.   [46] Josselin, *Diary*, 12.

[47] ERO, Q/SBa 2/58, Michaelmas, 1645; Q/SBa 2/59–60, Epiphany 1645/6; Smith *Ecclesiastical History*, 102–3.

The emergence and success of a sectarian group like the Quakers should be explained neither as the inevitable consequence of a pre-existing tradition of dissent nor solely as the work of their missionary preachers. The two factors are not in any case mutually exclusive. The anti-Laudian sentiment of the 1630s prepared the way, causing some parishioners to question the tenets of mainstream religion more extensively and to associate subsequently with sects like the Friends. Suspension of the restraining influences of the church courts and censorship does not alone account for the rise of Quakerism: it is possible that a movement of this sort would have emerged in any case, though it would not have met with such a marked degree of success. The significance of the radical dissenting tradition in the county of Essex was preparatory: it constituted a precondition which favoured the emergence of Quaker radicalism once there was freedom to preach and publish without restraint. It also provided a context in which Friends would meet with greater acceptance than elsewhere, for Essex society was probably more accustomed to accepting the novel and the radical than most other counties in England.

11

Dregs of the People

Christ was noble, sprung up of the noble seed, though of Nobles and great ones of the earth he was disdained, reproached and scorned to be the King of the Jews, because according to the world he was of low degree and supposed to be a Carpenter's sonne, so they spit upon him and disdained him, and crucified him . . .

James Parnel, *A Shield of the Truth* (1655), 24.

Ascertaining the social origins of early Quakers is one of the most important tasks facing historians of the sect, for knowledge about who joined it and whether one social group was to predominate over another in its composition is an important factor in considering the sect's relations with the world and its evolution over its first seventy years. The Friends' social origins can also throw light on broader issues with which historians of plebeian culture are concerned, such as the attractiveness of radical religious movements to the poor and those at the margins of parish society.

However, discovering the social constituency of Quakerism is no easy matter because Quaker documents do not always reveal the occupations of Friends, and the 'additions' or descriptions of occupations added to their names in, for example, court records have on occasion been shown to be inaccurate.[1] For this study I have compiled a nominal index of Friends in Essex, which includes as much detail as could be found about individual Quakers during their life-cycle. I derived this from a variety of Quaker and other sources. The index's primary purpose was to assist in the task of tracing the relations of Quakers with others in the local society, but many of the records examined revealed incidentally the occupations of Friends and I added this information to the personal index.

Because the nominal index draws upon a broad range of source material it enables inaccuracies or inconsistencies to be identified and amendments made. It has not been possible to discover the social origins of every Quaker in the county of Essex and the occupational index covers male Quakers only. None the less, we have a substantial profile of Quaker social

[1] See Appendix II for a discussion of how information on Quaker occupations was gathered and assessed for this study.

origins. Such important information about the lives and occupations of such ordinary folk is normally hidden from the gaze of the historian.

Contemporary descriptions of early Friends invariably locate them within the lowest ranks of society. The pretensions of humble Quakers to a spiritual calling were often a reason for scorn. However, one has to be careful about accepting this depiction of lowly Quaker origins at face value. Perhaps anti-Quaker pamphleteers deliberately set out to stigmatize the movement by suggesting that adherents derived exclusively from the 'dregs of society' and exaggerated plebeian elements within it. Before outlining the evidence compiled of the social origins of Quakers in Colchester and Essex let us first consider what previous studies have revealed about the movement's occupational base.

THE DEBATE

Quakers . . . had their *beginning* from the very *rabble* and *dregs* of the people, *uncatechised*, *undisciplined* and *ungoverned*.

John Gauden, *A Discourse Concerning Publick Oaths* (1662), 8.

The first systematic examination of the movement's social composition was published more than forty years ago. The pioneer in the field was Alan Cole, who based his research in a number of English counties, though mainly northern ones. There followed a thorough and more specific piece of work on Quaker social origins by Richard Vann, which differed from that of Cole in that it examined a wider set of original sources in a more limited geographical area. Vann surveyed the records for Norfolk and Buckinghamshire and his efforts gave rise to an important initial article and subsequently a major portion of his influential book on *The Social Development of English Quakerism*. Judith Hurwich was the final contributor to the initial debate. Her research project was based in Warwickshire, though its scope was wider than that of the other two scholars in that it looked at the nonconformist communities in the county. The originality of her approach lay in her use of tax records in order to get an idea of the social base of the early Friends. Over the years more scholars have warmed to studying the theme of Quaker social origins and have provided useful supplementary evidence, but in the main it is the work of these three pioneering historians which I have referred to when making comparisons with the social base of the movement in the county of Essex.[2]

[2] Alan Cole, 'The Social Origins of the Early Friends', *JFHS* 48 (1957), 99–118; Vann, 'Quakerism and the Social Structure in the Interregnum', *Past and Present*, 43 (1969), 71–91;

Cole's research was based principally upon a study of the sect's marriage registers, which were informative because grooms often revealed their occupation on their marriage certificates. Judging from the evidence sampled, Cole concluded that it was from among the 'more hardpressed sections' of society that Quakerism drew its support: the likes of weavers, tailors, shoemakers, and husbandmen who constituted the backbone of the society. The predominant occupational characteristic of the movement was, he wrote, that of an 'urban and rural *petite bourgeoisie*'.[3] A few years later Richard Vann forcefully challenged this view. His research was broader based and it proved, he suggested, that the better-off sector like yeomen and wholesalers formed the core of support for the Society in its earliest years. He argued that Quakers were drawn mainly from the ranks of what he termed the 'middle to upper-bourgeoisie'. Vann had a still more striking revelation, which was that the percentage of Friends drawn from the gentry class was not lower than that in the population at large.[4]

Vann explained the difference in results as due to the nature of the sources sampled; he maintained that by using marriage registers alone Cole had overlooked short-term changes in the sect's composition.[5] Judith Hurwich next joined the debate. Drawing on her research on Warwickshire, she argued that there was no gentry membership for the county such as was found for Buckinghamshire. Moreover, it was artisans and poor husbandmen who made up more than half the known Quaker occupations in 1662. The less-well-off were far from 'numerically insignificant' among the early Quakers. She introduced new evidence to support her thesis. From the ratings of Quakers for the 1662 Hearth Tax she discovered that over half the Friends included were exempt from the levy or lived in homes that possessed only one hearth, an indicator that they were near or below

---

id., 'Rejoinder', *Past and Present*, 48 (1970), 162–4; id., *Social Development*, chap. 2; Judith J. Hurwich, 'The Social Origins of the Early Quakers', *Past and Present*, 48 (1970), 156–61; ead., 'Dissent and Catholicism in English Society: A Study of Warwickshire 1660–1720', *Journal of British Studies*, 16 (1976), 24–55. There are also important contributions by: Margaret Spufford, 'The Social Status of Some Seventeenth-Century Rural Dissenters', in G. J. Cuming and Derek Baker (eds.), *Popular Belief and Practice, Studies in Church History*, 8 (Cambridge, 1972), 203–11; Alan B. Anderson, 'The Social Origins of the Early Quakers', *Quaker History*, 68 (1979), 33–9; Barry Reay, 'The Social Origins of Early Quakerism', *Journal of Interdisciplinary History*, 11 (1980), 55–72; and Bill Stevenson, 'The Social and Economic Status of Post-Restoration Dissenters, 1660–1725', in Spufford, *The World of Rural Dissenters*, 332–59.

[3] Cole, 'The Social Origins of the Early Friends', 117.

[4] Vann, 'Quakerism and the Social Structure in the Interregnum', 72 and his *Social Development*, 72.

[5] Id., 'Quakerism and the Social Structure in the Interregnum', 76–7.

the breadline.[6] Thus Hurwich's research seemed to support Cole's original proposition about the plebeian nature of the early movement.

There has also been disagreement about the change in the social constituency of the movement over time. According to Vann, Quakerism began as a movement of the 'better-off', but the proportion of the well-heeled among the sect's members dropped during its first century. He argued that the signs of this change were apparent as early as 1670; thereafter, those who joined the movement were of lower social standing for there appeared to be more petty tradesmen, labourers, and artisans. A corollary of this development was that there were fewer wholesale traders and professionals. Furthermore, Vann suggested that Buckinghamshire Friends who earned a livelihood from the land were more likely to be husbandmen and labourers than to come from the more prosperous yeoman class.[7] He concluded that it was only with the passage of time that Quakerism became the lower-class, plebeian movement which Cole had envisaged. However, Vann's hypothesis of change was also challenged by Hurwich, for though some of the features he described had also been discerned in Warwickshire, she argued that the evidence of occupations coupled with the Hearth Tax listings indicated that there was no decisive shift in the movement's social base. Her conclusion was that there was no definite trend of declining wealth among members between 1663 and 1689.[8]

ESSEX AND COLCHESTER

they betook themselves . . . to build and raise this kingdome which possibly may be the reason so many *Bricklayers* and *Carpenters* (and such like persons) turn *Quakers*, in the hope of imployment . . .

Ralph Farmer, *The Lord Craven's Case Stated* (1660), 42.

The social composition of the Friends in Essex is similar in many respects to that of the movement elsewhere, but there are also features distinctive to the county.[9] The Colchester sample has been analysed in its own right,

---

[6] Hurwich, 'Social Origins', 159–61. See also her 'Dissent and Catholicism', 54.

[7] Vann, *Social Development*, 78–9.

[8] Hurwich, 'Social Origins', 158–61; 'Dissent and Catholicism', 54.

[9] Ead., 'Social Origins', 161 on Warwickshire and the significance of different regional economies.

for the meeting in the town constituted a separate administrative unit from the rest of the county and it was felt that its importance as a Quaker centre was sufficient to justify individual attention. The figures discussed below represent, first, the known occupations of male Quakers in Colchester and then, separately, those in the rest of Essex.

The main body of Colchester Quakers in the decade from 1655, the years which saw the first Quaker outreach in the county, was drawn from the ranks of the lower middling orders, with 52.4 per cent of all Friends sampled belonging to the occupational category of artisans alone.[10] Despite the predominance of the lower middling orders among Friends—another 10 per cent of Friends had the description of retailers in addition to those in the artisan class—the figures also reveal that there was a significant number of wholesale traders and large producers in Quaker ranks with their numbers representing 26.2 per cent of the total sample (Table 6). The percentage of Colchester Friends who could be described as belonging to the gentry was 4.8 which is near to the level to be found in society at large, though not as large as the 6.3 per cent, 7.3 per cent, and 7.4 per cent that Vann found for Norwich, Buckinghamshire, and Norfolk respectively.[11] It should also be noted that local factors were probably influential in determining the types of employment undertaken by Friends. Colchester was an important centre for the textile industry and it is not then surprising to discover that most Quakers in the town had jobs that were in some way related to the woollen trade. Since it was also a port of some renown, the finding that 3 per cent of Friends were involved in the seafaring trade is to be expected.

However, the social profile of Friends in the county at large is significantly different from that in Colchester (Table 7). In Essex just over 3 per cent of Friends belonged to the gentry class. And the number of fairly prosperous Quakers, like yeomen, wholesale traders, and large producers compared with the more humble retailers, artisans, and husbandmen in the county are almost equal at around 38 per cent. There are also other significant features of the movement in the county. Many Friends in Essex relied for their livelihood upon farming; over 40 per cent in the county sample earned their income from working the land. The percentage of labourers in the movement was so small as to be almost

---

[10] The social origins of Essex Friends have been considered elsewhere but the conclusions of the present work are based upon a much larger sample of occupations. See Barry Reay, 'The Social Origins of Early Quakerism', 55–72; Felix Hull, 'More Essex Friends of the Restoration Period', 66.   [11] Vann, *Social Development*, 71.

unnoticeable.[12] The figures suggest that in the county in its first decade the movement won support evenly from across the ranks of the middling orders. What does the evidence about Colchester and Essex Friends tell us about the movement's social base? The Colchester evidence matches more closely the conclusions of Cole and Hurwich than those of Vann, but the figures for Essex fail to support fully the arguments of any of the contending parties.

What does an analysis of the occupational samples in Colchester and Essex reveal about the changing social composition of the movement over time? Certain features of the Essex and Colchester data confirm previous research (Tables 8 and 9). There is, for example, a gradual disappearance of the gentry from Quaker ranks. In Colchester only one member of that class remained in membership at the beginning of the eighteenth century. However, while the sect developed a broader constituency over the years, more striking is the lack of radical change in the movement's social composition. In Colchester the number of Quakers in the upper middling ranks of society peaked in the decade 1705 to 1714 at over 38 per cent of the total, though this percentage did not overtake the consistently high percentage of artisans among Friends in the town, which remained at over 40 per cent throughout the period. The number of artisan and retailer Friends in the county also increased, though not over-dramatically. By the end of the period they made up over 40 per cent of the total members, compared with a little under 30 per cent in the movement's first decade. In Essex, there was no change in social composition of the sort to warrant the conclusion that the social composition of the movement had narrowed significantly.

QUAKERS AND THE HEARTH TAX

. . . Both the post-Restoration episcopate's denigratory remarks, and the recent trend of interpretation which suggests that the literate 'middling' sort of the common people were much the most receptive audience to which piety and godliness appealed, are mistaken . . .

Margaret Spufford, *The World of Rural Dissenters, 1520–1725* (Cambridge, 1995), 19.

---

[12] But see Bill Stevenson, 'The Social and Economic Status of Post-Restoration Dissenters', 338, who has discovered a considerable number of labourers in the ranks of Friends in Bedfordshire. This group constituted 22.2 per cent of Quaker occupations between 1666 and 1676. Assuming the small sample has not skewed the results, this is a remarkable finding.

TABLE 5. *Distribution of Hearths in 1671 for Quakers and Inhabitants of Select Parishes in Essex*

	All Inhabitants		Quakers	
	Number	Percentage	Number	Percentage
8 +	46	2.4	3	2.9
4 + (large houses, prosperous)	441	22.9	31	30.1
2–3 (modest houses, comfortable)	672	34.9	45	43.7
Exempt–1 (small houses, poor)	766	39.8	24	23.3
Total	1,925	100	103	100

A valuable complementary source for measuring Friends' social status is the Hearth Tax, and this has been used to measure the social status of a sample of Essex Quakers. It is the assessment for the year 1671 which has been examined in preference to others because it is the most comprehensive account we have and includes parishioners who were too poor to make any contribution to the tax or were rated at just above the tax threshold. Friends' names have been checked against the entries for that year from a cross-section of parishes within the county. These were chosen to reflect parishes with small and large Quaker populations and different types of farming and economic structures.[13]

The results are illuminating, and modify an analysis based solely upon the evidence of 'additions' (Table 5). The number of Quakers who were exempt from paying the tax or were rated at only one hearth is remarkably high at 23 per cent of the total sample. It is a salutary reminder that the poorest members of English society were stirred by the difficult questions of human existence and were open to the answers that religious faith could provide.

Severe disagreement has been evident among historians about the extent to which strongly held religious convictions penetrated down the

---

[13] The parishes were Stebbing, Felsted, Great Horkesley, Boxted, Theydon Garnon, Cressing, Earls Colne, Witham, Halstead, Roydon, Steeple, Harwich, Great Sampford, Saffron Walden, and Barking. The Hearth Tax for this analysis was ERO, QRTH 5 (1671).

social hierarchy.[14] The Hearth Tax returns suggest that Quakerism was attractive to many in the lowest ranks of local society. However, the figures still confirm that in the main the sect relied on support from the middling orders. Indeed, a surprising and significant finding is that Friends drew followers disproportionately from this category, since those of middling degree constituted just over half of the residents in the select parishes sampled, whereas three-quarters of Friends came from this group. To date, scholars have debated whether the social constituency of members was broadly of one type or another. But rather than attempting to prove that the movement was composed predominantly of one social group we should perhaps instead be readier to recognize that the sect reflected distinctive and sometimes sharply contrasting occupational characteristics according to the locations in which it took root and flourished.

THE SIGNIFICANCE OF THE SOCIAL PROFILE

In pluralistic societies, new religious movements have shown a strong tendency to recruit their following from one particular constituency, and the appeal of the movement to one such constituency may undermine its appeal to other sections of society . . . Once a movement becomes type-cast in this way, the likelihood of recruiting effectively and widely outside the class which already predominates may well be limited.

Bryan Wilson, *The Social Dimensions of Sectarianism; Sects and New Religious Movements in Contemporary Society* (Oxford, 1990), 239–40.

What significance should we attach to the social profile of early Quakerism in Essex and does it reveal anything that can help us to understand the genesis of the movement (Tables 6 to 9)? The classic explanation for the origins of sects is that they compensate for the economic deprivation experienced by the lower orders of society,[15] but that does not square with the fact that many of the religion's early followers in the county were from the ranks of the comfortable or fairly prosperous. However, the

---

[14] A useful account of the current state of the debate can be found in Margaret Spufford, 'The Importance of Religion in the Sixteenth and Seventeenth Centuries', in ead, *The World of Rural Dissenters*, 1–102. See also Thomas, *Religion and the Decline of Magic*, chaps. 3 and 6; Ingram, *Church Courts*, 92–8; Keith Wrightson and David Levine, *Poverty and Piety in an English Village: Terling, 1525–1700*, 162. A valuable discussion on the nature of popular religiosity but in relation to another period can be found in Hugh McLeod, *Religion and Irreligion in Victorian England* (Bangor, 1994).

[15] For a discussion of the theories of Weber and Troeltsch see Michael Hill, *The Sociology of Religion* (1973), esp. chap. 3.

TABLE 6. *Occupations of Colchester Quakers, 1655–1664*

	Number	Category	Percentage
Gentlemen	4	(4)	4.8
Agriculture		(2)	2.4
Husbandmen	1		
Yeomen	1		
Professional		(1)	1.2
Schoolteachers	1		
Wholesale and large producers		(22)	26.2
Baymakers	5		
Chandlers	1		
Drapers	1		
Grocers	5		
Malsters	1		
Merchants	3		
Merchant tailors	1		
Millers	1		
Saymakers	1		
Staplers	1		
Tanners	2		
Retail traders		(8)	9.5
Bakers	2		
Glovers	1		
Shoemakers	1		
Shopkeepers	1		
Tailors	3		
Artisans		(44)	52.4
Bricklayers	1		
Butchers	1		
Carpenters	1		
Fellmongers	1		
Fullers	1		
Ship's carpenters	1		
Weavers	35		
Woolcombers	3		
Sea trades		(3)	3.6
Mariners	1		
Seamen	2		
Total	84		

TABLE 7. *Occupations of Essex Quakers, 1655–1664*

	Number	Category	Percentage
Gentlemen	6	(6)	3.3
Agriculture		(81)	44.3
Farmers	27		
Husbandmen	17		
Yeomen	37		
Professional			
Schoolteachers			
Wholesale and large producers		(34)	18.6
Clothiers	9		
Drapers	3		
Grocers	5		
Gardeners	5		
Malsters	2		
Merchants	1		
Millers	1		
Saymakers	1		
Tanners	7		
Retail traders		(29)	15.9
Bakers	3		
Chandlers	4		
Costermongers	1		
Glovers	1		
Shoemakers	9		
Shopkeepers	4		
Tailors	7		
Artisans		(24)	13.1
Basketmakers	2		
Blacksmiths	4		
Bottlemakers	1		
Brickmakers	1		
Butchers	1		
Carpenters	1		
Coopers	1		
Glaziers	1		
Joiners	1		
Masons	2		
Shipwrights	1		
Weavers	4		
Websters	1		

TABLE 7. (*cont'd*)

	Number	Category	Percentage
Wheelwrights	2		
Woolcombers	1		
Labourers and servants		(3)	1.6
Labourers	3		
Sea trades		(6)	3.2
Mariners	1		
Sailmakers	1		
Fishermen	3		
Oyster dredgers	1		
Total	183		

fact that so many of the middling orders found Quakerism attractive is significant. A thirst for personal salvation, growing literacy rates, and a greater economic independence meant that some in these ranks were now able to exercise a choice, and Quakerism, for a variety of reasons, fitted their aspirations.

That a substantial number of wealthy merchants, tradesmen, and the like were found in Quaker ranks is worth noting, for it probably encouraged a degree of integration with the wider community, since by virtue of the economic power they wielded and the social connections they developed, they were probably more likely to be sympathetic to worldly values and prepared to countenance a greater acceptance of association with the world. The wealth of the merchant classes and patronage of gentry members must also have afforded Friends some protection from their enemies. But, given the social diversity of those in Quaker ranks, a preponderance of followers from the middling ranks cannot explain the rise of the movement. It is significant that Quakerism attracted converts from both extremes of the social hierarchy, signalling to potential converts that the faith did not wish to draw its followers from a limited social range. A variety of factors—personal, religious, social, and psychological—coalesced to make Quakerism attractive.

That the sect's peculiar religious doctrines provided reasons for joining the Quakers is not to be doubted. One commentator found the breadth of the Quaker heresy to be remarkable, 'a Trojan horse of all Heresies', and saw this as responsible for the success of Quaker

TABLE 8. *Occupations of Colchester Quakers, 1655–1724*

	1655–64		1665–74		1675–84		1685–94		1695–1704		1705–14		1715–24	
	Number	Percentage	Number	Percentage	Number	Percentage	Number	Percentage	Number	Percentage	Number	Percentage	Number	Percentage
Gentlemen	4	4.8	4	4.1	4	3.3	3	2.1	2	1.5	1	0.7	1	0.9
Agriculture	2	2.4	4	4.1	3	2.5	4	2.8	2	1.5	2	1.5	2	1.9
Yeomen	1		2		1		4		2		2		1	
Husbandmen	1		2		2								1	
Professional	1	1.2	1	1.0					4	3.1	7	5.2	6	5.6
Teachers	1		1						4		4		3	
Doctors											3		3	
Wholesale and large producers	22	26.2	32	32.6	41	33.9	47	33.6	49	38.0	52	38.5	35	32.7
Baymakers	5		7		13		16		15		17		15	
Clothiers											1		1	
Distillers	1		1		1		1							
Drapers	1				1				1		1			
Gardeners	1		3		3		4		5		5		5	
Grocers	5		5		3		4		3		2		2	
Malsters	1		2		4		4		5		2		1	
Merchants	3		3		5		8		11		13		7	
Merchant tailors	1		3		2									
Millers	1													
Saymakers	1		4		5		5		6		2		2	
Staplers	1		1		1		1		1		5		2	
Tanners	2		3		3		4		3		1			
Pappers											2			
Retail trades	8	9.5	13	13.3	13	10.7	15	10.7	14	10.8	14	10.4	16	14.9
Bakers	2		2		1		1		1		2		2	
Clockmakers							1		1		1		1	
Glovers	1												1	
Shoemakers	1		7		7		9		8		8		8	

TABLE 8. (*cont'd*)

	1655–64		1665–74		1675–84		1685–94		1695–1704		1705–14		1715–24	
	Number	Percentage	Number	Percentage	Number	Percentage	Number	Percentage	Number	Percentage	Number	Percentage	Number	Percentage
Shopkeepers	1		1		1		1							
Salt refiners					1				1				1	
Tailors	3		3		3		3		3		3		3	
Artisans	44	52.4	43	43.9	58	47.9	69	49.3	57	44.2	58	42.9	47	43.9
Bricklayers	1		1						1		2		2	
Butchers	1										1			
Carpenters	1		1		1		2		2		1		3	
Ship's carpenters	1		1		2									
Cordmakers					1									
Curriers	1		1		2		2				1		1	
Dyers			1		1		4		3		3		3	
Fellmongers	1													
Fullers	1				1		1							
Glaziers							3		5		3		2	
Joiners							1		2		2		1	
Lastmakers					1		1		1		1		1	
Lathe cleaners					1				1		1			
Masons					1		2		2		1		2	
Rowers							3		2		2		1	
Rugmakers									1		1			
Weavers	35		34		34		34		27		26		18	
Websters					1		1		1					
Woolcombers	3		4		12		14		10		13		13	
Sea trades	3	3.6	1	1.0	2	1.6	2	1.4	1	0.8	1	0.7		
Mariners	1		1		2		2		1		1			
Seamen	2													
Total	84		98		121		140		129		135		107	

TABLE 9. *Occupations of Essex Quakers, 1655–1724*

	1655–64		1665–74		1675–84		1685–94		1695–1704		1705–14		1715–24	
	Number	Percentage	Number	Percentage	Number	Percentage	Number	Percentage	Number	Percentage	Number	Percentage	Number	Percentage
Gentlemen	6	3.3	6	2.6	6	1.8	4	1.3	4	1.3	2	0.8	1	0.5
Agriculture	81	44.3	94	41.4	119	35.2	99	32.3	109	36.8	82	35.0	58	30.4
Farmers	27		25		18		7		6		5		2	
Husbandmen	17		22		32		26		31		22		9	
Shepherds			1		3		3		1					
Yeomen	37		46		66		63		71		55		47	
Professional			1	0.4	4	1.2	2	0.6	8	2.7	8	3.4	5	2.6
Doctors			1		4		2		4		4		2	
Surgeons														
Teachers									4		4		3	
Wholesale and large producers	34	18.6	39	17.2	61	18.0	63	20.6	52	17.6	43	18.4	44	23.0
Baymakers			1		1									
Cheesemongers									1					
Clothiers	9		11		19		17		12		12		14	
Distillers											2			
Drapers	3		3		1						1			
Gardeners	5		4		3		4		2				5	
Grocers	5		3		12		15		13		6		6	
Lime burners					1		1		1					
Malsters	2		4		8		8		10		9		6	
Mercers									1		1			
Mealmen														
Merchants	1		1		1		3		4		4		5	
Merchant tailors													1	
Millers	1		1				2				1			
Saymakers	1		2		3		3		2		2		2	
Staplers					3						2			
Tanners	7		9		8		9		6		3		5	
Tobacconists					1		1							
Retail trades	29	15.9	37	16.3	50	14.8	54	17.6	51	17.2	44	18.8	41	21.5
Bakers	3		3		5		4		7		5		7	
Chandlers	4		4		4		5		4		3		2	
Clockmakers									1		1		2	
Costermongers	1													
Glovers	1		1		2		1		3		1		2	
Hatters							1		1		2		2	
Innholders			1		1		1		1		1			
Ironmasons			1						1		2		1	

TABLE 9. (cont'd)

	1655–64		1665–74		1675–84		1685–94		1695–1704		1705–14		1715–24	
	Number	Percentage	Number	Percentage	Number	Percentage	Number	Percentage	Number	Percentage	Number	Percentage	Number	Percentage
Sadlers							1						1	
Salesmen							1		2		1		8	
Shoemakers	9		1		1		19		14		11		7	
Shopkeepers	4		13		20		7		5		6		8	
Tailors	7		6		7		13		11		10		1	
Tallow chandlers			7		10		1		1					
Artisans	24	13.1	37	16.3	76	22.5	66	21.6	62	20.9	51	21.8	42	22.0
Basketmakers	2		3		4		5		4		4		5	
Bottlemakers	1		1		1				1		1			
Braziers													2	
Blacksmiths	5		6		8		5		2		2		1	
Bricklayers					1		1		1		3		2	
Brickmakers	1		1		1		1		2		3			
Butchers	1		2		3		8				3		4	
Carpenters	1				13		1		9		3		1	
Cardmakers					1		1		3		1			
Collermen														
Coopers	1		3		2		3		3		1		1	
Fellmongers					1		2							
Fanwrights														
Glaziers	1		1		1		1		1		2		3	
Joiners	1		1		2		1		2		1		1	
Locksmiths			1											
Masons	1		1		3		2		1		1		1	
Millwrights					1									
Shipwrights			1		1		1		1		1			
Thatchers							1		1					
Weavers	4		7		12		16		11		9		5	
Woolcombers	1		5		9		5		6		5		10	
Websters	1		1		6		6		8		6		3	
Wheelwrights	2		2		5		4		2		4		3	
Sea trades	6	3.3	10	4.4	15	4.4	12	3.9	7	2.4	3	1.3		
Fishermen	3		7		7		5		3		2			
Mariners	1		2		8		6		3		1			
Oyster dredgers														
Seamen	1		1											
Other trades	3	1.6	3	1.3	7	2.1	6	2.0	3	1.0	1	0.4		
Labourers	3		2		6		5		2		1			
Servants														
Coalmen	1		1		1		1		1					
Total	183		227		338		306		206		234		191	

proselytizing.[16] The degree of suffering and persecution experienced by the sect also distinguished it from the religion of other dissenters and this may have been another reason for its attractiveness. Richard Baxter remarked that 'many turned Quakers, because the Quakers kept their meetings openly, and went to prison for it cheerfully . . .'[17] The figures indicating Quaker numbers in the county suggest that the number of followers continued to rise in spite of severe bouts of persecution.

Aware that traditional theories do not wholly satisfy the diversity and complexity of sectarian groups, some sociologists have sought to support the thesis that 'deprivation' was at the root of decisions of followers to take up the faith by defining the term more widely so as to include any way in which individuals or groups felt disadvantaged in a society, that is, either in relation to others or to the predominant values or culture of that society.[18] According to this theory, religious movements like Quakerism did not remove 'deprivation', but they did act as a compensation. It might be objected that such a theory is so all-embracing that it lacks any distinctive quality and therefore explains nothing, but, while a broader understanding of deprivation cannot alone explain the genesis of Quakerism, it can go a long way to help to account for the reasons why parishioners from diverse walks of life were drawn to the new faith.

There is plenty of evidence that many, prior to joining Quaker ranks, were at odds with the ethos of the parish community. Perhaps the movement gave succour to those who felt excluded from the prevailing power structure or on occasion simply provided parish malcontents with a focus for their hostility. However, it should not be taken as read that the type of individual who would find membership acceptable was somehow predetermined; it was a matter of personal choice whether or not an individual sought out the new faith.

---

[16] J. Price, *The Mystery and Method of His Majesty's Happy Restauration* (1680), 31. I am grateful to Keith Thomas for this reference. [17] Baxter, *Autobiography*, 190.
[18] I am drawing here on the work of Charles Glock and Rodney Stark on modern sectarianism. See their *Religion and Society in Tension* (Chicago, 1965), 242–59. I am grateful to Peter B. Clarke for bringing this work to my attention.

12

The Growth and Decline of Quakerism

QUAKER MEMBERSHIP

If the church is to grow as fast as the population it must be able to recruit an expanding constituency; and if it grows at all, it must, given wastage, be able to recruit persons other than its own members' children. A church which can rely only on such *autogenous* growth—such recruitment from within 'church families', so to speak—must decline, unless those families are increasing very much faster than the total population, simply because no church can expect to recruit all its members' children.

R. Currie, A. Gilbert and I. Horsley (eds.), *Churches and Churchgoers*
(Oxford, 1977), 119.

There are no contemporary assessments of Quaker numbers in Essex during the period of this study. However, a fairly reliable picture of Quaker strength can be obtained by using the Quaker birth, marriage, and death registers. These sources, like their parish equivalents, are not problem-free, but if used carefully, and with the caveat that the figures derived from them constitute a guide to the Society's strength in the county rather than a precise measurement, their use can be most rewarding.[1] They provide clear evidence to explain why the authorities were so alarmed at the growth of Quakerism after the Restoration. Moreover, an examination of the figures detailing the movement's membership helps to explain why, from the 1690s onwards, so many of the official pronouncements of the Society emphasized the need to maintain Quaker children within the movement.

By the end of its first decade the Society had a sizeable following in the county: if we include in the total figure men, women, and children, there were 1,283 Quakers in Essex between 1655 and 1664. A contemporary put the national figure at over 30,000 by the Restoration, and the Quaker historian William C. Braithwaite calculated the number to have been as high as 40,000.[2] The largest rise in membership in Essex occurred in the decade

---

[1] See Appendices I and II below and Davies 'The Quakers in Essex', 46–7.
[2] John Gaskin, *A Just Defence and Vindication of Gospel Ministers* (1660), Fig. ARV; Braithwaite, *Beginnings*, 512; Barry Reay suggested the number of Quakers in the country was possibly near to sixty thousand; see his *The Quakers and the English Revolution*, 26–7.

1665–1674, when 600 new Friends were added. This was a significant increase when one considers that Friends were subject to prosecution under a variety of laws intended to suppress nonconformity. A general climb in membership was commented upon by the Colchester Friend Thomas Bayles. Writing in 1675 he noted that 'thousands' had in recent years opened themselves to the Quaker light. His words confirm the impression acquired from an analysis of statistics derived from the Quaker registers. About Colchester he wrote of the:

happy and blessed appearance of the Lord to the call and restitution of mankind . . . by his Servants, his Messengers and Minister, who here in this Town and Country have laboured for several years by past, both by word and writing: . . . and people come again, to partake of that heavenly blessed life . . . which hath been held forth in this place for the 20 years past.[3]

In the ten years up to 1684 the movement in Essex continued to expand, and although the addition of 452 Friends was somewhat less than the increases in the previous decade, this rise took the membership figure to a peak of 2,379. Much scholarly attention has focused on the opening years of the movement, which is perhaps not surprising given the militant behaviour of followers and the extreme doctrines they espoused. This attention has tended to obscure the fact that the movement grew vigorously in succeeding years. The numerical evidence alone perhaps puts a serious question mark against the view that 1660 was somehow the watershed in Quaker history.[4] Another striking feature of these membership figures is the proportion of the Friends who lived in Colchester (Table 10). After the movement's first decade the number in the town constituted over a quarter of all members in the county. Between 1675 and 1684 nearly seven hundred Friends were settled there. An extremely tentative estimate would put the Quaker following at around 7 per cent of Colchester's population, a figure which would have made them a highly visible group. For the county as a whole Quakers may have constituted about 2 per cent of the total population.[5]

---

[3] Thomas Bayles, *A Testimony to the Free and Universal Love of God* (1675), 3; Crisp, *Works*, 383.

[4] Reay, *The Quakers and the English Revolution*, 104–5; Christopher Hill, *The Experience of Defeat: Milton and some Contemporaries* (1984), 17–18.

[5] The population of Colchester was about ten thousand souls at this time. See T. C. Glines, 'Colchester Politics and Government, 1660–1693' (University of Wisconsin Ph.D. thesis, 1974), 13. K. H. Burley calculated the population of Essex around 1660 to be about 120,000 in his 'The Economic Development of Essex in the Later Seventeenth and Early Eighteenth Centuries' (University of London Ph.D. thesis, 1957), 11.

TABLE 10. *The Size of the Quaker Movement in Essex and Colchester, 1655–1724*

	Essex, including Colchester	Colchester	Colchester as percentage of total
1655–64	1,283	265	20.65
1665–74	1,927	546	28.33
1675–84	2,379	678	28.50
1685–94	2,118	629	29.70
1695–1704	2,254	600	26.62
1705–14	2,035	543	26.68
1715–24	1,649	439	26.62

After 1684 the number of Friends in the county began to decline. Between 1685 and 1694 the Society witnessed a loss of 261 members. The fall was arrested in the following decade, but the recovery was modest and was to be of no real or lasting significance. From 1705 to 1714 the pattern of decline was re-established; the movement lost another 219 members with a further significant haemorrhaging of 386 members between 1715 and 1724. The fall in Quaker numbers was consistent, though it masks significant variations in the strength and buoyancy of the movement within different towns and parishes.

The reduction in membership was accompanied by expressions of anxiety from local Quaker meetings and was probably connected to slackening of commitment among rank-and-file members. At Colchester in 1697 the meeting called upon its members to effect 'a Reformation' in their behaviour and urged Friends to devote themselves to God. Similar advice was given by the Society across the country. Earlier in 1694 the Quaker officials at the main meeting in Colchester town were shaken to discover that certain young Quakers married outsiders and that this trend was discernible even among Friends of more mature years.[6] By the 1720s the records indicate that the Quaker movement in the county was failing to win any new converts; members were then described by business meetings as being 'indifferent' or 'lukewarm'.[7]

---

[6] EUL, COLMM 34 (Copies of Yearly Meeting Epistles), 163 (3 June 1697); Supplementary Papers, 8 (1697); COLTW 1, 201.

[7] FHL, BARMM I (2 Mar. 1703). See also 3 June 1703. COLTW 2, 278 (1720); FHL, MYM, v. 418 (1720), MYM, vi. 17 (1721), 267 (1724).

Another symptom of lessened commitment from the end of the seventeenth century onwards was a greater preparedness of many members to pay tithes. It appears that there was either open neglect of the Quaker testimony or some kind of agreement with the tithe owner so that dues might be collected surreptitiously.[8] There were a number of complaints and in 1719 a response from Essex Friends to a query from the Yearly Meeting noted that 'many do not but plead for the upholding the anti-christian yoke, and yet call themselves members of the Monthly and Quarterly Meeting'.[9] The Society was not silent in the face of this waning commitment. Meetings castigated backsliders and focused attention on keeping children and youths loyal to the faith; the assumption was that retaining them would help stem the fall in numbers. The increased emphasis on the socialization of children coincides with the fall in membership from the 1690s.[10] For a brief period the strategy proved successful, but over time the movement failed to halt decline.

THE GEOGRAPHY OF QUAKERISM

It has become fashionable to attempt to account for the distribution of religious phenomena by explaining them in terms of the social and geographical backgrounds in which they flourish or wither away. There is no doubt much merit in this approach. It can also lead to over-simplification of an extraordinarily naive kind.

Margaret Spufford, *Contrasting Communities: English Villagers in the Sixteenth and Seventeenth Centuries* (Cambridge, 1974), 298.

Though we have so far considered the broad pattern of Quaker membership, this obscures the strength of the Society in certain areas. Historians have developed theories to account for the distribution of nonconformity and they are relevant to the topic under discussion. It has been suggested that Quakerism settled in those areas where Puritanism had never been strong[11] and for this reason Quakerism is believed to have had shallow roots in Essex. There were, it is admitted, exceptions like the towns of Colchester and Great Coggeshall, but the movement's strength in those places was determined by particular local circumstances. The evidence compiled for the present study does not support this analysis. Quakers resided in over 230 parishes in the county between 1655 and 1725. Moreover, when the parishes with Quaker populations are checked against the Compton

---

[8] Davies, 'The Quakers in Essex', 115–18.   [9] FHL, MYM, v. 371 (1719).
[10] Davies, 'The Quakers in Essex', 115.
[11] Barbour, *The Quakers in Puritan England*, 42, 86.

Census of 1676 and other sources which indicate the presence of dissent,[12] it is clear that Quakerism existed and prospered side by side with other forms of puritanism. Colchester and Great Coggeshall were not as exceptional as they at first seemed.

Of the theories explaining the distribution of dissent, the most interesting are those which focus upon the significance of land management and the economic structures of parishes.[13] Dissent, it has been suggested, was particularly strong in pastoral areas because large parishes which had farmsteads and small hamlets were less likely to be susceptible to the influence of local clergy or gentlemen. Quakers did indeed inhabit areas of meat and dairy production, but not to the extent that would be expected from this explanation. (See map, p. 4 above.) Of the total number of Friends only 7.3 per cent lived in pastoral areas. A further 8.9 per cent came from mixed farming land, and 27.6 per cent, a surprisingly high proportion, resided in the arable areas in the North-West of the County. The forest areas, usually considered to be natural breeding grounds for dissent, contained only 5.8 per cent of all Quakers. The bulk of the Friends, 47 per cent, were concentrated in the county's textile parishes. The significance of wool-producing and its relation with dissent has already been suggested. The tradition of nonconformity which prevailed in these areas made parishioners more willing to accept the Quaker message. The tendency of some areas in the County to be welcoming towards dissent was probably a major factor influencing the pattern of Quaker distribution.

Overall, the geographical spread of the Quakers in Essex appears to differ significantly from that of their brethren elsewhere. This is only one of several features which make the movement in the county distinctive when compared with the development of the sect in other regions.

URBAN OR RURAL

Friends . . . were not, as now, congregated in large towns but were generally engaged in agriculture, a pursuit from which they have gradually been driven by the vexations consequent on their strange scruple about paying tithe.

Lord Macaulay, *The History of England*, ed. C. H. Firth (1913), i. 499.

---

[12] ERO, T/A420 (Extract from Bishop Compton's Census); GL, MS 9583, Bundle 2; *The Compton Census of 1676: A Critical Edition*, ed. Anne Whiteman (Oxford, 1986), 37–65.

[13] Joan Thirsk (ed.), *The Agrarian History of England and Wales*, iv *1500–1650* (Cambridge, 1967), 109–12; Spufford, *Contrasting Communities*, chap. 12; Alan Everitt, 'Nonconformity in Country Parishes', in Thirsk (ed.), *Land, Church and People* (Reading, 1970), 185–97.

TABLE 11. *Essex Quakers: Urban and Rural Distribution, 1655–1724*

	Urban	Percentage	Rural	Percentage	Total number
1655–64	711	55.4	572	44.6	1,283
1665–74	1,147	59.5	780	40.5	1,927
1675–84	1,427	60.0	952	40.0	2,379
1685–94	1,260	59.5	858	40.5	2,118
1695–1704	1,443	64.0	811	36.0	2,254
1705–14	1,246	61.2	789	38.8	2,035
1715–24	988	59.9	661	40.1	1,649

The proportion of Essex Friends residing in urban areas is distinctive and runs contrary to the sect's settlement pattern elsewhere (Table 11). The consensus hitherto has been that Quakerism was predominantly a rural movement. A study of the sect in Warwickshire, for example, found that between 1660 and 1683 around 63 per cent of Friends were resident in rural parishes. Even between 1700 and 1720, half of Friends in that county still lived in rural locations. There is also a suggestion that Quakers were unique among the nonconformist groups in that they remained settled in rural areas until the early eighteenth century; other dissenting congregations abandoned the country for the town much sooner than Friends.[14]

However, the figures compiled for this study do not confirm the conclusions of other research. In Essex Quakers were settled in the main in urban parishes and townships. The extraordinary number of Colchester Friends may explain the unusual settlement pattern; the town harboured around a quarter of all members in the county. Another factor which helps to account for the preponderance of Friends in urban locations is that a large number were employed in the textile industry. A result of this urban bias may have been greater pressure upon Friends to become integrated into local society, since economic and social connections would surely have encouraged such a tendency. The closeness of ties between Quaker tradesmen and others is suggested by the inability of the authorities to root out dissent from towns. For example, an entry in state papers concerning the town of Yarmouth, Norfolk, in 1675 recorded the judgment of Lord Robartes about the difficulties of getting officers to subdue dissent:

[14] Hurwich, 'The Social Origins of the Early Quakers', 158–9; Vann, *Social Development*, 163–4.

in corporations it will never be carried through by magistrates or the inhabitants, their livelihood consisting altogether in trade, and their depending upon one another, so that when any of them may appear to act in the least measure, their trade shall decline and . . . their credit with it.[15]

The percentage of rural Quakers in Essex, however, was not negligible. In five of the seven decades under review rural Quakers comprised around 40 per cent of the total Quaker population. It was probably the Society's well-developed organizational structure, with its network of monthly and particular meetings, which enabled so large a following to be maintained in rural areas.

THE DECLINE OF QUAKERISM

The Spirit of Truth, not being minded to lead and guide, the spirit of the world gets in, and draws and leads into the earth and earthly things; and instead of labouring to be rich in faith and good works towards God such labour chiefly how to grow rich in the world, that they may have great substance to leave to they know not who.

8th September 1687

The comments by John Banks, quoted in Braithwaite, *Second Period*, 500.

Determining the reasons for the falling numbers in Quaker ranks is no easy matter, especially as the rate of decline in Essex varied in different parishes and was at odds with the vigour shown by the movement in other regions.[16] While there had been a decline in membership from the peak of the late 1670s and early 1680s to 1725 in Essex, this trend masked significant local differences in the strength of the movement. At Colchester, Great Coggeshall, and Witham membership declined after 1684 with no recovery in the decade 1695–1704. Figures for other parishes and townships tell a quite different story: in Great Dunmow the Quaker population peaked in the decade 1695–1704, practically maintaining its strength until 1724. The same was true of Thaxted, Burnham, and Great Burstead; while at Saffron Walden there were more Quakers in the parish between 1715 and 1724 than at any other time. There is no clear explanation for this variation. One might speculate that local factors, such as a

---

[15] *Calendar of State Papers Domestic, 1675–76* (1907), 1 quoted by Christopher Hill, *Some Intellectual Consequences of the English Revolution* (1980), 56.

[16] Morgan, *Lancashire Quakers and the Establishment*, 280–1.

well-organized meeting, the presence of a charismatic local Friend, a greater interest than normal in maintaining discipline or the movement of Friends to these parishes, contributed to the strength of numbers. Whatever the reasons, the success of these areas in holding on to and in some cases even adding to membership over time could not halt the over-all decline of the movement.

The reasons for this failure have often been debated. Toleration by the state and the growth of organization within the sect, it is suggested, para-lysed the missionary spirit and hastened the movement's decline.[17] Others point to another reason for failure which was evident elsewhere; the em-igration of Quakers to the New World, they suggest, was a significant rea-son for the depletion of the numbers in Quaker ranks.[18] It is often alleged that a frequent cause of decline of sectarian groups is that their Protestant virtues of thrift and avoidance of luxury resulted in a prosperity which undermined commitment and encouraged 'worldliness' among some fol-lowers. Members were seduced by worldly values and prepared to delight in goods and luxuries which the earliest converts would have disparaged.[19] It would be foolish to deny such an influence upon Quakerism, especially as so many in the movement and outside noted its effect.[20] Voltaire hinted in the eighteenth century that Quaker decline in London was due to mem-bers' involvement and success in commerce. He noted of Friends in 1734: 'They are reduced to the necessity of earning money through commerce, and their children, made wealthy by their fathers' industry, want to enjoy things, have honours, buttons and cuffs; they are ashamed of being called Quakers and become Protestants to be in the fashion.'[21] William Jones com-mented upon a trend among Quakers towards partial acceptance of worldly values and delights much earlier. He wrote in 1679:

But it must be confessed, their zeal is most extremely fallen and abated within these twelve or fourteen years . . . They use the good things of this World with as much fondness and delight as other sinners did: Nor does Righteousness alone serve to

---

[17] Rowntree, *Quakerism: Past and Present*, 22–3; Hurwich, 'Dissent and Catholicism in English Society', 45.

[18] I owe this point to Kenneth Carroll. See also Braithwaite, *Second Period*, chap. 15; Rowntree, *Quakerism: Past and Present*, 73; Frederick B. Tolles, 'The Atlantic Community of the Early Friends', Supplement 24, *JFHS* (1952), 24–5.

[19] This notion is described in Bryan Wilson, *The Social Dimensions of Sectarianism*, 120–4. Though Wilson's book is about modern sects and cults, it is full of insights and stimulating suggestions that may apply to sectarian communities of an earlier period. See also Wilson, *Religion in Sociological Perspective*, chap. 4. Also helpful on this is Hill, *The Sociology of Religion*, chap. 3.   [20] Braithwaite, *Second Period*, 499–500.

[21] Voltaire, *Letters on England*, 35–6.

cloath them, they wear (and will do) as good *Cloth, Silks and Camlets* as the proudest of mankind can do; offering freely to stand proof *that the sin lies only in the colour, or the broadness of the Ribbon.*[22]

In the late 1680s and early 1690s the faltering commitment of members in Essex had become apparent and it was a cause of considerable anxiety to the Society there. Attempts were made to reinvigorate the movement and greater emphasis was placed upon the outward symbols of the faith. Family visits were introduced in the early 1690s to bolster the commitment of individuals in this and other areas.[23] The contagion of the world as a factor undermining the movement may have been of more significance to Friends in a county like Essex than elsewhere, since the majority lived in urban areas and many were directly involved in trade and commerce.

These factors which had been of assistance to Quakers in reaching an accommodation with local society were also in time to prove weaknesses. For example, in Essex the predisposition to acceptance of dissenting ideas, the preponderance of Quakers in urban and textile areas, and the significant number of merchants and clothiers in membership, all worked in the movement's favour in the early stages. But these advantages proved in time to be double-edged since they enmeshed Quakers in local society and pulled them away from the sect. However, a slackening of resistance to worldly ways was not of itself sufficient to drive Friends into full-scale assimilation. The belief that they were uniquely God's people, a perception which was nurtured through the persecution Quakers suffered at the hands of the officers of the Church and State, countered for a considerable time the forces of assimilation.

The attitudes of London and South-Eastern Friends have been described as 'metropolitan', 'courtly', and 'urbane' in contrast with the more rigorous brand of Quakerism practised by the Society's Northern brethren.[24] Essex Friends may well have come to share the same mentality as their London counterparts. Debates in 1713 and 1714 about the manner in which the Society should respond to proposals for the renewal of the Affirmation Act—which permitted Friends in certain circumstances to use an affirmation in preference to an oath—indicate the precise brand of Quakerism to which members belonged. Friends at Colchester, where many members constituted an important part of the trading and business community, and for the most part elsewhere in Essex were in favour of

---

[22] Jones, *Work for a Cooper*, 14, 35–6.   [23] Braithwaite, *Second Period*, 505.
[24] Morgan, *Lancashire Quakers and the Establishment*, 281.

using the alternative to the oath agreed by Parliament. To threaten in any way the limited accommodation which was allowed Friends in their trading and daily lives was not acceptable here. In other areas, especially the North, opposition to the affirmation was resolute and Friends often refused to use it because it was considered insufficiently distinct from an oath.[25]

The movement had been successful but it had never, Colchester excepted, gained an unusually strong following in Essex. While many reasons can be adduced to explain decline it is contended here that the key lay in the decade of the 1670s. Then the Society began to seek a degree of social accommodation with the world which would have been unacceptable earlier. One motive for this was a desire to limit the suffering of members. It was then that the Society gave official sanction to new forms of intercourse with the wider world. So long as the threat of persecution remained, the Society retained a sense of being distinctly apart and separate which prevented Friends from being assimilated into local society. Once toleration was granted in 1689 the Quakers' sense of their own distinctiveness was to a degree removed. That, combined with other factors, sealed the fate of the movement in the county.

---

[25] See, for example, FHL, MYM, v. 14–17, 20–2, 24–5; Morgan, *Lancashire Quakers and the Establishment*, 144–6; Braithwaite, *Second Period*, 184–9, 195; Hunt, *Two Early Political Associations*, 44–6, 51–7.

PART IV

Quakers and the World

13
A Suffering People

The progression of mankind towards good is brought about by *martyrdom* not by tyranny . . . Good, meeting with evil and remaining untainted by it, can alone conquer evil.

Leo Tolstoy, What I Believe (1885), 47–8.

It was an excellent Observation of Jesus . . . that Gold is tried in the fire, and Acceptable Men in the Furnace of Adversity . . .

Besse, Sufferings, i, p. iii.

Before and after the Restoration, Friends bore the brunt of the penalties imposed upon dissenters by the officers of Church and State. And by contrast with many of their dissenting rivals, they remained unbowed when faced by their persecutors.[1] However, the image of Friends as suffering victims, which the Society liked to foster, ought not to be accepted without qualification. While on the whole Friends would not flinch from standing by their beliefs, they also took steps to limit the prosecutions to which they might be liable under the law. In this chapter an attempt will be made to chart the type of suffering to which Friends were subject. The endeavour is limited to the period 1655 to 1684, when a series of laws, mainly new, was used by the State in an effort to crush dissent. An analysis of the pattern of prosecutions of Quakers suggests that the peaks, by and large, match the periods of acute national political tension during which the State was most worried about the activities of dissenters. Officials were most active in prosecuting Friends during the Restoration of Charles II in 1660 and the early 1660s, at the time of the Second Conventicle Act in 1670, and following the struggle to exclude Charles's son from the succession in the early 1680s which gave rise to an acute period of suffering. It was at those times that the Quakers were most to feel the constable's arm or the discomfort of the gaoler's cell. The daily lives of Friends could hardly be described as tranquil at other times, but then at least most lived free of unrelenting harassment.

---

[1] Besse, *Sufferings*, *passim*; Baxter, *Autobiography*, 189. A useful discussion of Quaker attitudes to suffering can be found in Rosemary Moore, 'Reactions to Persecution in Primitive Quakerism', *JFHS* 57 (1996), 123–32.

The nature of Quaker suffering casts an important light onto the dynamics of local society, for it reveals the influence of different parochial networks in determining the persecution of dissenters. The dependence of the civil and ecclesiastical powers on the willingness of local officials to harass and prosecute is strikingly apparent. Constables and magistrates sometimes turned a blind eye to illegal activity and on occasion deliberately acted to prevent the prosecution of Friends. This growing sympathy for Friends was in part related to a changed attitude on the part of the Society towards outsiders, which was itself a consequence of the sect's strategy for dealing with the problem of the suffering experienced by its followers. At first the Society devoutly hoped that steadfastness in the face of their persecutors would induce them to desist. But this hope was to be unfulfilled, as Friends soon recognized after the passage of the Second Conventicle Act in 1670. As a result, from the mid-1670s the Society began to appeal more vigorously and in a more organized manner to the civil and religious authorities to lessen the imposition of fines, distraint, or gaol.

Individual Quakers had often maintained a pragmatic approach towards dealing with outsiders, so long as the principles of the faith were not undermined, but the Society itself had been far more suspicious of relations with the world. Ordinary Friends might have been fortunate enough to receive protection or at least sympathy from particular individuals in local society but they were now to benefit as a result of a coherent strategy pursued by the Society. The new approach amounted to a reversal of the narrow sectarianism of the sect's early years, since the measures employed by Friends to limit persecution constituted a major step towards accommodation with worldly institutions. However, it was in time to have the unforeseen consequence of hastening forward the assimilation and then the decline of the movement.

QUAKERS AND THE PENAL CODE

The *Anabaptists* and *Quakers* made more Noise than ever, and assembled together in a greater Number, and talked what Reformations they expected in all Particulars. These Insolencies offended the Parliament very much: and the House of Commons expressed much Impatience, that the *Liturgy* was so long in preparation, that the *Act of Uniformity* might without delay be passed and Published; not without some Insinuations and Reflections, that his Majesty's Candour, and Admission of all Persons to resort to his Presence, and his Condescension to confer with them, had raised their Spirits to an Insolence unsupportable; and that

Nothing could reduce them to the Temper of good Subjects, but the highest Severity.

Edward Hyde, *The Life of Edward Earl of Clarendon written by himself* (Dublin, 1759), ii. 282.

The events of the Civil War and Interregnum had taught the Restoration authorities a bitter lesson: that religious division could generate political turmoil and bloody conflict. As a result new legislation or laws already enacted were used to subdue Restoration dissent. A number of Elizabethan and Jacobean recusancy laws were brought into play sanctioning a twenty-pound fine upon those who absented themselves from church for a month or more, with the further option to seize two-thirds of the culprits' estates if they remained recalcitrant. Also utilized was a series of new and punitive measures which were to become collectively known as the 'Clarendon Code'. Of most relevance to Friends were the Corporation Act of 1661,[2] which disqualified them from holding municipal office, the Act of Uniformity of 1662, which set out what the state considered to be appropriate religious worship, and in the same year the so-called Quaker Act, under which it was possible to levy fines and pass verdicts of imprisonment and even banishment upon Friends and other extreme radicals who refused the oath of allegiance or attended illegal meetings for worship.

Of significance also was the Conventicle Act of 1664, which sanctioned a fine of five pounds or three months' imprisonment upon those who met in groups of five or more to worship illegally. Heftier fines and transportation could be imposed if offenders remained recalcitrant. The first Conventicle Act lapsed in 1669, but in the following year a more comprehensive version was passed. The new legislation made conventiclers subject to a fine of five shillings for the first offence and ten shillings for the second. Owners of the premises on which nonconformists gathered were subject to a twenty-pound fine for a first offence and forty pounds for a second. Furthermore, informers were permitted to claim a third of any fines, and magistrates who failed to enforce the law might have a hundred-pound penalty levied upon them.

These legal measures were formidable but Quakers openly flouted them. Moreover, the prosecution imposed was frequently sporadic and less than effective, often because the attitude of the authorities towards prosecution

---

[2] For a discussion of the laws passed to discourage dissent see J. P. Kenyon (ed.), *The Stuart Constitution, 1603–1688: Documents and Commentary* (1966), 376–86; Charles F. Mullett, 'The Legal Position of English Protestant Dissenters 1660–1685', *Virginia Law Review*, 22 (1936), 494–526; John Miller, *Popery and Politics in England, 1660–1688* (Cambridge, 1973), esp. chaps. 8 and 9, which contain a useful discussion of the issues raised here.

of dissent was itself confused. During the periods of political alarm magistrates, under direction from central government, attempted to crack down hard on attenders at Quaker meetings in Essex.[3] However, when the political situation moderated, if the central authorities showed any concern, it was only for those who were considered to be the 'ringleaders' or 'principal hearers' at Quaker conventicles in the county.[4] Perhaps a policy of mass prosecution was beyond the power of the county authorities or one which they did not in reality wish to carry through. Broader political factors were also significant. The battle for political supremacy between Parliament and Charles II prevented the full force of the laws being brought against dissenters.[5] And when the King issued in 1672 the short-lived Declaration of Indulgence in the hope of assisting his Catholic subjects, his dissenting subjects also benefited. There was a growing fear of Catholicism culminating in the discovery of the Popish Plot in 1679, which diverted Anglican attention away from dissenters.

Despite the uncertainty over which dissident religious group offered the greatest threat—Fifth Monarchist, Baptist, or Catholic—Quakers were still the most vulnerable to prosecution. An examination of the total number of indictments for non-attendance at church during two periods of heightened political tension from 1670 to 1672 and 1682 to 1685 reveals that Friends made up a sizeable proportion of those presented to the courts, even though they constituted a minority of nonconformists in the county of Essex. Of the citations between 1670 and 1672, 35 per cent involved Quakers, and for the years 1682 to 1685, the figure was 23 per cent.[6] The disproportionate number of presentments and indictments against Quakers is a reflection of the great threat which the sect seemed to represent to the social and religious order compared to most other dissenters. Though there were many offences for which Quakers were liable to be prosecuted, that for which Friends were most presented in the civil courts was absence from church.

---

[3] ERO, Q/SPbl (1682-5); Q/SR 448/121.

[4] HBR, 66/3 (Sessions Papers), 126/5 (Letter to the Mayor) (13 July 1669); ERO, Q/SO2, fo. 218ᵛ (1684); Besse, *Sufferings*, i. 195; EUL, EQ 22, 21; George Fox, the younger, *A True Relation of the Lamentable and Unlawful Proceedings of the Magistrates of Harwich in Essex* (n.p., 1660), 4.   [5] Miller, *Popery and Politics*, chap. 3.

[6] The number of indictments of nonconformists in the Quarter Sessions Courts was 1,955 between 1682 and 1685. Of these indictments 444 applied to Quakers. In the Assize Court for the period 1670-2, 377 of the 1,085 nonconformist presentments were for Quakers. For statistical purposes I have assumed that all absentees from church were nonconformists. But see Margaret Spufford, 'Can We Count the "Godly" and the "Conformable" in the Seventeenth Century?', *Journal of Ecclesiastical History*, 36 (1985).

There is a clear difference in attitude and behaviour between Friends and other dissenters in Essex. In a letter written in 1682 to Bishop Compton, a correspondent expresses some satisfaction at witnessing dissenting parishioners who had been disturbed at a Colchester conventicle[7] subsequently attending public worship: the inference is that some parishioners, despite being dissenters, were willing to have some contact with the established church probably to the extent of being occasional conformists. By contrast the Friends, unlike many of their dissenting rivals, were wholly uncompromising, and their obstinacy must have marked them out in local society. This is surely a major reason why Quakers were prosecuted more often than their nonconformist neighbours.

THE ENFORCERS OF THE LAW

Magistrates

What if Christ or any of his Apostles should have been in the body now outwardly, and come to the town and had a meeting to serve and worship God, would'st thou have asked Christ Jesus if he would swear allegiance to the King who shall swear not at all . . . wouldst thou have said to him as thou said to us, there is a law against meeting and by that we too must proceed against you, and I demand a fine of you which if you will not pay nor give security for ye good behaviour, you must go to prison . . .

Petition for release of Quakers in Harwich Gaol (24 July 1669), HBR, 66/3 (Sessions Papers).

Friends looked upon the institution of magistracy with ambivalence. They did not call for its outright abolition since they conceded the need for justices to enforce the law against genuine wrongdoers. However, they rebuked magistrates for harrying Quaker meetings and for complying with the contemporary social customs; for example, over hat honour, which required the paying of respect to superiors.[8] To most justices, Quakers seemed dangerous radicals who held the office of the magistrate and the judiciary in contempt. Friends claimed that magistrates acted in unison with the clergy to harass them; they turned a blind eye to illegal proceedings,

---

[7] Bodleian Library, Oxford, Rawlinson MS C 983, No. 26, fo. 59. From Sir John Shaw, the Recorder of Colchester.

[8] Parnel, *A Shield of the Truth*, 42, 19; Hallywell, *An Account of Familism*, 98, A2; Parnel, *Collection*, 466.

failing to check the sometimes violent actions of the mob against them.[9] In Essex a number of magistrates showed great determination and energy in prosecuting Friends; their names recur in the Quakers' records.[10] None the less, there is evidence that magistrates became progressively more under-standing of Friends and that even early on in the movement's history a minority showed them considerable sympathy.

It was usually current political circumstances which determined how serious were the perceptions of the Quaker threat to the body politic. At the height of the reaction to the Exclusion Crisis, the justices complied with the demands of central Government to search out preachers and conventiclers, and to ensure that recognizances and sureties were taken.[11] An independent spirit on the part of justices was unwise, especially as magistrates were aware that failure to enforce the laws against dissenters made them liable to prosecution. The Colchester Quaker, John Furly, intimated as much; when writing to London Friends in 1685 he noted that Colchester's magistrates proceeded against Quakers not on account of their own inclinations but 'through fear'.[12] The importance of the attitude of the central authorities in determining overall patterns of persecution or tolerance is again suggested by an appeal of Harwich Friends in 1685 to the Earl of Middleton, an official of the King, when a Justice was responsible for continually harassing a meeting in the town. It elicited the response that the justice was an 'impertinent fellow', since he had no order to act in that way.[13] In 1682 John Shaw, the Recorder of Colchester, hinted at the large degree of sympathy for nonconformists when he complained that there would be little hope of subduing the town's dissenting congregations until the magistrates showed more enthusiasm for the task.[14]

When a policy of harassment was applied locally it was not necessarily sanctioned by government. Certain magistrates were eager to fine, distrain, or imprison Quakers whatever the political circumstances of the time. The Quaker approach to the Earl of Middleton, already referred to, is indicative

---

[9] Tomlinson, *Seven Particulars*, 6; ERO, Assi 35/96/2 No. 6; Parnel *Collection*, p. xxvii; and id., *A Shield of the Truth*, 42.

[10] See, for instance, Dudley Templar: FHL, Great Book of Sufferings, i. 405–6.

[11] For example, ERO, Q/SO2 fo. 240ʳ (1685).

[12] For an account of a sympathetic justice see James Dickinson, *A Journal of the Life, Travels, and Labour of Love in the Work of the Ministry* (1745), 24; Gratton, *Journal*, 85–6; Sansom, *An Account of many Remarkable Passages*, 366–7; FHL, MMS, i. 102.

[13] FHL, MMS, iv. 126–7 (4 Aug. 1685).

[14] Bodleian Library, Oxford, Rawlinson MS C 983, No. 26, fo. 59. From Sir John Shaw, the Recorder of Colchester.

of such a situation. When distraining upon Witham Friends, another justice advised constables to take for a five shilling fine, what was worth five pounds.[15] Moreover, magistrates not only dealt with Friends at the regular civil courts, but also had authority to execute summary jurisdiction; and a number used this power as it pleased them. Often it was at the instigation of local officials who were particularly hostile to the sect that Friends suffered. For instance, it was during the mayoralty of William Moore in 1663 that troops were brought in to quell the Quaker ranks in Colchester and the sect's meeting house was boarded up. A similar situation prevailed in Thaxted in 1683, when a Colonel Turner and others nailed up the meeting house and burnt the benches and stools to prevent the congregation from assembling.[16]

There is evidence of a less hostile attitude on the part of some magistrates prior to the 1680s. In 1676 the Quakers' Yearly Meeting advised an approach to justices in the hope that they might be persuaded to hinder local officers who prosecuted Friends.[17] Earlier still, in 1659, for instance, the Society drew up lists of sympathetic justices, and during 1664 the Quakers in Colchester recognized that some magistrates had been lenient when applying the law against them.[18] That magistrates were not all of the same opinion is suggested by the complaint in 1662 of the imprisoned Colchester Friend Stephen Crisp. Confined in Harwich gaol for refusing the Oath of Allegiance, Crisp appealed in 1663 to John Eldred, a Colchester magistrate, to get him freed. He explained that most Justices felt no antipathy towards him or the other Quakers in the town but that one JP, Daniel Smith, was bent on intimidating Friends.[19]

Magistrates had increasingly learned to tolerate what they considered a band of sincere if somewhat misguided Christians. A less aggressive method of evangelizing from the mid-1660s also helps to account for the magistracy's more lenient treatment of Quakers. In addition, their suffering must have earned the sympathy of some justices who were themselves Nonconformists. From the mid-1670s Quakers were to appeal to justices in order to limit their sufferings.

---

[15] EUL, EQ 22, 20–1.   [16] Besse, *Sufferings*, i. 199–201, 208.
[17] EUL, EQ 27 (17 May 1676).
[18] [Anon.], *A True and Faithful Relation of the Proceedings of the Magistrates from the People of God (called Quakers) in Colchester* (1664), 5; *Calendar of State Papers Domestic 1640–1700*, lviii. 35 (21 May 1659). See also Davies, *An Account of the Convincement*, 60–1, 82.
[19] FHL, Portfolio MS, 32/27 (23 Aug. 1663); EUL, Crisp MS fo. 303ʳ; [Anon.], *A True and Faithful Relation*, 6; *FPT*, 101.

Constables

While we were talking, came by several poor creatures, carried by the Constables
for being at a conventicle. They would go like lambs, without any resistance. I
would to God they would either conform, or be more wise and not ketched.

7 August 1664.

Samuel Pepys, *The Shorter Pepys*, ed. Robert Latham (Harmondsworth,
1987), 413–14.

Despite Pepys' observations, of all the local officials given responsibility
for prosecuting Quakers, parish constables usually showed Friends the greatest sympathy. They are known to have returned goods that had been distrained, and the excess on goods already taken to pay fines;[20] and even on
occasion to have paid fines themselves rather than execute warrants[21] or
distrain Quakers.[22] And when constables did present Friends, this was often
after several warnings that they should conform. That some constables made
a positive decision to shield Quakers and other dissenters from the full
effects of the law is clear from the remarks of contemporaries. In 1682,
for example, Sir John Shaw, the Recorder of Colchester, complained that
officers in the borough were loath to execute warrants 'without many and
great threats',[23] and in 1684 a local correspondent of Bishop Compton's
noted that there was 'a general connivance at conventicles in this town'.[24]

Earlier, in 1670 at Great Coggeshall, the constables brought in presentments indicating that there were no Quakers in the parish. In turn,
the Assize Court prosecuted the constables as it was recognized that 'several parishioners did not go to church'. Further evidence of reluctance to
present nonconformists is suggested by the large numbers of constables
who appeared in the Court of Assize and Quarter Sessions for wilfully
misleading the authorities regarding the number of nonconformists in
their respective parishes. The presentments of constables in Essex for
this failure peak in 1670 and in the years 1682 and 1685, when the state
demanded a strict enforcement of the laws against nonconformity. The
implication is that the allegiance of officers was possibly greater to the local-
ity and its inhabitants than to the State. The query of one constable in

[20] FHL, Great Book of Sufferings, v, pt. 1, 203 (1690); ibid., ii, pt. 1, 217 (1705); EUL,
EQ 22, 15 (1671).
[21] Besse, *Sufferings*, i. 204; FHL, Great Book of Sufferings, i. 100 (1670–4), ibid., ii,
pt. 1, 73; EUL, EQ 22, 15 (1671); FHL, Great Book of Sufferings, v, pt. 1, 203 (1690).
[22] Besse, *Sufferings*, i. 207; EUL, COLMM i. 189 (1670s), EQ 22, 15 (1677); FHL, Great
Book of Sufferings, ii, pt. 2, 480 (1678).
[23] Bodleian Library, Oxford, Rawlinson MS, C 983, No. 26, fo. 59.
[24] Ibid., No. 32, fo. 187, from William Shelton; ERO, Q/SR 435/53 (1677).

1677 as to whether action should be taken against dissenters, whom he termed 'harmless people',[25] probably represented a widespread sentiment.

There is also other evidence of support by constables for Quakers.[26] This is suggested by a comparison of the names of those Quakers notified to the Quarter Session and Assize Courts in Essex between 1670 and 1672 with a list of known members at this time.[27] In 1670, the returns from eighty-seven parishes were entered at Quarter Sessions. Quakers were noted by nineteen constables, though the returns from twenty-one other parishes where Quakers are known to have resided make no reference to Friends at all. Forty parishes made returns in 1671; eight constables mentioned Quakers, but the officers from nineteen parishes with Quaker populations reported that there were no nonconformists present. Finally, in 1672 there were presentments covering forty-three parishes; the returns from thirteen of these parishes note Quakers, but in ten parishes known to include Quaker inhabitants their presence was not mentioned.

One needs to sound a note of caution, for an inconsistency in record-keeping or mere administrative incompetence may account for the omission of Quaker names. None the less, it seems more likely that some constables deliberately excluded the names of Friends from their returns. Ties to kin and neighbours and a broad range of social and economic relationships often influenced the actions they were prepared to take against fellow parishioners. By their actions they may also have been reflecting the consensus in the parish and wishing to maintain a climate of harmony within.[28] How should we interpret this evidence? Is it indicative of widespread though tacit support for Quaker activities, or are these presentments of constables symptomatic of the attitudes of no more than a significant minority? We ought not to accept that this sentiment was universal. Many officers still calculated that the Quaker heresy would wreak untold harm on the community if left unhindered, and were prepared to execute the laws with harshness. It is unlikely that any individual Quaker

---

[25] For example, ERO, Assi 35/112/9 No. 32 and Assi 35/112/10 No. 22; Q/SR 432/53–4 (1677).   [26] EUL, EQ 22, 19 (1683), 55.

[27] The figure for 1670 is taken from the returns of a series of petty constables' presentments. See ERO, Q/SR 423, 8–41 and also, ERO, Assi 35/112/2 Nos. 22–62 and Assi 35/113/2 Nos. 16–49.

[28] J. A. Sharpe, 'Enforcing the Law in the Seventeenth-Century English Village', in V. A. B. Gattrell, Bruce Lenman, and Geoffrey Parker (eds.), *Crime and the Law: The Social History of Crime in Western Europe Since 1500* (1980). Keith Wrightson, 'Two Concepts of Order: Justices, Constables, and Jurymen in Sixteenth-Century England', in John Brewer and John Styles (eds.), *An Ungovernable People: The English and the Law in the Eighteenth Century* (1980).

avoided all kinds of hardship, though the extent of it varied according to the attitudes of the different parish authorities.

THE PROSECUTION OF FRIENDS

for they (Quakers) were so resolute, and gloried in their constancy and sufferings, that they assembled openly . . . and were dragged away daily to the common gaol . . . so that the gaol at Newgate was filled with them. Abundance of them died in prison, and yet they continued their assemblies still.

Baxter, *Autobiography*, 189.

The obvious sympathy of some magistrates and constables does not mean that great suffering was not undergone by many ordinary Friends. Indeed, in the seventeenth century more than four hundred Friends died as a result of harassment or imprisonment and thousands more were imprisoned on account of their faith.[29] But it is legitimate to ask what was the nature of the persecution most Friends endured and how widespread was it among rank and file believers? To date historians have utilized the Quakers' own 'Suffering Books' and published literature as a guide to the matter, but reliance on these records alone is unsatisfactory. The 'Books' are sometimes uneven in the types of prosecutions they record, with some sufferings ignored altogether. Moreover, the published literature emphasizes the most sensational aspects of the cruelty to which Quakers were subject. This is not surprising, given that accounts were often laid before those in authority in a bid to obtain clemency. Like other historians I have used the suffering records of Friends, for they are an indispensable source, though where possible they have been supplemented with other records of prosecution.

The purpose of raising the matter of Quaker suffering is not to question the sometimes horrific treatment meted out to Friends. The intention here is to consider whether evidence in local archives can reveal more about the pattern of prosecutions. Did the changing perceptions about Quakers in local society and the sect's own campaigns to limit prosecution

---

[29] Figures on Quaker deaths and imprisonments derived from Joseph Besse's *Sufferings* and quoted by W. A. Speck, *Reluctant Revolutionaries* (Oxford, 1988), 30. For a questioning approach to the degree of suffering experienced by Quakers and the steps taken to influence the authorities see Craig Horle, *The Quakers and the English Legal System 1660–1688* (Philadelphia, 1988), chaps. 2–5. On the pattern of Quaker prosecutions see David M. Butler, 'Friends' Sufferings 1650–1688: A Comparative Summary', *JFHS* 55 (1988), 180–4.

have any effect on the type of suffering experienced by members during the periods of maximum suffering?

Quaker and other sources have been analysed to get an idea of offences for which Friends were prosecuted and imprisoned and how the nature of this persecution varied between 1655 and 1684. The figures are revealing in that they reflect how the authorities resolved to deal with Quakers and how the relations between Quakers and local society evolved.

Fines and Distraints

There is scant direct evidence of the type of fines imposed by the civil authorities, but it is often possible to calculate indirectly the exactions the courts wished to make, for under the recusancy laws Friends were penalized according to the number of weeks they absented themselves from church. Failure to attend for up to three weeks earned a penalty of twelve pence per Sunday; a month's absence incurred the much larger fine of twenty pounds. Quakers, of course, refused to attend church at all. The size of the fine ought to indicate the degree to which the authorities were worried about the sect. During the 1660s the presentments of Quakers in Essex were mostly for absence from church for a month, thus incurring the more onerous fine of twenty pounds.[30] Among the large number of presentments which survive for the period 1670 to 1672 information on the length of absence from church is in the majority of cases not given. Where the length of absence is indicated, almost half of the Friends concerned were subjected to the larger fine.[31] Colchester appears to provide an exception: Friends detained for attending conventicles there during the early 1660s suffered the lesser fine for three weeks' absence at twelve pence per Sunday.[32] A striking finding is how lenient on the whole the civil authorities were towards Friends in the town.

Evidence worthy of a more systematic analysis is available for the years 1682 to 1686 in the Quarter Sessions records for the county.[33] The figures derived from them do not include prosecutions of Quakers in towns like Colchester and Harwich, which had their own civil courts. The prosecutions are analysed in such a way as to reflect the penalties imposed upon

---

[30] Of the 93 Friends presented to the Courts of Quarter Sessions between 1660 and 1667, over 90 per cent were subjected to the larger fine.

[31] Of the 152 presentments which give length of absence from church, 74 were for four weeks or more. ERO, Assi 35/111/7 to Assi 35/113/2.

[32] CBR, Depositions Relating to Quaker Conventicles, loose leaf.

[33] ERO, QSPb 1 (Process Book of Indictment).

TABLE 12. *Indictments of Individual Quakers at Essex Quarter Sessions, 1682–1686*

Fines	Number	Percentage
12*d.*	90	45.7
12*d.*/£20	68	34.5
£20	39	19.8
Total	197	

individual Quakers (Table 12). Almost 46 per cent of Friends indicted suffered only the lesser fines of twelve pence per Sunday; a little under 20 per cent had the larger sum of twenty pounds alone imposed upon them. There was a mixture of fines imposed upon the remainder, with the twenty-pound levy being imposed normally after a succession of lesser fines.

It is significant that during what is widely considered a period of political turmoil almost half of the Friends indicted were spared the worst penalties that could be levied upon them. The statistics suggest a good deal of sympathy for Quakers in local society. Even so, the civil authorities were eager to ensure that those who disobeyed the law were punished in some way. Indeed, some Justices consistently imposed fines on the poorer brethren in the movement, presumably in order to force them to relinquish membership of the sect.[34]

In contrast, the records of the church courts during the 1670s hardly register the presence of dissenters. Perhaps the religious authorities had chosen to focus their attention elsewhere or there was a recognition that the apprehension of nonconformists was better dealt with by the secular courts. Compared to the capability of the secular courts to distrain and imprison with almost immediate effect, the church authorities seemed impotent. Except in a few parishes only Quakers and a few other nonconformists were presented during some years of that decade, though the presentation of Quakers was still rare; a form of toleration had been established. During the 1680s the church courts stepped up their campaign against dissent, but by then the sect was well established and the likelihood of its eradication slim.

Yet, however lenient the authorities were towards Friends, the sect considered any imposition upon members to be unjustified. Recalcitrant

---

[34] In 1686 a number of Essex Friends were said to be paying fines of twelve pence per week. FHL, MMS, v. 245.

Quakers who did not pay up became liable to distraint of their goods. Some public officials sought to protect Friends or at least to carry out their duty with a degree of fairness when distraining. The goods taken from Colchester Friends in the 1670s hardly exceeded the value of the fines imposed upon them.[35] A picture of distraints in the rest of the county is provided by the sect's suffering books. Between 1660 and 1684 hundreds of Quakers found themselves at the mercy of local officials for preaching, holding, or attending meetings. Hundreds of pounds' worth of goods were taken from Quakers as the process of distraint proceeded. The less scrupulous took far in excess of that to which they were entitled when distraining, but these may have been exceptions. The alternative for some Friends was a term of imprisonment which might be preferable to the distraining ravages of parish officials. Gaol sentences in place of fines and consequent distraint ranged from as little as ten days to two months.[36]

Quaker records indicate that as a result of fines the suffering of individuals could be severe, especially in the early years of the movement, but that this had moderated by the 1680s. In respect of fines Colchester Friends seem to have been treated with some leniency throughout.

Imprisonment

There were several hundred imprisonments of Essex Quakers in the thirty or so years from 1655 to 1684 for periods lasting from a few days to several years. Over eighty Essex Quakers were gaoled in the first years of the movement, indicating the terrible menace that sect members were thought to pose at that time. The most common reasons for the imprisonment of Quakers during the 1650s were the disturbance of ministers at public worship and refusal to pay tithes. Such behaviour was viewed by many in local society with deep disapproval.

Friends were particularly reviled by the clergy for speaking in church. They certainly acted in an extremely provocative manner. In 1660 George Ede announced in church that participating in the Lord's Supper was equivalent to partaking in 'the table of divells'. On other occasions Friends interrupted services of baptism and burial, and the mere presence of Mary Bourne and Zachary Child at the parish church was sufficient provocation to justify their being beaten by some of the congregation.[37] Ralph Josselin was troubled on more than one occasion by the activities of parish

---

[35] EUL, Crisp MS (May 1670).   [36] ERO, Q/SR 405/180 (1665); 402/26 (1664).
[37] FHL, Great Book of Sufferings, i. 407; Besse, *Sufferings*, i. 193; EUL, EQ 22, 8.

Quakers. In 1659 he recalled in his *Diary* how 'a Quaker wench came bois-
terously into the church up almost to the deske, I perceived persons expected
some disturbance, but she staid the end and then went out quietly,
blessed be god'. Earlier in 1656 he noted:

Sam Burton, and lame Buyat, while I was reading the chapter, were sitting in the
maids seate, and made a disturbance, the justice commanded the Constable to take
them forth to the cage, the mother went out of the church and tooke her son from
the Constable and said her housband paid scott and lott in the towne, and her son
should sitt any where.[38]

From the mid-1650s to the decade's end thirty-seven Friends in
Essex are recorded as having been incarcerated for speaking in church,
though this probably under-represents the number of such incidents.[39]
Prosecution and imprisonment of Quakers for disorderly behaviour in
church almost ceased as the practice declined from the early 1660s. This
was the first sign that Quakers were prepared to moderate evangelizing
activity in the face of official disquiet.

The Quaker practice of refusing tithes constituted an equally robust challenge to the authority of the Church, for thereby the economic security
of the ministry was undermined. An entry in the Archdeacon's court records
for 1663 is a reminder of the eagerness of many clerics to take action against
Friends. Under the names of John and Joseph Pollard of Steeple (both
of whom owed the local incumbent tithe and church rates) are the desig-
nations 'incarcerati'.[40] However, it was not just clergy who abhorred Quakers
on this count; lay impropriators were as much disturbed. The measure of
official anxiety at Quaker tithe refusal is evident from the number of Friends,
over fifty, imprisoned on this account between 1655 and 1664. The pressure did not cease as imprisonment or seizure of property for tithes persisted. Crisp's account of imprisonment from 1656 to 1659 notes that
imprisonment for tithe refusal varied from nine weeks to three months,
six months, twenty months, and two years or more.[41] Though clerical sentiment largely determined the pattern of imprisonment for resistance to
tithe payment, a spell in gaol appears not to have been an inevitable consequence of refusal to pay. Towards the end of the seventeenth century
the level of prosecutions and subsequent imprisonment for tithe offences
declined sharply; a change in the law simplified the action necessary for a

[38] Josselin, *Diary*, 450, 377.
[39] Besse, *Sufferings*, i. 192 (1656–9); FHL, Great Book of Sufferings, i. 405–6 (1656).
[40] ERO, D/ABA 10, fo. 30ʳ (17 Mar. 1663); D/AEA 44, fo. 96ᵛ (June 1666).
[41] EUL, Crisp MS, fos. 300ᵛ–301ᵛ.

claimant to recover tithes. The decline was also indicative of greater willingness on the part of Friends to pay dues surreptitiously against the will of the Society.[42]

Since Friends believed that the swearing could not be justified, the law which required the taking of an Oath of Allegiance to the crown became a convenient instrument of restraint. At the Restoration officials decided that the more extreme forms of dissent had to be subdued. Over eighty Friends were imprisoned for refusing the oath alone, an indication of how serious the need to contain dissenters was considered.[43] Friends arrested at East Ham, for example, were charged 'with a house meeting amongst a multitude of other people, and a pretence of God's worship and refusing to take the Oath of Allegiance'.[44] Those Quakers at Harwich gaol in 1662 were likewise placed there 'for holding an illicit conventicle, and refusing to take the Oath of Allegiance, or attending the Church of England'.[45] The intention of magistrates was probably to warn Friends about their unruly behaviour rather than to extirpate the sect root and branch. The variations in length of imprisonment from a matter of days to the more usual two or three months seem to confirm this.[46]

Though confinement in gaol was a regular occurrence throughout the period, the number of imprisoned Friends varied. After the first decade the numbers of incarcerated Quakers were not significantly high again until the early to mid-1680s when the authorities targeted the sect's 'ringleaders'. Quaker arrests on these occasions were due mainly to Friends' refusing the Oath of Allegiance or failing to provide sureties for good behaviour. Over fifty Friends were gaoled between 1682 and 1684, presumably in order to disable the movement at a politically troublesome time.

The number of imprisonments over the decades reflects the general pattern of prosecutions indicated earlier. Quaker incarcerations peaked in the 1650s, the early 1660s, 1675 to 1679, and 1680 to 1684 (Table 13). However, the imprisonments for tithe refusal were not related to wider developments in the body politic but were more dependent on the prejudice of the local incumbent or other litigant. In the 1650s a remarkably high number of Friends were incarcerated for committing disturbances in church. Informal actions taken against Friends such as beatings or being held in

---

[42] Davies, 'The Quakers in Essex', 115–18.
[43] Besse, *Sufferings*, i. 197–8; EQ 22, 9–10 (1661); FHL, Great Book Of Sufferings, i. 415–16. [44] ERO, Q/SR 396/125.
[45] HBR, 98/15 (Sessions Book), No. 121.
[46] ERO, Q/SR 407/69 (1666), 406/110 (1665); Besse, *Sufferings*, i. 202; EUL, EQ 22, 11 (1665) and 19 (1683).

TABLE 13. *Quaker Imprisonment: Derived from Suffering Records, 1655–1684*

	1655–9	1660–4	1665–9	1670–4	1675–9	1680–4
Absence from church		8			4	
Not swearing		87	2			21
Teaching unlicensed		1				
Non-payment of church rate					7	1
Disturbing ministers	37	8				
Non-payment of tithes	29	24	4		13	6
Meeting illegally	6	32	14		3	7
Refusing sureties	2					24
Excommunication		8	3			1
Miscellaneous	9			7		
Total	83	168	21	9	27	60

Sources: FHL, The Great Book of Suffering; EUL, Essex Sufferings; and Besse, *Sufferings*

the stocks disappear from the suffering books after the 1650s. The new and re-enacted legislation was considered to be more effective in containing the movement.

Although the number of prosecutions experienced by Friends increased at times of political crisis, there are indications that the severity of prosecutions lessened over time and was never to reach the height that it did in the 1660s. Even in the 1680s, when Quaker prosecutions were again at significant levels, they were not pursued with the same ferocity as earlier. The main reason for this was the petitioning and negotiating activities of Quakers themselves, who sought accommodation with the world to limit their suffering.

THE RESPONSE TO PERSECUTION

The behaviour of the Quakers . . . had something in it that looked bold . . . they would not petition to be set at liberty, nor would they pay their fines set on them, nor so much as the jail fees, calling these the wages of unrighteousness. And as soon as they were let out, they went to their meeting-houses again; and when they found they were shut up by order, they held the meetings in the streets, before the doors of those houses. They said, they would not disown or be ashamed of their meeting together to worship God; but in imitation of Daniel, they would the more publicly, because they were forbidden the doing it. Some called this obstinacy, while others called it firmness; but they carried their point: for the government grew weary of dealing with so much perverseness, and so began to let them alone.

Bishop Gilbert Burnet, *History of his Own Time* (1838), 184.

Friends would have welcomed Burnet's assessment, since it supported the sect's contention that it was Quaker steadfastness in the face of persecution which alone led government to desist. But in this regard Burnet was surely mistaken, for the changed attitude was not the result of a passive, albeit determined, resistance on the part of the sect but due to more complex reasons. A variety of factors coalesced to the benefit of the Quaker sect. There was a latent sympathy among some magistrates, constables, and neighbours for Friends, and over time a familiarity with Quakers in local society made some feel that the sect was not the pernicious presence that it had once seemed. But one factor stood out above all others in determining attitudes in the local community and that was the changed stance of the Society itself towards local officials and those in authority.

Friends had petitioned central government for clemency towards suffering members since the days of the Commonwealth, but up to the mid-1670s this petitioning had been unsystematic, and was not entered into with the full resources and support of the wider Society. In 1676 a 'Meeting for Suffering', based in London, was instituted with the purpose of surveying the extent of suffering in general and offering advice to persecuted Friends in each county. This was to be a major and significant change in the way that Friends related to worldly people and their institutions. In Essex Quaker meetings appointed two local Friends who were given the task of recording and passing on to London the accounts of suffering in the county.[47] Officials at the Meeting for Suffering were aware of the persecution of Friends across the land and with this accumulated knowledge were well placed to advise their county brethren of the best course of action.[48]

Friends' counsel was diverse, giving recommendations on matters ranging from the best course to follow over disputes concerning land that backed onto the railings of the parish church to whether sureties should be given for good behaviour, whether attorneys should be employed when a Friend was sued for debt, or whether Friends should go to prison when a writ had been issued from the Exchequer.[49] The Society cautioned suffering Friends about seeking legal remedies because of the danger of

[47] PRO, RG6 1379, 1; FHL, MMS, iv. 20 (1686).
[48] FHL, Book of Cases, i. 47–9.
[49] FHL, MMS, vii. 262 (1690); MMS, iv. 123 (1684); MMS, iii. 35–6; MMS, iv. 226 (1685).

compromising the movement's principles, though it left the final decision to individuals.[50] There was none the less a sea change in attitudes from the mid-1670s. From then on the Society offered not only advice but encouraged members to seek redress by visiting and negotiating with those in authority over the present suffering of some Friends and the future punishments to which others might become subject. Craig Horle has illustrated the ways in which the use of the law constituted a major step towards accommodation, for previously the Society had called for reform of the law and considered its representatives little better than pariahs.[51] This change was part of a wider shift in perception among Quakers as to how their goal could best be met. The most probable reason for this fresh approach was the vicious persecution of Friends following the passage of the second Conventicle Act. The records indicate that many ordinary followers were fined and then had distraints imposed upon them that were far in excess of the expected levy. A combination of renewed persecution and a realization that the State might seek to impose a blanket persecution at its whim forced Friends to develop a new strategy for limiting suffering which involved them in a greater interaction with the world.

The Meeting for Suffering advised county Friends to avoid antagonizing the authorities unnecessarily. In 1681, for instance, Friends were recommended not to pass any public comments upon the magistrates who prosecuted them.[52] Friends were also advised not to discuss matters relating to government in taverns and other social venues.[53] The methods by which Quakers challenged the application of the recusancy laws illustrated the degree of coordination and discipline that permeated the Quaker movement. From 1678 meetings dispatched representatives to all Assize and Quarter Sessions to discover whether Friends were to appear in court. If prosecution was imminent, Friends approached grand jurors in the hope of persuading them to dismiss the prosecution on the grounds that the laws were framed to apprehend Roman Catholics and not Quakers.[54] Magistrates were approached to stop prosecutions and hinder the activities of lesser officials.[55] The statistical evidence on recusancy fines suggests that

---

[50] EUL, EQ 26, 161 (1670s); FHL, MYM, i. 26 (1685).

[51] See Horle, *The Quakers and the English Legal System*, 162–73, 215. Horle dates the decisive year for the changing of Quaker attitudes to the law as 1673. See also his 'Changing Quaker Attitudes toward Legal Defence: The George Fox Case, 1673–5, and the Establishment of the Meeting for Sufferings', in J. William Frost and John M. Moore (eds.), *Seeking the Light: Essays in Quaker History in Honor of Edwin B. Bronner* (Pennsylvania, 1986), 17–39.

[52] FHL, EQ 27 (24 May 1681).   [53] FHL, Book of Cases, i. 98 (1681).

[54] EUL, COLMM 34, 62, EQ 27 (6th 4 m 1682); FHL, MYM, i. 110–11.

[55] EUL, EQ 27 (17 May 1676); FHL, MMS, iv. 164 (1686).

Friends' campaigns in this respect were successful. When Quakers were prosecuted under the recusancy laws in the 1680s, some Justices overlooked the normal requirement of swearing an oath and refrained from imprisoning or fining Friends on condition that they signed a declaration of loyalty.[56]

Petitioning was extended beyond the county to representatives of central authority. Appeals were made to the Attorney General in 1686 to free imprisoned Quakers, and judges were approached in the late 1670s before they joined the circuit in order that the injustice to and consequent hardship of Friends might be laid before them.[57] Quakers were also advised to take what steps they were able locally to ensure the election of Members of Parliament sympathetic to the dissenting cause.[58] Besides issuing recommendations to petition the judiciary, the Meeting for Suffering in London also gave valuable advice on how to avoid certain legal penalties. Quakers under a charge of a month's or more absence from church on the word of an informer, for example, were advised not to attend court.[59] The Meeting calculated that an informer would be unlikely to proceed, since the cost of undertaking action for arrest, which would be the next step, was considerable. Friends may have remained at liberty because of such advice. From the mid-1670s the Society's new approach to the civil authority was the chief reason for the fall in the number of imprisoned Quakers and for the reluctance of some in authority to impose the stiffest of fines upon most county Friends.

Friends also exploited with a remarkable degree of skill the network of communal ties and allegiances that enabled local society to run smoothly. This is evidenced from the certificates drawn up by some parishioners who wished to procure the release of Quakers from prison. In 1685 several inhabitants of Harlow described Mathew Clare, a Quaker from the parish, as 'a man of a quiet behaviour'.[60] Anthony Pennystone and John Surridge, both from Saffron Waldon, possessed certificates describing them as 'quiet and peaceable',[61] which were signed by neighbours, the local overseers, and constables. The Friends exerted pressure not on the judiciary alone, but also within the local community to ease the burden of persecution.

Friends were prepared to go to great lengths to achieve their goals. There are accounts in Quaker records of visits during the 1680s to the clergy in

[56] FHL, MMS ii. 94 (1681), Book of Cases, i. 96 (1681).
[57] EUL, EQ 27, 2 May 1678; COLMM 34, 62; FHL, MSM, iv. 25.
[58] FHL, MMS, iv. 271 (1686); MMS, iv. 25 (1686); Book of Cases, i. 82 (1681).
[59] FHL, Book of Cases, i. 47–9. EUL, EQ 27 (June 1682), COLMM 34, 34.
[60] FHL, MMS, iv. 167 (1685); Horle, *The Quakers and the English Legal System*, 220–2.
[61] FHL, MMS, iv. 153–4 (1685).

order to press for leniency towards their co-religionists. Two Friends attended the Bishop of London in 1686.[62] In the same year an appeal was made to the Bishop to procure the freedom of several Harlow Friends gaoled upon a writ of excommunication.[63] There are also several other examples of clergy being solicited to intervene on behalf of beleaguered Friends.[64] When all else had failed, a final recourse was an approach to a cleric's relative or other sympathetic individual in the parish in the hope that he might mediate on behalf of Quakers.[65] The charitable actions of some bishops can probably be accounted for by doubts as to whether persecuting Friends was the best method of winning them back to the Church. The bishops more than others were aware that a harsh policy hardly satisfied the Gospel's teaching of love to one's neighbours, especially when Quakers had become peaceful and reliable members of the local society.[66]

The most striking evidence of a radical reversal in the relations of Quakers with the world was the Friends' desire to reach some form of accommodation with the church courts. Once the object of Quaker contempt, the courts were acknowledged by the sect from the mid-1690s onwards and members were advised to attend when cited.[67] Pragmatism was one reason for doing so, since non-appearance enabled a prosecutor to commence proceedings and excommunicate a Friend for contempt. The Colchester Friend Thomas Kettle was advised in 1706 to plead the excuse of sickness or being away from home on unavoidable business, and when the reason for absence was genuine, Friends were told to employ a proctor to plead on their behalf.[68] There was a further change in that the plea of personal conscience was more often than previously given as the primary reason for refusing tithe payment or for non-attendance at church.[69]

During the reign of James II William Penn was active in seeking sympathy for Friends at Court. His friendship with the king was clearly significant.[70] But this was part of a wider strategy among Friends to diminish their persecution. The accommodation reached with the institutions of the world suggests a radical departure from the strict sectarianism of

---

[62] FHL, MMS, iv. 114 (1686), 133 (1690).
[63] FHL, MMS, iv. 233 (1686); Horle, *The Quakers and the English Legal System*, 179.
[64] FHL, MMS, xxiii. 394 (1724); MMS, iv. 163 (1685).
[65] FHL, MMS, ix. 116, 122 (1693).
[66] Davies, *An Account of the Convincement*, 61–7.
[67] FHL, Book of Cases, ii. 7 (1696), 36 (1695).   [68] FHL, MMS, xviii. 148.
[69] EUL, EQ 26, 249 (1703).
[70] See Hunt, *Two Early Political Associations*, 13 who suggests that the Society relied mainly on the relationship of Penn and Robert Barclay with James to limit the persecution of Friends from 1681 to 1689. This alone is not sufficient to account for the attitudes of the authorities towards Friends in Essex. See also Penn, *Writings*, pp. xxx–xxxi.

the movement's early years. Given what we know of the types of prosecution experienced by Friends in the 1660s and early 1670s compared with the 1680s, the approach appears to have paid dividends. Evidence on fines in the 1680s shows a clear diminution in the levels levied compared with earlier. The most plausible explanation for this is the negotiating activities of Friends. The process by which the Society sought to influence the policies of Church and State in their favour also casts doubt upon the notion that Friends had retreated from politics after the Restoration. To be sure, by the end of the century they had shed many of the ideas and much of the behaviour which had earlier distinguished them as subversives. But it would be inaccurate to describe them as having relinquished involvement in all forms of political life. Indeed, they showed themselves to be extremely effective in manipulating opinion in their favour. The Quakers' changing response to suffering also suggests the degree to which the sect began to take on some of the characteristics of a formal denomination. Gone was the aggressive proselytizing of the early years and the zeal which made them want to turn the world upside down.

The experience of Quakers can be contrasted with that of another harassed minority at this time, the Roman Catholics. Catholics were able to avoid the worst of the penalties sanctioned by the law, much of which was framed to penalize them. A study of the Catholics in Wiltshire found that local officers preferred to impose the lesser fines for recusancy of a shilling per week's absence rather than prosecute Catholics with the larger and more damaging fine. Most Catholics also avoided the imposition of a writ of excommunication which rendered offenders liable to seizure of two-thirds of their estates. However, in the years from 1681 to 1683 Catholics too suffered larger fines.[71] None the less, Quakers suffered more than Catholics, who were able to rely more upon the sympathy of neighbours and the patronage of landed gentry to protect them. Reliance on the local society for support was an approach that Quakers too adopted.

However, the Quakers' search for accommodation was to have an unforeseen consequence that constituted one of the principal reasons for the decline of the movement. Suffering engendered among the Friends a sense of uniqueness which gave rise to a tension between them and others in external society. Once the reality or the prospect of suffering was diminished, this tension was dissipated. This development was gradual and not on its own responsible for the decline of the movement. But the

---

[71] J. A. Williams, *Catholic Recusancy in Wiltshire, 1660–1791*, Catholic Record Society (1968), 3–5, 15, 25, 33, 69–72; Miller, *Popery and Politics*, chap. 8.

accommodation that Friends reached with the world in order to avoid suffering assisted the process by which Quakers were assimilated into local society. Sympathy for suffering on the part of Quakers and attempts made to limit it by local officials, kin, and neighbours imply a real tolerance of Friends and were a significant indication of how far the process of Quaker integration had advanced. Further evidence of this is examined in the final chapter.

14

The Quakers in Society

my poor wife was sore grieved that I went among *Friends* . . . and the People of our town began to rage, some disputed with me, some cursed me, as I heard, some pleaded for me, some derided and mocked me, calling after me 'Quaker', 'Quaker' . . .

John Gratton, *A Journal of the Life of that Ancient Servant of Christ* (1720), 42, *c.*1671.

This is the land of sects. An Englishman, as a free man, goes to Heaven by whatever route he likes.

Voltaire, *Letters on England*, tr. Leonard Tancock (1734; repr. Harmondsworth, 1980), 37.

There was a consensus among historians that the social fabric of English society was rent in the second half of the seventeenth century by religious division. In a pioneering study Margaret Spufford set out to chart the effects of religious diversity on local society and concluded that the parish community was 'divided in a way previously unknown', 'split from top to bottom on ideological grounds for the first time in its existence'.[1] In a stimulating study of seventeenth-century Lincolnshire, Clive Holmes reached conclusions similar to those of Spufford. The separating congregations both before and after the Civil War, he suggests, were communities based 'not upon ties of geography or status but on spiritual kinship'. Holmes identified Quakers as the most extreme of the Interregnum sects; as a group they were 'differentiated from the larger society and seeking to minimize contacts with it'.[2]

However, the relation of Quakers to local society ought not to be regarded as being characterized by division and segregation alone, for, as we have seen, when faced with the prospect of suffering, Friends were sometimes able to rely for assistance upon those in positions of authority such as local constables and magistrates. To get a better understanding of the social

---

[1] Margaret Spufford, *Contrasting Communities: English Villagers in the Sixteenth and Seventeenth Centuries* (Cambridge, 1974), 347, 341. Dr Spufford has now revised her views on this point: see ead., *The World of Rural Dissenters*, 20 n. 7, 360 n. 1.

[2] Clive Holmes, *Seventeenth Century Lincolnshire* (Lincoln, 1980), 45, 44.

interaction between Quakers and the world it is necessary to place Friends more fully in their local context by using a broad range of local source material. This suggests that there was a greater degree of cooperation between the early Quakers and their contemporaries than has hitherto been appreciated. However, this is not to deny that normal kin and neighbourly relations could be fractured by the arrival of Quakerism in a parish nor to question the view that Friends' failure to follow conventional social mores prevented them from qualifying fully as members of local society.

The Society advised members that they should avoid spiritual pollution by spurning worldly associations, but this was a goal more easily attainable in theory than in practice. As a group Quakers were not geographically isolated and economically self-sustaining and were unable therefore to live sharply segregated social lives like, for instance, the original religious communities of the Mormons in Utah or the present-day Amish in Pennsylvania.[3] Friends lived in proximity to and were obliged to intermingle with family, neighbours, and parishioners on a more than occasional basis and also entered into social and economic relations with those around them. Even so, to accept that relations between Quakers and the world were not universally hostile and were conducted at times in a spirit of moderation is not to suppose that they were uniformly rosy. One must be wary of arguing that religious belief had little direct or practical effect on social relations in local society.[4]

To throw light on the relations of Quakers with the world a number of topics have been studied. These include an examination of the difficulties Friends encountered over the need to swear oaths, the turbulence caused within families by conversion to Quakerism, the ideals of neighbourliness and how these were adhered to by Friends and others in local society, the role of Quakers in the parish, and the extent of economic relations between Quakers and the world.

THE SWEARING OF OATHS

Swear not at all; neither by heaven; for it is God's throne: Nor by the earth; for it is his footstool.

Matthew 5: 34-5.

[3] On these religious groups see T. F. O'Dea, *The Mormons* (Chicago, 1957); J. A. Hoestetler, *Amish Society*, 3rd. edn. (Baltimore, 1980). On the Amish and outsiders see Donald B. Kraybill, *The Amish and the State* (Baltimore, 1993), esp. chaps. 1–2.
[4] Patrick Collinson urges caution on this line; see his essay 'The Cohabitation of the Faithful with the Unfaithful', in O. P. Grell, J. I. Israel, and Nicholas Tyacke (eds.), *From Persecution to Toleration: The Glorious Revolution and Religion in England* (Oxford, 1991), 76.

Oath taking was an important social ritual in the seventeenth century which was normally used to signify loyalty on the part of the swearer or a commitment to be truthful when giving testimony in court.[5] Quakers refused oaths, citing and taking literally the biblical injunction 'swear not at all'. However, there is considerable evidence that the local community was prepared to assist Friends in surmounting the everyday problems they faced as a consequence of their unwillingness or failure to swear. Below are set out some of the strategies Friends pursued to overcome the difficulties that the swearing of oaths presented to them.

The second Act for Burial in Woollen was passed in 1678 in order to stimulate the wool trade. The Act decreed that an affidavit had to be sworn confirming that woollen cloth had been used to wrap the deceased before burial. The document was then submitted to a Justice of the Peace. This placed Friends in a difficult position, for failure to procure an affidavit resulted in a heavy fine. Some Quakers simply refused the oath and paid the fine.[6] But the normal practice of Friends was to draw on parishioners, neighbours, and kin to swear in their place. When Stephen Holman's son died in 1684, the wife of a fellow cordwainer swore the affidavit for him.[7] The evidence from parish burial records indicates that while it was sometimes neighbours or close family members who swore, the task was more often performed by poor parish women for a fee. Records of these payments also form frequent entries in the Quakers' own poor relief accounts.[8] Friends were thus prepared to seek the support of 'the world' to execute duties which they were unwilling to perform.

Another requirement to swear came from the imposition of an Association Oath which was promulgated in the wake of a plot to assassinate William III. The purpose of the oath was to expose opponents of the regime. At first only citizens who held office were required to pledge the association, but so great was the fear for the King's life that there was a campaign to secure the association among ordinary citizens. The oath was first taken in London in 1696, and the requirement to swear it applied throughout the country. The Privy Council required county lieutenants to procure the signatures of 'gentlemen and any other persons of consideration', focusing particular attention on those who were unwilling or

---

[5] Christopher Hill, *Society and Puritanism in Pre-Revolutionary England* (1969), 371–2.

[6] ERO, D/P 209/1/4 (Earls Colne), James Potter (10 Sept. 1680); D/P 231/1/2 (Feering), John Raven (11 Feb. 1709). For a thoughtful and pioneering discussion of Quaker expedients see Forde, 'Friends and Authority', 115–25.

[7] ERO, D/P 115/1/1 (Hornchurch).

[8] ERO, D/P 152/1/2 (Theydon Garnon); D/P 19/1/2 (Boxted); D/P 307/1/10 (Little Horkesley). ERO, T/A 261/1/1 (Thaxted Monthly Meeting) (31 Jan. 1712).

neglected to sign.[9] Such a demand was potentially very threatening to the security of Friends.

Quakers refused to take the oath, though proclaiming that they felt no enmity towards the King or his government. In Colchester a separate roll was drawn up by Quakers in which they substituted for the oath a formula acceptable to themselves. One hundred and twenty-five Quakers signed the pledge, which was accepted by the authorities as an alternative testimony of loyalty. A copy of the document is entered with other rolls in the town's Assembly Book without any hostile comment.[10] In other parts of the county Friends signed the parochial Association Rolls without taking an oath. The Earls Colne Quaker Henry Abbot signed the parish roll and added after his signature, 'I cannot fight, I am subject to the king and his Government and to them I freely subscribe'.[11] Friends also signed the rolls at Cressing, Felsted, and Rayne in the presence of the local constable.[12] There is no evidence from the sect's books of discipline that members were failing to live up to their testimonies regarding oaths. It appears that a considerable degree of tolerance was permitted to Friends, enabling them to sign the roll without taking an oath.

Prior to the Affirmation Act of 1697, which did away with the need for Quakers to swear, the chief and most frequent difficulty they encountered was over probate of wills. Friends had to swear an oath before probate could be granted. Prior to affirming, Friends were expected to get wills proven at the church court. Given Friends' objections to church doctrine and hierarchy and the court's well-known animosity to Quakerism the situation seemed ripe for conflict. One option open to Friends was simply to ignore the formalities of probate and we know that some took this course.[13] But there was always the danger when an oath had not been sworn that a testator's intentions might be successfully challenged by non-Quaker relatives or other interested parties.[14] Alternatives to established practice were probably resorted to when it was known beforehand that there was little hope of getting a will proved in a particular court. On the whole, though, Quakers appear to have turned up at the church courts for this purpose. In the decades of the 1670s, 1680s, and 1690s Quaker executors numbered 75

---

[9] Cressy, *Literacy and The Social Order*, 97.

[10] PRO, C/213/264/3; CBR, Assembly Book 1693–1712, 88–9.

[11] ERO, Q/RRO 2/1/14.

[12] ERO, Q/RRO 2/1/17, 20, 32. At Kelvedon the Quakers signed a separate roll Q/RRO 2/2. This procedure was probably repeated in a number of parishes.

[13] GL, MS 9853, Bundle 2 (Sept. 1664). John Adams, Parndon; ERO, D/ABV2, fo. 140r (25 July 1684), James Webb, Braintree.   [14] FHL, MMS, iv. 205 (1685).

per cent, 79 per cent, and 77 per cent respectively for the total number of Quaker wills proven.[15] Next to the executors' names in the probate records are notes to the effect that an oath had been taken. It is improbable that Friends were avoiding the Quaker taboo regarding oaths and there is no evidence that this happened. It is likely that some form of accommodation had been reached with the ecclesiastical authorities which enabled Quakers to pass wills through the probate procedure without compromising Quaker principles.

In the 1660s, however, the position was rather different; the executors of Quaker wills in the ecclesiastical courts were in the main not Quakers. During what is recognized to have been a decade of intense ill-feeling between Quakers and the Church, probate was undertaken only with immense difficulty. Friends looked for assistance outside the religious group to prove their wills. The figures indicate that of those chosen to act as executors during the 1660s, 79 per cent were not followers. Further analysis indicates that Friends drew on their non-Quaker children (41 per cent), non-Quaker brothers and sisters (25 per cent), or personal friends and neighbours (13 per cent) to perform the task.

This assessment of will probates suggests that some form of *modus vivendi* was reached between Quakers and church officials only after the early 1670s. This arrangement probably reflected an increasing recognition of Quakers as peaceable people, and the Friends' own desire to reach some form of accommodation with the courts, since before this date members were forced to rely on sympathetic family, friends, or neighbours. The manner in which Quakers overcame the requirements of oath swearing suggests that the notion of their being an alienated group needs significant modification. Of course, the official representatives of the Society would probably not have welcomed the tactic adopted by rank-and-file members of allowing others to swear in their place. However, it appears that so long as Friends did not personally default, many local meetings considered such a practice acceptable.

FAMILY DIVISION

And now is the Separation, the Sheep from the Goats, the Wheat from the Tares, and Christ is come to set at Variance, Father against Son, and Son against Father,

[15] The number of extant Quaker wills is 24 from the 1660s, 38 from the 1670s, 46 from the 1680s, 22 from the 1690s.

and Wife against the Man, and Man against the Wife and to turn the World upside
down, and this is the Cause why the world rages, this is His condemnation of the
world.

> James Parnel, *A Collection of the Several Writings given Forth from the Spirit*
> *of the Lord, through the Meek, Patient and Suffering Servant of God, James*
> *Parnel* (1675), 67–8.

According to contemporary moralists the family was the bedrock of
seventeenth-century society; within it the father held absolute power and
the behaviour of wife and children was subject to his authority.[16] Related
to this was the conviction that the patriarchal household formed a nursery
of Christian socialization within which obedience to Church and State was
fostered. What would today be accepted as merely private, familial concerns with no wider bearing were regarded in the seventeenth century as
crucial to the welfare of society.[17] Because they spurned the normal filial
courtesies and pressed for equality of respect, Quakers were considered
to be undermining paternal authority and with it the very idea of the family. Hostile pamphleteers jeered at Friends for forging disunity within the
household and chipping away at the ideal of parental authority.[18]

One can discern more than a hint of generational conflict in the disputes between conforming parents and their Quaker children, for the religion undermined the accepted notion that respect was to be accorded to
age and that parents were without question deserving of youthful respect.
It was subservience to the inner light and loyalty to the social testimonies
of the Society which earned respect among Friends, and these cut across
contemporary assumptions regarding age and authority.[19] Indeed, Friends
admitted that family division was a consequence of conversion to the Quaker
faith.[20]

The Society feared that the ties of kinship which bound the family
together might also draw new converts away from the Quaker faith. Stephen
Crisp warned Friends in 1666 to beware of turning away from truth for
the pity of a wife, children, or other relatives; they were, he said, 'instru-
ments of Satan' who would attempt to 'seduce' Friends back to the world.[21]

---

[16] Christopher Durston, *The Family in the English Revolution* (Oxford, 1989), 4.

[17] Collinson, *Birthpangs*, 61.

[18] Say and Sele, *Folly and Madness*, 18; [Anon.], *The Quaking Mountebanck*, 19; Baxter,
The Quaker's Catechism, 16; Bourne, *A Defence of the Scriptures*, 30; Penington, *The Memoirs
of the life of Isaac Penington*, 52.

[19] W.P., *An Answer According to Truth*, 1, 4; Parnel, *Collection*, p. xxi; Keith Thomas, *Age
and Authority in Early Modern England* (1976), 6, 32–3.

[20] Parnel, *A Shield of the Truth*, 8.

[21] Stephen Crisp, *An Epistle to Friends Concerning the Present and Succeeding Times* (1666), 11.

Earlier the response of James Parnel to his family's efforts to persuade him to relinquish links with the Society was a rebuke in which he described them as his 'adversaries'.[22] On occasion, the requirement of unfailing loyalty to the Society hardened familial divisions. When James Barret's parents withheld permission for his betrothal to a member in 1675 on the grounds that they disapproved of his taking a Quaker wife, the local meeting was bound to overrule the objection since marrying into the Quaker faith hardly qualified as a legitimate reason for refusal.[23] This is a clear example of the religious group overriding parental authority when it was considered appropriate to do so. Indeed, members were to distinguish between their 'natural' parents and elders in the faith whom they termed 'spiritual parents'. The elders were approached when it was thought appropriate: Thomas Ellwood, for instance, consulted Isaac and Mary Penington on spiritual matters and sought their advice in the 1660s when he entertained thoughts of marriage.[24]

When a member married outside the Quaker faith, a testimony disowning that action was required. This inevitably caused unwelcome tension between spouses: one wife complained in 1704 that the action expected of her 'should displease her husband', but the meeting insisted on a declaration admitting wrongdoing before readmission into fellowship was permitted.[25]

There were occasions where a Friend was excluded from membership while the rest of the family remained in the Society. Benjamin Danks was disowned in 1708 for burning his wife's Bible, though his spouse remained a loyal follower.[26] When the issue of poor relief arose, Quaker members of a family applied to the local meeting for support, while other kin were dispatched to the parish overseer.[27]

However, relations within families divided by Quakerism were not persistently sour. By the beginning of the eighteenth century kin frequently paid the amounts owed by Quakers for tithes and church rates. The Society disapproved, but it was a practice over which it had little control.[28] During the 1680s Harwich Friends were bailed out of prison by relatives, and in 1670 one Friend transferred property to a brother to escape the ravages of the informer.[29] In the 1650s on two occasions non-Quaker brothers

---

[22] Parnel, *Collection*, 233–4.   [23] ERO, COLTW 1, 51.

[24] Thomas Lawrence and George Fox, *Concerning Marriage* (1663), 12, 5–6, and Thomas Ellwood, *The History of the Life of Thomas Ellwood* (1714), 249.

[25] ERO, T/A 261/1/1 (27 Mar. 1704); PRO, RG6 1335, fo. 174 (1692).

[26] EUL, Supplementary Papers, 203 (1708).

[27] EUL, T/A 283/1/1 (13 Oct. 1719); Waltham Abbey Monthly Meeting Minutes (Feb. 1688).

[28] EUL, COGMM 27 (10 Nov. 1701); FHL, Portfolio MS 16/37 (1685).

[29] EUL, EQ 22, 19 (1683); FHL, Great Book of Sufferings, i. 400.

acted to secure the release of Quaker kin from gaol.[30] The existence of
different faiths within a marriage might prove advantageous. The courts
summoned husbands to account for the conduct of wives absenting
themselves from church.[31] Husbands and wives naturally could and
did pay the fines of their Quaker spouses in order to prevent possible
imprisonment.[32]

No matter how shocking and deplorable conversion to Quakerism
seemed, parents and other kin often sought to maintain contact with their
erring relatives. Indeed, there is some evidence that ties of affection and
genuine concern for family members carried greater weight than dislike
of the new religion when calculations were made about cutting ties with
children or spouses who had converted. Richard Davies, though practically disowned by his father, recalled after joining Friends the first meeting with his mother in 1657, who 'looking on my face . . . said that I was
her child, and I was not as they said bewitched or transformed into some
other likeness'.[33] John Gratton described in his *Journal* how he and his
non-Quaker wife had many disputes about religious observance 'till we both
wept but still we loved dearly'.[34] In the 1660s the father of Elias Osborn
sought at first to persuade his son to relinquish his attachment to
Quakerism, though he eventually allowed him to take a Quaker wife despite
his disapproval of the faith.[35] That religious disagreements within families did not always precipitate bitterness is suggested by the example of
Elias's aunt, who wrote to him saying that 'Differences in judgement should
not cause differences in Affection'.[36] Moreover, a family's dislike of
Quakerism was not always based upon hostility to doctrine alone; sometimes objections of kin were determined as much by pragmatic concerns.
Many feared imprisonment for their offspring who converted to Quakerism and the harm that might then befall them and their children.[37] Parents
were also anxious that membership of the sect might hinder the advance-
ment of children, and limit their prospect of employment.[38]

---

[30] EUL, Crisp MS fo. 295 (1658); FHL, Great Book of Sufferings, i. 412 (1657).

[31] ERO, Q/SR 448/178, 199, 201 (1685); GL, MS 9853, Bundle 2 (Sept. 1664), Felsted.

[32] EUL, EQ 22, 16 (1677); FHL, Great Book of Sufferings, i. 401 (1675); ERO, Q/SR
429/7 (1675).   [33] Davies, *An Account of the Convincement*, 18.

[34] John Gratton, *Journal*, 50 (c.1672).

[35] Elias Osborn, *A Brief Narrative of the Life, Labours, and Sufferings of Elias Osborn* (1723),
21.   [36] Ibid.

[37] Ibid., 28; Sansom, *An Account of many Remarkable Passages*, 16; Tompkins, *A Faithful
Warning*, 4.

[38] *Journal of the Life of Thomas Story*, i. 107, 132; Davies, *An Account of the Convincement*, 80; Edward Coxere, *Adventures By Sea*, ed. E. H. W. Meyerstein (Oxford, 1945), 90
(c.1661).

Instances of kin intervening to help Quaker relatives certainly confirm the impression that division within families was not so pervasive as critical pamphleteers suggested. Moreover, the hostility of the Society towards non-Quaker kin was not as unyielding as it at first appears. For example, when it was decided that a young man who 'seemed inclined to truth' should be apprenticed among Friends, the meeting first authorized an approach to his father to obtain approval.[39] If such sanction was not forthcoming, representatives of the meeting would seek to persuade him.[40] Ultimately, of course, the meeting was prepared to overrule parental objection. However, the Society appears to have been far more sensitive to the feelings of non-Quaker parents than one might infer from perusing the published literature alone. While the convictions of Quakers prevented their agreeing to certain conventions such as the removal of the hat as a sign of deference to parents, other filial duties were, where possible, accepted as obligatory.

What then is to be made of this contradictory evidence? Did Quakerism encourage family divisions or not? The answer is not straightforward. It is best to distinguish between the behaviour of individual Quakers and the attitude of the Society as represented by the local meeting. The attitude of the Society evolved; during the 1650s and 1660s the movement was wary of the pull which family ties might exert on newly converted Friends. In this regard the Society can be said not just to have encouraged but also to have maintained division within families. But by the 1670s the perception was rather different; the wider community and non-Quaker kin were no longer looked upon with such distrust. An indication of this is the presence of non-Quaker parents and relatives at the weddings of Quaker children. To judge from Quaker marriage certificates it appears that prior to the 1670s they were rarely present at the marriage declaration, for Quakers alone mainly acted as witnesses.[41] But thereafter they attended the marriage ceremony and their names were subscribed on the certificate.[42]

The Society's attitude to the burial of non-Quaker kin also modified. Grounds were purchased to avoid interment in the parish graveyard, but Quaker graveyards were not reserved for sect members alone. Interment of non-Quakers could proceed so long as permission had first been

---

[39] EUL, COLTW 1, 51, 44 (1674).

[40] EUL, COLMM 1, 87 (1690); COLTW 1, 249 (1700).

[41] Lawrence and Fox, *Concerning Marriage*, 14; PRO, RG6 1335, 159 (1659); RG6 999, 58 (1669).

[42] For example, PRO, RG6 1382, 10 (1673); EUL, COLTW 1, 59 (1674). By the 1680s relatives attended regularly.

acquired from the meeting.[43] From the period before 1670 there are few examples of non-Quaker burials in Friends' grounds; afterwards burial of non-Quaker spouses, parents, grandchildren, and brothers was a common occurrence. Even disowned relatives were permitted a burial in Friends' grounds. The change in burial practice suggests that by 1670 the Society looked more favourably upon non-Quaker kin and the wider community.[44]

An analysis of inheritance customs reveals that the Quakers did not usually discriminate against their kin on grounds of religion when deciding upon disposal of their estate. Throughout the period of this study Friends bequeathed money, goods, and property to non-Quaker children, brothers, cousins, and other kin. Samuel Burton from Earls Colne is not untypical. In 1663 he left his son of the same name, who had married in church and served in the office of churchwarden, 'all those utensils which belong to my trade of a chandler'.[45] That family division was not the inevitable consequence of membership is also suggested by the manner in which Quakers proved their wills during the 1660s. In that decade Friends looked to non-Quaker kin to serve as executors. They chose non-Quaker children (41 per cent), and non-Quaker brothers or sisters (25 per cent). At a time when Quaker leaders warned Friends against too close a contact with relatives, help was not only sought from them but it appears given, on occasion, without question.

It is certainly true that Quakerism was capable of generating deep familial division, but that was not an inevitable consequence of this brand of sectarianism. The relationship between Quakers and conforming kin may well have been more agreeable than has hitherto been appreciated. Friends maintained informal relations with their families probably because of a genuine affection but also because the assistance of non-Quaker

---

[43] EUL, EQ 30 (Deed of Halstead Burial Ground, 1660), 201.

[44] ERO, D/NF 1/3/10 (Witham Monthly Meeting Burial Ground, at Billericay, 1715); EUL, COLTW 1, 104 (1683); PRO, RG6 1382, 211 (1663); RG6 675, 10 (1674), spouses; RG6 1262, 181 (1679); RG6 331, 179 (1704), brothers; RG6 1262, 181 (1677); RG6 1382, 224 (1699), 228 (1703); RG6 1262, 189 (1679), parents and children.

[45] ERO, D/ACW 16/185. For recognition of non-Quaker brothers see, for example, D/AEW 23/252, Edmund Blatt of Barking (1665); D/ACW 17/176, John Pilborough of Colchester, (1664); D/AER 22/222, David Shonk of Barking (1667); D/AER 23/319 Thomas Debbett of Barking (1679); D/ABR 13/32, William Swan of Halstead (1694). For children see PRO, PROB 11, 342/42, John Guyon of Great Coggeshall (1672); ERO, D/ACR 10/78, Ann Burton of Earls Colne (1678). For cousins and other kin see ERO, D/AEW 26/243, Stephen Dennis of Barking (1677); D/AER 23/219, Thomas Debbett of Barking; D/ACW 21/119, Stephen Crisp of Colchester (1692); PRO, PROB 11/357/70, Theophilus Wimple of Harwich (1681). There are many other examples of testators recognizing non-Quaker kin.

kin allowed them to circumvent potential troubles arising from their faith in their everyday lives.

NEIGHBOURLINESS

Our Saviour hath reduced all the Law and the Prophet, to these two Heads viz. *To Love God above all and our Neighbour as ourselves.*

William Crouch, *Posthuma Christiana* (1712), 216.

The criticisms levelled against Friends for being unneighbourly were discussed in earlier chapters. Quakers were accused of fracturing the bonds of love and charity which held together local society because they railed savagely at ministers and spurned established codes of civility.[46] Moreover, their religious inclinations rendered them incapable, a critic wrote in 1676, of satisfying even the most basic of neighbourly obligations; it was said that Friends would be unwilling to give evidence in support of a fellow parishioner at court because it required the swearing of an oath.[47]

Opponents pressed home the attack by claiming that it was mistaken to behave in a charitable manner towards Friends since this would achieve nothing but to stiffen them in their obstinate ways.[48] Indeed, there were parishioners who practised what they preached and refused any form of communion with Quakers.[49] But an ambivalence was apparent as to what was the appropriate neighbourly response, for while Quaker disruption of communal harmony was deplored by many, those who criticized Friends and wanted them excluded from parish life were themselves then judged to be guilty of failing to satisfy the duties of charity and good neighbourliness. How could adversaries accuse Friends of violating the principle of 'Love thy Neighbour', when it was an obligation they themselves so manifestly failed to satisfy?[50] The ideals of communal harmony which governed behaviour in the parish may well have limited the hostility directed

---

[46] Jeremiah Ives, *The Quakers Quaking* (1656), 45; Haworth, *The Quaker Converted to Christianity*, A2v, 105; Ralph Farmer, *Satan Inthron'd in his Chair of Pestilence* (1657), 53; Charles Gataker, *An Examination in the Case of the Quakers Concerning Oaths* (1675), 5–6.

[47] [Anon.], *The Anti-Quaker; or, a Compendious Answer to a Tedious Pamphlet* (1676), 32.

[48] Ibid., 46–7; Thomas Moore, Jnr., *An Antidote Against the Spreading Infection of the Spirit of Antichrist* (1655), 66–7; John Faldo, *A Vindication of Quakerism No Christianity* (1673), Preface, A3v.   [49] Crisp, *Works*, 98–9.

[50] Charles Marshall, *Sion's Travellers Confuted* (1704), 274; Benjamin Bangs, *Memoirs of the Life and Convincement of that Worthy Friend* (1757), 33; Ambrose Rigge, *Constancy in the Truth Commended* (1710), 21; George Whitehead, *The Christian Progress of that Ancient Servant and Minister of Jesus Christ, George Whitehead* (1725), 486–7; William Crouch, *Posthuma Christiana; or, a Collection of Some Papers of William Crouch* (1712), 216.

at Friends. Moreover, Quakers sought to redefine the ideal of neigh-
bourliness. The doffing of the hat, the saying of 'Good Eve' and 'Good
Morrow' were not a genuine reflection of good neighbourliness, they argued.
John Whitehead wrote in 1663:

And for Courteousness to all, both to Superiors and to Equals, where is the Man
or Woman, among all our Neighbours, that have been conversant with us, that
can justly accuse us, and show where we have not been Courteous and Amiable
to them . . . where is the Man that can say, we Refuse or are discourteous and
unneighbourly? And from whom have we witholden, either Rents, Debts or other
Customs . . . which in righteous Reason and Conscience is due.[51]

Evidence from local sources indicates that informal cooperation and contact between local Quakers and their neighbours were considerable during the period of this study. Between 1660 and 1700 over 80 per cent of the
witnesses to Quaker wills were not Friends.[52] In the Essex township of
Halstead, for example, Quaker wills were signed by nonconformists and
Anglicans alike.[53] Some parishes contained Quaker alehousekeepers;[54] in
others non-Quaker scribes wrote the wills of local Friends.[55] Ministers who
prosecuted Quakers in the Exchequer Court sometimes discovered that
parishioners refused to give evidence against Friends in court and on occasion joined with them in evading tithe payments.[56] Neighbours also paid
tithes and church rates in the place of Friends, and sometimes acted as
sureties when they were imprisoned, or even paid the fines to obtain their
release.[57] They also testified as to the amount of tithe taken from members (and these accounts served as the basis for the reports entered in Quaker
'Suffering Books'), refused to purchase distrained goods, and ostracized
informers.[58] Quakers were evidently not wholly alienated from other

---

[51] John Whitehead, *The Written Gospel Labours*, 144, 145.
[52] Eighty five per cent in the 1660s, 80 per cent in the 1670s, 93 per cent in the 1680s,
82 per cent in the 1690s.
[53] Evidence of nonconformity was deduced from entries in the records of the church courts
and Quarter Sessions.
[54] John Weir at Colchester in 1663, CBR, Tradesmen Recognizances, 1648–89. The Terling
Quakers Cyprian Corwall, John Chandler, and Judith Spring were all alehousekeepers. I am
indebted to Keith Wrightson for this information on the parish.
[55] John Child (son of the Quaker of the same name), a conformist, wrote Quaker and non-
Quaker wills. At Terling the will of Thomas Perry, a Quaker, was written by the parish clerk.
I am once again indebted to Keith Wrightson for this information on Terling.
[56] See, for instance, PRO, E 112/397/151 (1668).
[57] EUL, EQ 26, 422 (1703); HBR, 98/11 (Court of Pleas with Recognizances,
1662–1689), 1662, 1669, 1679, 1683.
[58] EUL, EQ 22, 18 (1682), 29 (1689); FHL, Great Book of Sufferings, 2, 335 (1697); Crouch,
Posthuma Christiana, 186 (*c.*1670).

village inhabitants. However, the attendance of neighbours at Quaker weddings[59] and at interment in Quaker burial grounds[60] was not common until the 1670s and later. The Society was more fearful of the consequences of intermingling with neighbours than were individual Friends; it was not until the 1670s that the sect sanctioned greater openness on the part of members. And while the sect was careful about welcoming strangers into its midst, Quakers did perform their professional duties in wider society. Quaker midwives were much sought after in some communities, though Essex Friends were at first reluctant to permit the use of the midwives of the world among their own sort.[61]

Quaker religious beliefs, of course, prohibited the use of ordinary courtesies, but insofar as they were able, Friends mixed with parishioners. The charitable bequests made by them to the parish poor also imply that the Quaker sense of community was not limited to their own sort. Gifts in wills to the poor range from a few shillings to several pounds: John Woodroffe of Colchester gave twenty shillings in 1666[62] and Thomas Writtle a much larger sum of seven pounds in 1698.[63] Elizabeth True indicated in her will of 1706 that five pounds were to be given to the poor: half was to be distributed among Quakers, the rest to be put into the hands of the churchwardens and overseers for the use of the parish.[64] John Freeborne, a Quaker clothier, bequeathed in 1674 to Witham's poor 'four score sixpenny loaves'. He willed that on the day of his funeral the loaves were to be handed over to the parish overseer at whose discretion they were to be distributed among the 'needy poor'.[65] To Friends poverty constituted a threat to spiritual well-being and as such had to be combated whether among the Quaker or the parish poor.[66]

Ordinary Quakers felt obligations towards members of parish society and did not wish to be wholly set apart. The number of non-Quaker

---

[59] PRO, RG6 1391, 35, 'friends and people present' (1678); 27, 'neighbours' (1680); 47, 'friends and friendly people' (1689); 573, 71, 'friends and neighbours' (1704). See also FHL, Kelsall, *Journal*, 37.

[60] See, for example, PRO, RG6 999, 130, John Hatch of Earls Colne (1675), 153 Mary Reay (1703). Edward Abbot of Coptford, a non-Quaker, gave a piece of land to the Quakers in 1668 with the condition that a burial plot be reserved for him. S. H. G. Fitch, *Colchester Quakers* (Colchester, 1962), 23.

[61] 'At a Meeting of the Midwives in Barbados', *JFHS* 37 (1940), 22–5; see also p. 38 above.

[62] PRO, PROB 11/321/258.   [63] ERO, PROB 11/448/254.

[64] ERO, D/ACR 12/78.

[65] ERO, D/ACR 9/159. Isaac Dallam of West Ham stipulated in his will of 1665 that twelve pence should be given to poor people who were of 'innocent life and conversation', D/AER 21/154.

[66] Five per cent of Friends made bequests in their wills to non-Quaker poor. See also Livingstone, *Selections*, 189; Crouch, *Posthuma Christiana*, 16.

parishioners who signed Quaker wills and the bequests in Quaker wills to the poor in the parish suggest that Friends did not strive for total separation in local society.

QUAKERS AND THE PARISH

Quakers were not expected to take part in the administration of the law, nor to exercise authority over others. Just as they were to renounce worldly honours, they were not to accept official position; they were a people gathered and separated from the world.

E. D. Bebb, *Nonconformity and Social and Economic Life, 1660–1800* (1935), 79.

It is often claimed that Friends' religious principles led them to spurn any form of public office, but from the Restoration onwards followers of the sect in Essex held positions of responsibility within the parish administration, serving as overseers of the poor, surveyors of the highway, vestrymen, vermin destroyers, and, at the end of the seventeenth century, constables. Overseer of the poor was the office most often held. Parish records reveal the wide range of duties Quakers fulfilled. Friends bound out pauper apprentices, collected and distributed funds for the poor, and inquired into the paternity of illegitimate children. They also decided who was eligible for poor relief, determined what was the best method of helping the poor, gave judgment when disputes arose over parochial jurisdiction for supporting the poor, and proceeded to take legal action against those who refused to pay the rate. Most of these duties were performed with the assistance of another parochial overseer and the local churchwardens, though Friends who undertook the task of overseer were themselves often in a state of excommunication. After 1670 Quakers served in the office of overseer of the poor with greater regularity. At Halstead Friends served in this office on at least seven occasions between 1658 and 1689.[67]

As overseers, Quakers had a considerable amount of discretion to determine day-to-day policy in a parish, and sometimes found themselves out of pocket when discharging their office. In 1677 Henry Haslum, the Quaker overseer from Southminster, distributed money to the sick and the lame, to the widows and nurses, paid for stockings and coats, and for laying out bodies and carrying them to burial.[68] Earlier, in 1664, it was the Quaker overseer at Harwich who was left to administer the goods of

---

[67] ERO, D/P 96/14/1 (Apprenticeship Papers, 1648–1812).
[68] ERO, D/P 259/12/2.

the widow Dorothy Vinyard on her death and arrange an apprenticeship for her son.[69] The discovery that Quakers held important parochial offices is something of a puzzle. It hardly fits in with their reputation as a deviant group in local society. Moreover, whoever was chosen by the vestry to serve had also to be approved by a local magistrate. Could it be that Friends so elected were in some sense 'lukewarm' or perhaps only transitorily associated with the sect? From checking the names of Quakers who held office against the nominal index created for this study it appears that such Friends were normally of some importance within the Society, often being elders; they also appear in the Society's suffering records, which is normally a sign of watertight commitment. When the parish community agreed to Quakers' holding office there was no misunderstanding about the character of their religious allegiance. Of course, since the duty of overseer was considered onerous, parishioners might have insisted that Friends should take their turn. None the less, by holding positions of authority in the parish Friends were surely recognized as trusted members of local society. For example, a High Constable remarked in support of Theophilus Green, a northern Friend, who was indicted in 1675 on account of his Quakerism:

he is as honest a man, of a Quaker as was about us, and he was lately in office for the poor and behaved himself as well as any has done the last twenty years.[70]

There is no evidence that early Friends were appointed as constables in Essex and some were distrained upon for refusing to take the oath of office.[71] The position was one which required the swearing of an oath and the consent of a magistrate had also to be obtained before service was permitted. We cannot say that sympathy for Friends among the local community in Essex stretched to allowing Quakers to hold the office of constable. It has been established with some certainty elsewhere in England that Quakers held this important position from the early 1660s.[72]

On some occasions Friends, normally people of exceptional means, attended the local vestry where parish business was decided upon. At All Saints vestry in Colchester in 1688 three Quakers were present when money was allocated to relieve the suffering of the French Huguenots,[73] and at

---

[69] HBR, 98/1 (Church Book with Vestry Minutes, 1550–1718), fos. 307ᵛ, 308ʳ (30 Aug. 1664).

[70] Theophilus Green, *A Narrative of Some Passages of the Life of Theophilus Green* (1702), 22.

[71] For example, ERO, 375/46. Janet Gyfford informs me that a Thomas Richmond, possibly the Quaker, was a Witham constable in 1670.

[72] Stevenson, 'The Social Integration of Post-Restoration Dissenters', 369–71.

[73] ERO, D/P 208/8/1 (All Saints) (28 Nov. 1688).

the same vestry in 1693 two Quakers, William Havens and Thomas Bayles, voted ten shillings a week to the overseer of the neighbouring parish of St Giles.[74] Surprisingly, the attendance of Friends at vestry sometimes coincided with that of the local minister.[75]

Quakers often employed servants and apprentices who were not of their faith. Colchester Friends who became freemen of the borough before converting to Quakerism during the 1650s continued to take non-Quaker apprentices throughout the remainder of the century: John Furly, William Havens, and Solomon Freemantle, wealthy merchants and clothiers, are just a few of the masters who did so.[76] Other instances of Friends taking non-Quaker apprentices are common and are to be found, for example, in the Essex townships and parishes of Barking, Buttsbury, and Coggeshall.[77] Some youths who were apprenticed to Quakers swore oaths in order to become freemen, which raises the issue whether religious observance was enforced within the household. The probable answer is that it was not; there is evidence that Quakers were permissive in this matter.[78]

Some Friends made personal agreements with parish officials to lodge members of the parochial poor in their households. William Hownell, a Quaker from Great Coggeshall, reached an agreement with the two overseers Thomas Guyon and William Cox in the 1660s to place a poor woman in his home for two shillings per week.[79] At Barking in September 1675 Robert Smart's children were lodged with a Quaker,[80] and from then up to 1682 Ann Shonk, a widow, and John Salter took in pauper children from the parish.[81] Similar cases can be found at Feering and Colchester in the 1680s, Finchingfield in the 1690s, and Great Bentley in the early eighteenth century.[82]

---

[74] ERO, D/P 208/8/1 (All Saints) (28 Nov. 1688).

[75] HBR, 98/1 (Church Book and Vestry Minutes), fo. 334ʳ (13 Apr. 1691), fo. 351ʳ (5 Aug. 1701) (Harwich).

[76] For Solomon Freemantle see CBR, Thursday Court Book, fo. 322ʳ (29 June 1677), Monday Court Book, fo. 230ᵛ (1681). For John Furly see Thursday Court Book, fo. 210ʳ (11 Oct. 1678). For William Havens, Monday Court Book, fo. 300ᵛ (1660); fo. 293ʳ (1682). There are several other Quaker masters with non-Quaker apprentices.

[77] PRO, IR1 No. 4, fo. 162 (1716), No. 1, fo. 64 (1711). For non-Quaker servants in Quaker households see, for example, FHL, BARMM 1 (7 Sept. 1704, 2 Aug. 1705). See also the reference to non-Quaker servants in the wills of John Woodward in 1666 and John Guyon in 1683. PRO, PROB 11/321/258, PROB 11/374/295.

[78] See n. 75 above, and FHL, MS Box 10 (10), 6–7. Josiah Langdale.

[79] ERO, D/ACW 16/262.

[80] ERO, D/P 81/8/1 (in reverse poor children and pensioners settled, 1675–1694).

[81] Ann Shonk bequeathed fifty pounds to her foster child in 1682, ERO, D/AEW 27/20.

[82] ERO, D/P 231/12/10, Feering. John Bilifield kept a child in 1685 and 1686. CBR, Order Book, 120 (Oct. 1684). ERO, D/P14/8/1, Henry Lagden took an adult and children

The Quaker movement in Essex was not one that spurned relations with the wider community. Far from seeking isolation, Friends took an active part in parochial life. However, they were prepared to integrate into the wider community only to the extent that this would not compromise their religious faith and the social practices it demanded.

BUSINESS AND ECONOMIC LIFE

Every one of you abide in your calling, waiting upon God where he hath called you. And take heed of reasoning with flesh and blood, for there disobedience, pride and presumption will arise . . .

George Fox, *Epistles*, vol. i, No. 79, p. 88 (1654).

Friends were able to act with a degree of discretion when deciding whether to associate with neighbours or kin, but in the sphere of economic life the scope for picking and choosing trading partners and associates was more limited. This is evident from debts recorded in Quaker wills and occasions when Quakers were cited at the borough courts in Colchester regarding disputes over trade.[83] None the less, Friends' religious convictions were to influence their economic activity in external society, for in the work or market place the peculiar social testimonies of the Friends collided with the customs of the world. The Society's instruction that members should eschew the common practice of haggling over the price of goods was often remarked upon and was taken initially as yet more evidence of Quaker eccentricity.[84] To Friends, of course, it was proof of their having reached a state of comparative innocence and cast off some of the attributes of fallen man. James Parnel wrote that those who did not follow Quaker business practice were living 'in the Fall, cursed from God in the first nature in lying and cheating and dissembling, and striving to ensnare and abuse one another'.[85]

---

in 1693, 1694, and 1695. At Finchingfield D/P 14/8/1, Henry Green of Great Bentley agreed to take Elizabeth Hunt at ten shillings for the year 1707. By the end of the seventeenth century some parochial authorities placed pauper apprentices with Quakers. See, for example, ERO, D/P 94/8/1 (30 Aug. 1690), Thomas Elcock of Chelmsford; William Stout, *Autobiography*, 154.

[83] ERO, D/AER 16/88, John Raven of Feering (1708); D/AEW 30/54, Joseph Wright of Mundon (1704); CBR, Thursday Court Book, fo. 374ʳ (Jan. 1664); Monday Court Book fo. 285ᵛ (Jan. 1666/7); fo. 285ᵛ (24 Mar. 1674); fo. 287ᵛ (20 June 1682); fo. 294ʳ (28 Aug. 1682). For joint ownership of ships see PRO, PROB 11/366/58 (1686); Richard Gay of Chich St Osyth; PROB 11/375/70, Theophilus Wimple of Harwich (1681); ERO, D/ABR 11/42; Dorothy Hunt of Harwich (1681); D/ACW 21/237, Edward Feedum of Wivenhoe (1692).

[84] Parnel, *Collection*, 429 (correct pagination is 411).   [85] Ibid.

Friends considered that 'truthfulness' assisted them in business since they were acknowledged in time as honest and dependable tradesmen. Indeed, exceptional integrity was expected in all areas of social life. Moreover, the sect's religious beliefs did not necessarily lead to members being ostracized or suffering unduly in business. Failure to take oaths prevented Friends from assuming the status of freeburgesses which carried important trading rights. But some Quakers seem to have bypassed the regulations which permitted only freemen to trade; at Colchester and Harwich, for instance, they paid 'foreigners'' fines which allowed limited trading rights. Later, when the passage of the Affirmation Act enabled some of the problems caused by oaths to be bypassed, Friends on occasion took the freedom of the borough and the trading rights that came with it, and some served as common councillors in the eighteenth century.[86]

As to occupations, certain callings were prohibited. The Society did not allow followers to partake in business that in some way transgressed the Quaker peace testimony.[87] Involvement in the manufacture, trade, or transport of armaments, for example, was disallowed. At the same time, Quaker prescriptions regarding plainness and simplicity applied to business. Quaker tailors and cobblers were not to fashion goods in such a way as to satisfy human pride. Moreover, the pursuit of profit was not to be uppermost when a calling was followed.[88]

Despite their peculiar faith and the stigma associated with it, Quaker tradesmen and artisans seem to have prospered, with some finding employment at the behest of the parish. At the turn of the seventeenth century the work of John Bayles, a Quaker bricklayer from Kelvedon, raised eyebrows among Coggeshall Friends when it was discovered that he had repaired the parish church in the town.[89] In 1672 and 1681 at Southminster, the Quaker cordwainer, Edward Sewell, made and mended the shoes of poor children in the parish. In 1685 a Robert Ludgater, perhaps the Quaker clothier, supplied skins for the use of the poor at

[86] CBR, Foreigners' Fines (1634–67), which includes the names of Quakers Arthur Condor, Giles Tayspill, Thomas Cole, and Daniel Studd; HBR, 98/15 (Quarter Session, 1670), which includes the names of Quakers William Bramham, John Vandewall, and Daniel Vandewall. See also 99/2 fo. 57 (1664) and fo. 39 (1686). For Quaker fee burgesses in the eighteenth century see the Monday Court Book from 1700, CBR.

[87] On Quakers and business practice see Arthur Raistrick, *Quakers in Science and Industry* (Newton Abbot, 1968), 42–4, and James Walvin, *The Quakers: Money and Morals* (1997).

[88] I owe this point to the kindness of Kenneth Carroll. See also Robert Barclay, *The Inner Life of the Religious Societies of the Commonwealth* (1876), 491–4; Kendall, 'The Development of a Distinctive Form of Quaker Dress', 58; Braithwaite, *Second Period*, 505.

[89] EUL, COGMM 27 (13 Oct. 1701).

Feering.[90] In Harwich in 1666 a Mr Smith, the Quaker draper, mended the sergeant's clothes and the Quaker chandler, William Marloe, supplied locks and nails for the council chamber.[91] John Vandewall supplied bread to the town's poor and with his brother Daniel reached an agreement in 1674 with the borough's churchwardens to rent the windmill from which most of the town's inhabitants procured their bread.[92] Quakers bought, rented, and sold freely among parishioners no matter what their religious persuasion. Richard Reery, a Quaker of Terling, Essex, owned extensive property and had nine tenants, none of whom was a Quaker and only one a nonconformist.[93]

Remarkably, there are also instances of economic relations between Friends and ministers of the established Church. In Harwich and Kirby in the 1680s Quaker cobblers mended the minister's shoes.[94] In Stanstead in the North-East of Essex John Day, a Quaker chandler, supplied the vicar John Leighs with candles and paper for sixteen years from 1692.[95] Friends who held office as overseers of the poor from the 1660s discovered on occasion that ministers refused to pay the poor rate and gave as the excuse that payment was withheld to meet the tithe and other customary payments owed by the Friends.[96] Economic links with ministers or churchwardens enabled dues to be paid surreptitiously, though Friends, of course, claimed to be unwitting participants in such affairs. However, the occasions when Friends paid tithes in this manner in the movement's early years were rare. Nevertheless, what these examples indicate is the existence of a far wider degree of economic cooperation between Quakers and the wider community than has hitherto been appreciated.

QUAKERS IN LOCAL SOCIETY

We should contemne them, that is, we should avoid their society, we should not make them men of our countenance, Counsel, Company, our familiar friends; we

---

[90] ERO, D/P 259/1/2 (Southminster Vestry Minutes) (10 Mar. 1673, 24 Apr. 1681, 5 Oct. 1687); ERO, D/P 231/1/2 (Feering Overseers Accounts).

[91] HBR, 99/1 (Chamberlain's Accounts, 1608–1737) (25 July 1666, 18 Dec. 1674).

[92] HBR, 99/2 (Chamberlain's Accounts, 1673–1708) (5 Mar. 1709); 98/1 (Church Book with Vestry Minutes) fo. 317ᵛ (16 Mar. 1674).

[93] I owe this point to the kindness of Keith Wrightson. For other examples of property transactions between Quakers and others see, for instance, CBR, Monday Court, Roll 203, membrane 5 (13 Jan. 1686). See also the Monday Court Book, fo. 271ᵛ (16 Oct. 1671), fo. 415ʳ (4 Mar. 1674).   [94] FHL, Great Book of Sufferings, iii. 481 (1684).

[95] ERO, D/P 109/3/1 (Tithe Account, 1682–1818), the entry for 29 Apr. 1708.

[96] PRO, E 134/21/22 (1670), John Bundock of Stanaway. FHL, Great Book of Sufferings, viii, p. 2, 340 (1698); BARMM 1 (3 Mar. 1702).

should withdraw from them and show our dislike of their wayes, and reprove them. *Have no fellowship with their unfruitful works &.*

[Anon.], *Querers and Quakers Cause* (1653), 19.

Despite the impression derived from the literary sources there is evidence of a considerable degree of interaction between Friends and the world across a range of social situations. Moreover, the findings outlined so far contradict the standard assumption about the evolution of the sect, which is that from the 1670s, as power passed from the individual to the group, there was a corresponding withdrawal of Friends from local society.[97] This was not so in Essex, where Friends increasingly became integrated into the parish community. Indeed, there may have been a connection, for the greater the integration of Friends, the more importance the Society attached to members' good behaviour in local society.

The level of Quaker integration varied according to time and place. There is inevitably an overlap but it is suggested that there are three distinct periods during which particular approaches to integration prevailed. These are from 1655 to 1670; from the 1670s to 1689; and from the 1690s to the end of the period under review. A complex series of factors and events influenced tendencies towards integration and accommodation within the Society and there was never to be universal agreement among Friends on the degree to which one strategy or another should prevail. Some form of interaction between Quakers and other parishioners existed from the earliest years of the movement. The informal relationships between Quakers and family members and neighbours discussed earlier are indicative of that. This is significant because it suggests that ordinary Friends were prepared to accept a degree of social interaction that was not openly sanctioned by the Society. Indeed, not until the early 1670s does the Society appear to have accepted more readily some form of integration with the wider community.

One of the major factors influencing this change was the Society's decision in the early to mid-1670s to try to limit the extent of suffering to which followers were liable under the law. This was not an isolated factor, for the shift in emphasis also coincided with a growing belief that maintaining the purity of the faith and participating in worldly affairs were no longer irreconcilable. The Society treated outsiders in a more welcoming manner. There was a belief that individual conviction, if held sufficiently strongly, could protect Quakers from the world's pollutions. Perhaps the sect became more confident as its numbers grew. Robert Barclay, for instance, assured Friends in 1678 that they might mix and converse with the world because

---

[97] Vann, *Social Development*, 201.

they were 'inwardly redeemed out of it'. 'True godliness', wrote William Penn in 1682, 'does not turn men out of the world, but enables them to live better in it, and excites their endeavours to mend it'.[98] It was no longer acceptable to hold that allegiance to Quakerism was synonymous with withdrawal from the world other than for the purpose of proselytizing. The parish community responded favourably to the change within the movement: appointment of Friends to parochial office, the relative ease with which probate was achieved from the 1670s, and the frequent lodging of parish apprentices with Quakers by the end of the century all indicate the growing tolerance with which local society viewed the movement. However, it should not be assumed that social interaction was approved of if it compromised Friends' religious beliefs. Members were expected to integrate only to the extent that their religious convictions were not undermined. It appears that Friends moved cautiously towards greater social involvement with the world while accepting its inevitability.[99] From the 1690s onwards the Society adopted a stricter attitude towards members associating with the world. There was a greater stress upon outward appearance and loyalty towards the doctrines and social principles of the faith. But by then it was too late to reverse the decline in membership in a radical manner, especially as integration of members with the world was so advanced.

The pattern of interdependence between Quakers and the local society was more marked in certain parts of north-east and central Essex than elsewhere in the county. Early in the movement's history Friends here played a significant role in the administrative life of some of its parishes, where it was not uncommon for Quakers to hold parochial office before the 1670s. The textile industry which predominated there was in some way conducive to dissent.[100] The northern textile parishes were densely populated with a large labour force which lived in or close to poverty. In the 1671 Hearth Tax returns, for instance, 58 per cent of households were shown to be exempted and over half the tenants farmed land of less than five acres in size. Dr Hull has suggested that these inhabitants constituted 'a wage earning class divorced from the soil and relying entirely on the clothiers for their employment and livelihood'.[101]

---

[98] Barclay, *Apology*, 372; Penn, *No Cross, No Crown*, 62–3.

[99] Isaac Penington, *The Memoirs of the Life of Isaac Penington*, 16–17.

[100] See Chap. 10 below.

[101] K. H. Burley, 'The Economic Development of Essex in the Later Seventeenth and Early Eighteenth Centuries' (University of London Ph.D. thesis, 1957), 343–4; Felix Hull, 'Agriculture and Rural Society in Essex, 1540–1640' (University of London Ph.D. thesis, 1950), 480.

The economic forces which helped shape attitudes to dissent in Essex can be gauged by examining the relationship between the Quakers and the community in the township of Great Coggeshall. If outlying rural areas are included, it has been calculated that the township employed over five thousand people in the textile trade. Sixty per cent of the town's two thousand inhabitants were exempt from the hearth tax.[102] In Great Coggeshall Quakers were elected to parochial office on thirty occasions between 1660 and 1700.[103] Four Friends also served on the town's employers' body; their duties included controlling the number of apprentices in the town and ensuring that terms of indenture were satisfied and that only local youths took up apprenticeships.[104]

The level of integration in the parish probably explains why the tide of persecution which swept over the movement touched Friends in Coggeshall in no more than a limited way. It is difficult to find instances of hostility to the sect in the town. The prosecution and distraint of Friends for meeting illegally in 1670 took place only after the intervention of two informers who reported the Quakers to local justices. More often it is possible to discover evidence of constables refusing to harass Friends. In 1665 John Dawes and John Sampson, both clothiers, refused to arrest and escort to prison the Quakers Robert Ludgater, William Clarke, Daniel Fann, and his wife for attending conventicles.[105] Sampson had earlier joined with Friends in resisting tithe demands.[106] In 1670 two constables were prosecuted for submitting a false presentment to the Assize, knowing full well that parishioners absented themselves from church and attended illegal religious meetings.[107] In the same year eight parish officers (a churchwarden, three constables, and four overseers) were fined for refusing to distrain Friends' goods.[108]

The reluctance to prosecute was probably in part because Friends had proved themselves responsible and reliable parishioners. Moreover, since the middling ranks in parish society seem to have dominated office-holding, officials may have been reluctant to proceed against villagers who were from the same social rank and with whom they possibly had business

---

[102] Burley, 'Economic Development', 101–3.

[103] ERO, D/P 36/8/1 (Coggeshall Vestry Minutes Book).

[104] ERO, T/A 156, John Bufton's Diary (*c.*1659–*c.*1700).

[105] ERO, Q/SR 402/76.

[106] In 1658 some of the constables joined with the Quakers in refusing to pay impropriated tithes. PRO, E112/299/112.

[107] ERO, Assi 35/113/10, No. 22 (July 1670); Assi 35/112/9, No. 32 (Winter 1670/1). See also Assi 35/117/3, No. 17 (Winter 1675/6).

[108] Besse, *Sufferings* i. 204; EUL, EQ 22, 15.

ties. The parish authorities would also have been uneasy about imprisoning Friends, especially the more prosperous, who employed many parish
paupers.[109] It was widely argued by the sect that prosecuting Friends, and
thus endangering their trade, would be likely to increase the number of
poor families and thus the burden on the parish poor rate.[110]

Perhaps a significant reason for the lack of enmity to the movement in
Great Coggeshall lay in the county's tradition of religious radicalism, which
may have predisposed the local authorities and local society (especially from
the 1660s when the Quakers on the whole abandoned their aggressive proselytizing) to a greater tolerance of Quakerism than was the case in other
areas. Isaac Hubbard, the deacon of the Congregational Church in Great
Coggeshall, who served on several occasions in local office, sometimes along
with Quakers, was said to be 'never so unchristian as to make any anti-
Christian who differed from him; as if none could get to heaven but went
in his congregation'.[111]

Whatever the sympathy of parishioners for Quakers in Coggeshall, it
was not shared by Thomas Jessup, the local incumbent. In the early 1660s
and later Jessup summoned Quakers and other parishioners to the
Exchequer Court for non-payment of tithes.[112] However, when it came
to parish affairs Jessup's authority was limited, since he could nominate
only one churchwarden.[113] The majority of the parochial officials were
appointed by the vestry, who, presumably ignoring his counsel, appointed Quakers and other nonconformists to serve in parochial office.
The experience of Quakers in this township suggests that Friends were
not wholly segregated from the larger community. Indeed, their election
to office in Great Coggeshall may not have been unusual: at Witham and
Halstead, townships with similar economic profiles to that of Coggeshall,

---

[109] In Great Coggeshall 18 per cent of known Quaker occupations between 1660 and 1700
were clothiers. See also ERO, D/ABR 3/299 (1694): Solomon Freemantle bequeathed money
to weavers who worked for him; D/ABR 13/321 (1694): William Swan of Halstead did the
same. When Coggeshall clothiers petitioned the King for assistance in 1642 they claimed
that through their actions 'many thousands of poor people are employed'. Seven clothiers
who were to become Quakers signed their name to the petition, PRO, S/P 18/25. The economic significance of the clothiers in respect of employment is suggested by the example of
the poor who begged for clothiers' release in 1627 because their imprisonment meant additional hardship. Hunt, *The Puritan Moment*, 203. See also G. D. Ramsay, *The English Woollen
Industry 1500–1700* (1982), 50; Thirsk and Cooper, *Seventeenth-Century Economic Documents*, 324.　　　　　　　　　　　　　　[110] George Whitehead, *Christian Progress*, 583.
[111] Quoted by Bryan Dale, *The Annals of Coggeshall* (n.p., 1863), 204.
[112] PRO, E 112/396/75, 396/168, 396/11, 401/367, 401/53, 579/64.
[113] ERO, D/P 36/8/1 (Vestry Minutes) (27 Mar. 1676, 21 Apr. 1679, 20 Apr. 1685). On
the social composition of office-holders see Wrightson, *English Society*, 36.

Quakers served in parochial office and were integrated to a similar degree in parish life.[114]

GOOD NEIGHBOURS OR DEVIANTS?

a generation most pestiferous in their Doctrine, and dangerous in their Seduction and so ought of all men to be avoided.

Richard Blome, *The Fanatick History* (1660), Preface.

How does the experience of Quakers in one English county match up to current assumptions about the development of the movement? In Essex Friends achieved a far greater level of integration than has previously been thought. Integration was to have its limits. Friends were unlike the early Stuart dissenters examined by Professor Collinson who, while exercising a strict ecclesiastical separation, were none the less prepared to countenance all social contacts.[115] To the Society, integration was acceptable only to the extent that it did not compromise religious conviction, and this gave rise to a complex pattern of interdependence between Friends and the world. As we have seen, from the earliest years of the movement in the county, kin and neighbours showed sympathy to ordinary Friends, which contradicts the impression given by hostile pamphleteers and the Society that Quaker sectarianism gave rise to only deep familial and societal divisions. Moreover, there were areas of the county, the textile parishes to the north, which appear to have developed a particularly strong pattern of integration. Not, however, until the decade of the 1670s did the Society itself adopt a more conciliatory approach to the world.

It is difficult to reconcile the position of Quakers in local society as outlined here with the account of Friends reported in part one of this study, where much of the evidence suggested that the sect was disliked and distrusted by others. Are we to disbelieve the invective of anti-Quaker pamphleteers and sometimes the words of Quakers themselves? One must be careful in interpreting evidence about early Quakers. A dispute between Quakers, a local minister, and some parishioners is not necessarily evidence that the whole parish was of a single view or that it was symptomatic of what prevailed elsewhere. And some sources with which historians deal— for instance, court records and the recollections of the persecuted—will inevitably suggest conflict; when consensus existed the evidence is more

---

[114] Davies, 'The Quakers in Essex', 306–7.   [115] Collinson, *Birthpangs*, 144–5.

difficult to come by. To overcome the inherent bias of some sources a wider range of local materials such as will and parish records can prove useful. Even so, some Essex Friends balked at the prospect of holding parochial office and wanted to remain aloof from the wider community.[116] Moreover, there is no doubt that in Essex and across the country Friends could be subjected to harsh treatment. One is reminded of the churchwarden's accounts for Saffron Walden, which recount that in 1682 a payment of 4*d.* was made for nailing up the doors of the Quaker meeting house in the parish.[117]

There were disagreements as to how dissenters should be treated in local society. In those instances where persecuting clergy and magistrates got the upper hand, the result for Quakers could be misery. But by and large in Essex a number of factors seem to have coalesced to protect Friends over time. Less militant evangelizing by Quakers and greater familiarity with their ways certainly contributed to growth of tolerance of the sect. The tradition of dissent in the county of Essex, the importance of Quakers in the textile economy, and the Society's decision after the early 1670s to seek greater accommodation with the world were the main reasons for Quakers becoming more readily accepted. Nevertheless, given the mass of critical literature that was published against Friends, it is probably correct still to refer to them as 'deviants'. In the county of Essex hostility towards Friends was restrained by local factors. How typical the experience of the movement in the area was will become clearer in the light of further research on the movement and dissenting communities in this and other regions.

---

[116] ERO, D/ACA 44, fo. 217ʳ (Dec. 1668), Thomas Fretton of Great Stambridge; D/P 81/8/1 (13 Apr. 1680), Robert Bailey. FHL, Portfolio MS 13/22 (1726).
[117] Mary Whiteman, *Friends in Saffron Walden* (n.p., n.d.), 1.

Conclusion

religions which partake of enthusiasm, are, on their first rise, more furious and violent than those which partake of superstition; but in a little time become more gentle and moderate . . . When the first fire of enthusiasm is spent, men naturally, in all fanatical sects, sink into the greatest remissness and coolness in sacred matters.

> David Hume, *Of Superstition and Enthusiasm* (1771), reprinted in *Selected Essays*, ed. Stephen Copley and Andrew Edgar (Oxford, 1993), 41.

For many of them have really gone off from the height of *Blasphemy* and *Madness* which was professid among them at their first setting up, in the Year, 1650 and so continud till after the Restauration *Anno* 1660. Since which time they have been coming off by degrees, especially of late . . . they have in a great measure, Reform'd from the Errors of the Primitive *Quakers* . . .

> Charles Leslie, *The Snake in the Grass* (1696), 4–6.

1660 is the crucial year in Quaker history, the commencement of what has been accurately termed the 'second period' of Quakerism.

> Barry Reay, *The Quakers and the English Revolution* (1985), 104.

Hume's remarks are directed mainly at the changed attitudes of his Quaker contemporaries when compared with those of the fanatical brethren who first propagated the Quaker gospel. Coolness and formality were to be characteristics of the movement by the close of the period of this survey. Indeed, behaviour which seemed commonplace and unremarkable to Friends in the 1650s and the early 1660s was later severely disapproved of by the Society. When in the early 1720s the maverick 'Quaker' Benjamin Lay disturbed the assemblies of the established and nonconformist churches in Colchester in the manner of the earliest converts, he was not only charged at the local Quarter Sessions for his actions but also testified against by the Quaker meeting in the town.[1] In the early eighteenth century George Whitehead had queried how many early Friends had 'gone naked', saying that 'very few . . . many years since were concerned

---

[1] CBR, Q/SR 136 fo. 49 (12 Aug. 1723), Order Book, 306. See also *JFHS* 33 (1936), 3–19.

therein', adding that 'I cannot excuse everyone in that case to have a Divine Calling to make themselves such spectacles to the world'.[2]

A transformation within Quakerism has been identified quite early in the sect's development. Some argue that 1660 is the watershed, the dividing line in Quaker history. Soon after that point, it is contended, a clear and universal commitment to pacifism, and a withdrawal from militant and political campaigning marked an end to the aggressive radicalism which had characterized the sect during the 1650s. The movement was thereafter transformed 'ideologically, organisationally, culturally'.[3] Others point to the establishment of a network of monthly and quarterly meetings in 1667 as the key date.[4] From then on corporate approval was necessary to legitimate the guidance of the spirit. Though some Friends expressed anxiety about the growing institutionalization of Quakerism and resisted such development,[5] on the whole individual Quakers no longer looked to God alone to test the leadings of the heart. How the Society was transformed and even when the process began are debatable. Should we be looking for a year, an event in Quaker history, or a change of heart in Quaker perceptions?

While accepting the weight of the arguments outlined above, the perspective of this study, based heavily upon local sources, leads one to a different emphasis. The crucial period in early Quaker history was the 1670s, for then the Society set out upon a path of accommodation and integration which ultimately sowed the seeds of its own decline in the next fifty years. Quaker strategies for the avoidance of suffering and a willingness to associate more with the world have been identified as two key factors encouraging integration, but they must be considered in the context of the social make-up of Quakerism, the wealth of its members, the history of dissent in the county of Essex and the moderate size of the Quaker movement there; all of which were factors to explain the decline of the movement.

One of the objectives of this study was to consider how far Friends in Essex conformed to the pattern of the sect's development described by Quaker historians and others who have studied the evolution of sectarian

---

[2] George Whitehead, *Christian Progress*, 226; Kenneth Carroll, 'Early Quakers and "Going Naked as a Sign" ', *Quaker History*, 67 (1978), 69–87.

[3] Reay, *The Quakers and the English Revolution*, 107, 104–5; Christopher Hill, *England's Turning Point: Essays on 17th Century English History* (1998), 326–7.

[4] David Scott, *Quakerism in York, 1650–1720*, University of York, Borthwick Paper, 80 (1991), 11.

[5] Kenneth Carroll, 'John Perrot: Early Quaker Schismatic', 44–5, 51–64; Braithwaite, *Second Period*, chap. 11. For a succinct summary of the issues see Watts, *The Dissenters*, i. 302–3.

groups. While many of the features described here are familiar to students of religion there are aspects of the movement's evolution in Essex which do not easily fit the conventional picture of sectarian development. For instance, it has been suggested by Richard Vann that the drive for uniformity and standardization in the behaviour of members which occurred a generation or so after the Society first emerged was accompanied by a move towards greater sectarianism, in the sense of greater social separation. After 1670, and more so after 1689, the Friends, it is suggested, charted a course whereby they deliberately separated themselves from their host community. It has also been argued that the isolation of Friends in local society was accentuated by their becoming concentrated in a narrower social and geographical range.[6] It is reasonable to speculate that a stronger discipline and integration were in some sense related, but the conclusions of research in Essex do not support the view propounded by Vann.

From the 1670s the Society in the county was prepared to countenance greater levels of integration between Quakers and others. It may be that as Friends were more fully integrated into local society, the more important it became for their lives to seem free of blame so as not to bring reproach upon the wider Quaker community. Moreover, the view that the social composition of the movement narrowed is not supported by the local evidence; the figures on social origins point to a wider range of wealth among Essex Quakers at the end of the seventeenth century than earlier. Friends interacted with members of local society to a far greater degree than has hitherto been realized. Evidence of a dissolution of the traditional hierarchical structures of daily life during this period, a feature of which was the transferral of allegiances from the parish community to the sect, was not as great as had been anticipated.

The pattern of social interaction found in Essex was to some extent repeated elsewhere. Quaker converts were drawn from communities where they were already a part of familial and neighbourhood networks and were not able to sustain a high level of social isolation.[7] It is likely then that there was some degree of integration wherever the movement took root, though the amount of interaction between Quakers and others may have varied with time and place. Other local studies of Quakerism tend to support this view. In York, for example, Quakers appear to have been able to go about their business activities relatively unhindered in the 1650s and 1660s. The marriages of several leading Quakers were entered

---

[6] Vann, *Social Development*, 201, 164.

[7] Stephen Brook, *The Club: The Jews of Modern Britain* (1989), chap. 31 for a useful comparison.

in the parish registers for these decades in order, it appears, that they might avoid the damaging charge of illegitimacy. And twenty York Quakers were found not guilty of 'illicit' meeting at Quarter Sessions in 1662 and in turn promised to keep the peace. The Quaker townsfolk in York were not involved in the disruptive evangelizing which Friends practised in Essex and this may account for the sympathetic response they received.[8] In Bedfordshire, Hertfordshire, and Huntingdonshire there is also evidence of considerable social integration, with Quakers serving as constables from the 1660s. Some were known on occasion to have refused to distrain upon their own brethren or break up dissenters' meetings.[9] It is no longer possible to accept the view that the evolution of the sect involved a retreat into greater social isolation.

The experience of Essex Quakers raises some serious questions concerning aspects of the conventional explanations for the evolution of sectarian groups. At one time most attention was focused upon how the sect was transformed into a church. But more recently scholars have gone on to examine the ways in which, with the passage of time and an increase in prosperity, sects become denominations. While the characteristic of a sect is seen to be social withdrawal and hostility to the world, the process of denominationalism is one whereby the sect becomes reconciled to worldly values.[10] There were developments within Quakerism which conform to this model of change. For instance, there was a shift in emphasis from a personal to an institutional religion and by the end of the seventeenth century the Society exhibited a greater concern with educating the faithful in the values of the Society than acquiring new converts. While it is true that the Society held fast to the principle of a priesthood of all believers and did not develop a professional ministry as such, the steps to achieving leadership and the opportunity to preach did become more formal.[11]

The extent to which the Society had moved towards denominationalism is most evident from the changing relations of the Society and the established Church. We have already mentioned how in the 1650s and early 1660s Quakerism was infamous for its disturbance of church services and supposed miracle cures effected by its strident preachers. By the mid-1660s

---

[8] Scott, *Quakerism in York*, 5–6.

[9] Stevenson, 'The Social Integration of Post-Restoration Dissenters', 369–70.

[10] Though concerned with Victorian Quakerism, Elizabeth Isichei's, 'From Sect To Denomination among English Quakers', 161–81 is a perceptive account of sectarian change. See also Michael Mullett, 'From Sect to Denomination: Social Development in Eighteenth-Century English Quakerism', *Journal of Religious History*, 13/2 (1984), 168–91.

[11] Ibid., 172–3, 176.

this frenetic behaviour was discontinued on the whole, though relations with the Church remained distant, as is evident from the difficulties encountered by Quakers in getting their wills proved. In the mid-1670s the Society mounted a campaign to win new allies so as to lessen the persecution, or the threat of it, to which members were liable under the laws directed against dissenters, but though probate was more easily achieved, neither the payment of church dues nor clerical discipline was recognized as legitimate by Friends. The result was numerous prosecutions of Quakers for tithe evasion, for most parish clergy felt no sympathy with Quakers on this count. However, by the 1680s the Society was prepared to petition church representatives for leniency during bouts of severe persecution, and in the 1690s it even encouraged members to attend the church courts and plead conscience as the reason for non-payment of tithes. The days had gone when a judge's remark would meet with derision or the response that Anglican ministers were the agents of Satan. We know from the records of the Quaker movement in Essex that by the early eighteenth century many Friends paid tithes surreptitiously.[12] Moreover, a simplification of the law for the recovery of tithes afforded the clergy more straightforward legal remedies for getting their dues, thus reducing tension between them and the Friends.[13]

The clergy continued to harbour resentment against Quakers: after all, Friends still failed to attend church and the large majority persisted in not paying their dues. And while the clergy and parishioners would have welcomed the cessation of social disruption and the fracturing of communal harmony which made Friends such a disagreeable feature of local society, followers in the opinion of many still remained despicable heretics. Francis Bugg, a renegade Quaker who turned 'apostate' in the early 1680s, was a notorious and unyielding thorn in the Quaker flesh. In 1703 he wrote perceptively about the changed image of Quakerism and how the religion was still to be distrusted. The changed outward appearance of Quakerism—a deliberate change thought Bugg in order to 'turn men's eyes from this blasphemous faith'—ought not to mislead people about the reality of the Quaker faith.

As to their *Conversation*, we have in some measure *considered* this too. We know what they were at first about fifty years ago; we know likewise what they are *now*, and we see how different they are *now* from what they were then. Then they dis-

---

[12] Davies, 'The Quakers in Essex', 116–18.
[13] Eric J. Evans, ' "Our Faithful Testimony": The Society of Friends and Tithe Payments, 1690–1730', *JFHS* 52 (1969), *passim*.

tinguished themselves by the extraordinary Fasting, and Quaking; now they do not *Quake*, because they do not *Fast*: Then they ran naked about the street: now they walk cloathed, though not in the Fashion: then in a literal sense, they *called No Man Master on Earth*; now in some degree they have left off that way of *Levelling* ... But let the *Conversation* be what it will as long as their Doctrines are Heretical and Blasphemous, they ought to be *Censured* and *Condemned* by us.[14]

But despite Bugg's condemnation, the sting had been removed. To most, the changed social behaviour of Friends and the Society's deliberate policy of accommodation meant that Quakers were now accepted as an oddity, more a band of annoying eccentrics who could more or less be subsumed in parish culture than a potent threat to the Church and State.[15]

However, the drift to denominationalism was not inevitable nor final. The Society still maintained a sectarian posture in many respects. It continued to insist that the payment of tithes and church dues should be resisted and its members were expected to hold fast to the social practices of the faith. The Society was also keen that the pursuit of wealth did not become an obsession and warned those who were attracted by the seductive lure of covetousness. The new emphasis on plainness in clothes and deportment in the 1690s also sharpened the dividing line between sect followers and others. Indeed, as the eighteenth century progressed, the movement deliberately jettisoned members who failed to heed the Society's injunction to practise endogamous marriages, thus sharpening boundaries with the world in a sectarian fashion.[16] Thus the progress to denominationalism was not, then, unqualified or unilinear. It could be argued that it was not until the middle of the nineteenth century that Quakerism finally surrendered its sectarian status and truly assumed the mantle of denominationalism. In 1860 it was decided by Yearly Meeting that Quaker distinctions in dress and speech should be optional for members, and in the previous year the Society ruled that choosing partners from within the Quaker faith was no longer compulsory.[17]

One of the advantages of a local study is that it provides an opportunity to compare general explanations of sectarian change against actual

[14] Francis Bugg, *Quakerism Drooping* (1704), 43–4.

[15] Quakers were not exactly popular and were often the subject of jibes in the nineteenth century. See, for example, the comment of Sydney Smith, who confessed to 'one little weakness, one secret wish—to roast a Quaker ... One would satisfy me, only one. I hope you will pardon my weakness ... but it is one of those peculiarities I have striven against in vain'. From Stuart J. Reid, *The Life and Times of the Rev. Sydney Smith* (1884), quoted in A. N. Wilson (ed.), *Church and Clergy* (1992), 259.

[16] Isichei, 'From Sect to Denomination among English Quakers', 161–2.

[17] Ead., *Victorian Quakers* (Oxford, 1970), 158–9, 162–3.

developments on the ground at a local level. Traditional analyses of sectarian radicalism consider sectarian development almost exclusively from the perspective of the group's leaders. Here again local evidence suggests that we should be careful about accepting without qualification conventional accounts of sect development. Local sentiments were important in deciding how policies were implemented, and they did not always accord easily with the broad theories. Friends within each county were able to exercise a considerable amount of discretion in day-to-day matters affecting followers, a factor which deserves greater recognition. There were, of course, centralizing forces such as the Yearly Meeting and Meeting for Suffering, and their significance in imposing national uniformity on the sect should not be underestimated. In Essex, rank and file members were influential in determining the direction of the movement. They played an essential role in establishing the sect in the county and seem to have been more sympathetic than Friends elsewhere towards backsliders. In addition, ordinary Friends were prepared to interact socially with others in the local community before accommodation was sanctioned officially by the Society. They therefore provide a quite different perspective on the sect and its development. Indeed, ordinary Quakers reached accommodation with kin and neighbours early on, setting a course the Society was to follow.

What has been learned about Friends in this study has a wider bearing on the changing nature of English society at this time than might perhaps appear. The years from the Restoration to the Act of Toleration are sometimes referred to as the 'Period of the Great Persecution'.[18] Recent studies of judicial records and local societies have questioned the view that persecution was rigidly and ubiquitously enforced.[19] Quakerism was certainly capable of generating a hostile response from the inhabitants of local society, and the comportment of Friends was such that they were always likely at least to be mocked or shunned and therefore not accepted as full members of the community. But the actions of some parish constables and an analysis of the court records confirm the impression that persecution was not uniform. The main pressure for mass persecution appears to have originated from the central authorities and that mainly at times of political instability. This raises important issues about the origins of persecution.[20]

---

[18] Gerald R. Cragg, *Puritanism in the Period of the Great Persecution, 1660–1688* (1957).

[19] T. C. Curtis, 'Quarter Sessions Appearances and their Background', in J. S. Cockburn (ed.), *Crime in England, 1550–1800* (1977), 144–5; Miller, *Popery and Politics*, chap. 3. See also Chap. 13, above.

[20] The issue is thoughtfully discussed in another context in R. I. Moore, *The Formation of a Persecuting Society* (Oxford, 1987), 5 and *passim*.

Save possibly during the sect's early years, the persecution of Quakerism was not on the whole a spontaneous outburst by local communities against hated sectaries, but in the main a policy that was pursued by certain elements within the ruling elite and imposed from above because of political necessity or the political advantage it promised. The chief and perhaps most surprising finding of this study, from evidence mainly drawn from the county of Essex, is that local society in the seventeenth century was far more pluralistic and tolerant of deviant opinion and behaviour than has been appreciated hitherto.

An examination of sectarianism in its local context also raises important questions about the degree to which the presence of Friends altered the nature of attitudes in local society. In today's world Quakers are mainly remembered for their advocacy of the peace testimony, philanthropy, penal reform, and anti-slavery campaigns. Their important legacy to science and industry is also noted.[21] But possibly just as important were the attitudes of the Quakers and the reactions provoked by them for they helped remove barriers which had acted as brakes upon new modes of thinking and behaviour. The incursion of Quakerism, and the changing reactions towards them in local society, contributed to a revolution in attitudes towards authority, society, and daily relationships which constituted the roots of Enlightenment tolerance.[22] It may be that the climate of tolerance which Quakerism fostered and the fragmentation it encouraged assisted these broader social and economic changes.[23] When John Locke published his famous essay advocating religious toleration in 1689, he urged a freedom limited to spiritual matters alone.[24] But changes in attitudes to religion, encouraged by religious pluralism, possibly fostered broader social changes. A mood of greater tolerance and an acceptance of diversity in daily life informed people's relations with one another and resulted in part from a greater preparedness to recognize freedom of conscience in religious matters. Seventeenth-century Quakers played no small part in that process.

---

[21] Barbour and Frost, *The Quakers*, 118–34, 164–6; Arthur Raistrick, *Quakers in Science and Industry* (Newton Abbott, 1968), chaps. 3–10.

[22] On this see Roy Porter, *The Enlightenment* (1990), 5–6, 11, 28.

[23] For example, on the loosening of moral and religious control because of the transformation of the apprenticeship system and the softening of attitudes towards suicide see K. D. M. Snell, *The Annals of the Labouring Poor: Social Change and Agrarian England, 1660–1900* (1985); Michael MacDonald and Terence R. Murphy, *Sleepless Souls: Suicide in Early Modern England* (Oxford, 1990), p. 2.

[24] John Locke, *A Letter Concerning Toleration*, 1689, ed. John Horton and Susan Mendus (1991), which contains the original text of Locke's letter 12–57, and discussion of its implications, 2, 70, 99–100.

Appendix I
A NOTE ON SOURCES

Some of the chief sources utilized are worth noting. Particularly useful have been the records of the church courts in ascertaining the attitudes and behaviour of Friends in local society. Though suspended at the onset of the Civil War, the courts operated again after the Restoration. For the purpose of this study the courts may be described as being of two types. First, there were the Archdeaconry courts, which were a step up from the level of parish administration and had responsibility for enforcing conformity in the county. Above them were the Bishop of London's Consistory and Commissary courts, which also had jurisdiction over Essex. Though effectively different bodies, they served much the same purpose. Churchwardens were expected to return to the courts accounts of parish affairs which included the state of the church, whether the local minister conformed to the prescriptions of the Book of Common Prayer, any evidence of bastardy, adultery, or fornication in the parish, and the incidence of religious nonconformity. A principal source for this study has been the Archdeaconry courts' Act Books where offences by parishioners were entered. The names of offenders were presented in the courts and judgment reached as to what action should be taken against them. The decision of the church authorities was entered at the side of the original presentment. Much the same procedure applied in the Archdeaconry as in the Bishop's courts.[1] Quakers, of course, refused to accept the validity of either and failed to appear when summoned. The result for most Friends was excommunication.

The most valuable records of the secular courts for revealing official local attitudes towards Friends are those of the Quarter Sessions. These covered similar offences to those dealt with by the church courts, but also had jurisdiction over other areas of parish life such as poor relief, the building and maintenance of bridges, highway repairs, and weights and measures. Moreover, the court could levy a fine or commit culprits to gaol where judged appropriate. Every three months constables, magistrates, and jurymen submitted to the Quarter Sessions presentments, which are an important source for learning how nonconformists were dealt with. Like Quarter Sessions, the Assize court was independent of the Church but it was a national court that had local authority. Essex, for instance, was part of the Home

---

[1] For a description of church records see Dorothy M. Owen, *Records of the Established Church in England*, British Record Association (1970); Alan Macfarlane, *A Guide to English Historical Records* (Cambridge, 1983), chap. 5; G. Worley, *Essex: A Dictionary of the County Mainly Ecclesiological* (1915); F. G. Emmison, *Guide to the Essex Record Office*, 2nd. edn. (Chelmsford, 1969), 67–71.

Circuit, with the court visiting the county twice a year. The Assize was considered to have a superior authority, dealing with cases of a more serious nature such as felonies, while misdemeanours were limited to the lesser Quarter Sessions. In reality, the remits of the courts overlapped and the activities of religious nonconformists were investigated in both.[2] For Essex the indictments have survived only from the Assize court and these only for certain periods, though they still provide a useful guide to attitudes to dissent.

Records of Quaker business meetings contain much of the source material for this study.[3] While Quaker meetings for worship welcomed all comers, the business meetings were exclusive to members, who were normally of some standing in the community. Besides offering opportunity for worship, they looked after administrative matters such as arranging apprenticeships for poorer members and also acted as the disciplinary body within the movement. The principal forum of Quaker government was the Monthly Meeting, which was itself serviced by four to six more locally based Particular Meetings. However, above all these in local importance lay the Quarterly Meeting, whose authority stretched across the county. This meeting also dealt with disciplinary matters and was the primary route for communicating matters with the centrally located Quaker administration in London. There was an exception to this pattern in Essex, since at Colchester, because of the large Quaker population in the town, there was a Two Weeks Meeting which possessed an importance equivalent to the Quarterly Meeting.

Preserved in the Friends' archives are registers which detail the births, marriages, and deaths of members. There are also published diaries and journals which recount the experiences of early Friends and much other material that is of significance to a local study of the movement.[4] In addition there is a mass of relevant literature in the form of books and pamphlets, though not always originating from Essex, that is extremely valuable. Much of this was issued by Friends and has been useful for charting the course of the movement. Literature critical of the movement, of which there is a considerable body, is also revealing, though it has to be read with care since its authors were surely not motiveless when attacking the sect.[5]

A key ingredient of this study has been a nominal index of Friends in Essex. The index was compiled principally by using references in the Friends' own birth, marriage, and death registers alongside other records of the sect like books of suffering and discipline. Civil sources, such as presentments in the Assize and Quarter Sessions courts, provided useful supplementary evidence. Extensive use was also

[2] Macfarlane, *A Guide to English Historical Records*, 59–64; id., Sarah Harrison, and Charles Jardine, *Reconstructing Historical Communities* (Cambridge, 1977), 60–3; F. G. Emmison and I. Gray, *County Records*, Historical Assoc. (1973), 5–16; *Emmison, Guide*, 1–50.

[3] Hugh L. Doncaster, *Quaker Organisation and Business Meetings* (1958).

[4] Owen C. Watkins, *The Puritan Experience* (1972). The bibliography provides a useful guide to the journals and diaries of Quaker and other dissenting authors.

[5] Pamphlets critical of the Quaker movement are listed in Joseph Smith, *Bibliotheca Anti-Quakeriana: or A Catalogue of Books Adverse to the Society of Friends* (repr. New York, 1968).

made of wills and parish records. The index was compiled during research in national and local archives. A considerable amount of cross-checking was undertaken in local archives to avoid confusion of identity. The index has provided the key to unlocking the lives of the ordinary men and women in the local community whose actions and words are the basis of this work.[6]

---

[6] The definition of community is much disputed. For a discussion of the various views see Richard R. Beeman, 'The New Social History and the Search for "Community" in Colonial America', *American Quarterly*, 29 (1977), 422–42; Colin Bell and Howard Newby, *Community Studies* (1971).

Appendix II
SOCIAL ORIGINS

The greatest challenge in compiling an occupational index of Friends has been in assessing the reliability of the information available on this subject. The problem is twofold. First, how accurate is the occupation or 'addition' given?[1] Second, are sources such as wills biased in such a way as to reflect the occupations only of those from the better-off social groups?

There are indeed occasional inconsistencies in the 'additions' of Essex Quakers.[2] One Friend was said to be a yeoman at one time, a sawyer at another, and a labourer on a third occasion.[3] However, a clear social profile of the movement can be compiled by using a wide variety of Quaker and non-Quaker sources, thus allowing discrepancies in the 'additions' of individual Quakers to be spotted. Sources useful for discovering social status are Quaker registers, minute books, deeds of property, suffering books, and pamphlets. Other relevant sources are wills, parish, borough, Quarter Session, and Assize records. Not all give specific occupations, but where there is some doubt over a Friend's occupation they provide useful complementary evidence.

Compiling the statistics for Friends employed in agriculture proved the greatest difficulty. Encouragingly, however, there is a remarkable degree of consistency between additions and other indicators of occupation. Where no addition has been discovered, other evidence has been relied upon to identify social origins. Vann has suggested that if a Quaker was liable to pay four pounds or more a year in tithes, this was equivalent to having the status of a yeoman. Those who owed less in tithes are assumed to have been husbandmen. This formula has been adopted here in order that a comparison might be made with the work of Richard Vann. However, this methodology has been questioned.[4] Those who plainly relied on the

---

[1] Vann, *Social Development*, 64, 53.

[2] Stephen Holman of Hornchurch, a husbandman, according to his addition lived in a house rated at five hearths. John Sewell from Gestingthorpe, described as a yeoman, was rated at one hearth. However, additions do on the whole correspond to Hearth Tax assessments: the tax listings of 131 Quakers were checked. The average Hearth Tax ratings for the categories used here were as follows: gentry (8.0), professionals (3.0), yeomen (4.3), husbandmen (2.0), wholesalers and large producers (4.9), retailers (3.0), artisans (1.9), mariners (2.5), fishermen (2.7), labourers (1.3).

[3] John Pearce of Billericay. Information derived from nominal index of Essex Quakers.

[4] Vann, *Social Development*, 65. This formula has been questioned by Stevenson, 'The Social and Economic Status of post-Restoration Dissenters', 352 n. 94. However, the number of times the formula is used to determine social origins in this study is limited and has a minor effect on the whole sample.

land for their main livelihood, but whose exact status is uncertain, have been designated as farmers.

Some of the inconsistencies in occupational description may reflect more than the whim of a scribe. Different occupations were held by individuals in a lifetime, or even at the same time. Thomas Lark, a Great Coggeshall Quaker, was described as a woolcomber in his will, but we also know that he traded as a locksmith in the parish.[5] Henry Haslum, according to the description in his will, seems to have traded as a grocer and woolcomber simultaneously.[6] Another Friend was said to be a schoolmaster and a tailor, and yet another a yeoman and cheesemonger.[7] Moreover, many Friends seem to have kept a foothold on the land. James Allen, a cordwainer from Halstead, kept sheep and Robert Tibball, a wheelwright from Great Birch, grew hay and kept cattle. At Wimbish the brothers James and Michael Pettit shared a farm, though James' main occupation seems to have been that of a blacksmith.[8]

The tables indicating social origins have been compiled so as to reflect the changes in occupational history. However, if a Friend held more than one occupation simultaneously, his primary occupation has been used. When this is not certain, the addition that occurs most frequently has been used in the tables.

[5] ERO, D/ACW 19/89 (1678). Lark was described as a locksmith. John Bufton's Diary, ERO, T/A 157. Like Vann, I have counted as gentry those who were described as gentlemen in more than one source, or who were university graduates, or who held the positions of Mayor or Common Councillor (*Social Development*, 61–3).

[6] ERO, D/ABR 115/178 (1708).

[7] For example, Joseph Besse of Billericay and William Drewett of Abberton. Information on their occupations was acquired from the nominal index.

[8] ERO, D/ABR 13/99 (1662); PRO, E112 400/456 (1680); E112/396/19 (1663). See also E112/396/208 (1662); E112/599/64 (1684). See also D. C. Coleman, *Industry in Tudor and Stuart England* (1974), 24–5.

BIBLIOGRAPHY

MANUSCRIPT SOURCES

ESSEX RECORD OFFICE, CHELMSFORD

Ecclesiastical Records

Archdeaconry of Essex

Act Book, 1626–1640	D/AEA 36–42
Visitation Books	D/AEV 6–21

Archdeaconry of Colchester

Act Book, 1540–1666	D/ACA 1–55
Deposition Books, 1587–1641	D/ACD 5–7
Visitation Books, 1666–1721	D/ACV 5–14

Archdeaconry of Middlesex

Acts/Visitations, 1662–1724	D/AMV 1–12

Bishop of London's Consistory Court

Visitation Book, 1631–1639	D/ALV 2
Deposition Book, 1633–1639	D/ALV 1

Bishop of London's Commissary Court in Essex and Herts.

Act Books, 1628–1670	D/ABA 4–12
Visitation Books,	
1633–1639	D/ABV 1
1676–1684	D/ABV 2
1687–1725	D/ABV 3
Miscellaneous Book, 1660–1770	D/AXD 3
Deposition Books, 1618–1665	D/ABD 1–8

Quarter Sessions Records

Rolls, 1630–1714	Q/SR 269–560
Bundles, Early Series, 1621–1687	Q/SBa 2
Bundles, Late Series, 1694–1725	Q/SBb 1
Order Books, 1651–1724	Q/SO 1–6
Process Book of Indictment	
1681–1694	Q/SPb 1
1709–1714	Q/SPb 2
1714–1773	Q/SPb 3

Association Roll for Essex, 1696   Q/RRO 2/1–58
Quaker Association Roll for Kelvedon, 1696   Q/RRO 2/2
Hearth Tax, 1661   Q/RTh 1
Hearth Tax, 1671   Q/RTh 5

Maldon Borough Records

Original Series of Presentments for Absence from
    Church, 1669–1705   D/B3/3/520–2
Court Books, 1658–1740   D/B3/3/12–17
Session Book, 1664–1716   D/B3/1/21–4

Saffron Walden Records

Session Book, 1657–1673   T/A 419/1
List of Apprenticeship Indentures in
    Saffron Walden Corporation   T/A 419/19

Quaker Records

Witham Monthly Meeting, 1672–1712   DNFI/1/1
Witham Monthly Meeting, 1701–1753   DNF1/1/2
Register of Births, Marriages and Deaths   DNF1/2/1
Original Certificates of Removal, 1717–1781   DNF1/2/3
Chelmsord Preparative Meeting, 1676–1725   DNF1/3/1
Billericay Preparative Meeting, 1704   DNF1/3/9
Declaration of Trust, 1710   DNF1/3/10
Thaxted Monthly Meeting, 1692–1722   T/A 261/1/1
Women's Monthly Meeting, 1697–1719   T/A 261/1/11
Felsted Monthly Meeting, 1712–1720   T/A 283/1/1
Deed of Coggeshall Meeting House   T/A 425/1/1

Parish Records

Barking Parish Registers, 1600–1715   D/P 81/1/1–7
Vestry Book, 1666–1695 (In Reverse, Poor Children
    and Pensioners Settled, 1675–1694)   D/P 81/8/1
Boxted Burial Registers, 1678–1711   D/P 19/1/2
Chelmsford Parish Registers, 1649–1753   D/P 94/1/1–10
Settlement and Apprenticeship Papers, 1645–1851   D/P 94/8/1
Great Coggeshall Parish Registers, 1600–1715   D/P 36/1/1–3
Vestry Minute Book, 1609–1777   D/P 36/8/1
Colchester, All Saints Parish Registers, 1689–1715   D/P 200/1/1–4
Vestry Minute Book   D/P 200/8/1
Colchester, St Mary's at the Wall, 1600–1750
    (Parish Registers)   D/P 246/1/1–4
Earls Colne Burial Registers, 1678–1755 and 1653–1671   D/P 209/1/3–4
Felsted Parish Registers, 1600–1753   D/P 99/1/1–4

Feering Parish Registers, 1600–1750	D/P 231/1/1–2
Overseers' Accounts, Rates and Burials, 1684–1714	D/P 231/12
Finchingfield Parish Registers, 1671–1750	D/P 14/1–15
Minutes of Town Meeting	D/P 14/8/1
Halstead Parish Registers, 1600–1750	D/P 96/1/1–5
Apprenticeship Papers, 1648–1812	D/P 96/14/12
Little Horkesley, Burial in Woollen Certificates, 1680–1767	D/P 307/1/10
Hornchurch Parish Registers, 1650–1750	D/P 115/1/1–2
Apprenticeship Indentures, 1702–1764	D/P 115/14
Southminster Overseer's Accounts, 1666–1740	D/P 259/12/2
Overseer's Notes, 1660–1740	D/P 259/12/3
Stansted Mountfitchet, Incumbent's Tithe Account, 1682–1818	D/P 109/3/1
Theydon Garnon Burial Registers, 1643–1685 and 1648–1774	D/P 152/1/1–2
Witham Apprenticeship Papers, 1671–1814	D/P 30/14/1–2
Papers relating to Barnardiston's Charity	D/P 30/25/42

Other Records

Typescript Calendar of Essex Assize Files in the Public Record Office, 1519–1774, ed., N. McNeil O'Farrell	
John Bufton's Diary, *c.*1659–*c.*1700	T/A 156
Extracts from Bishop Compton's Census	T/A 420
Wills indexed by	
F. G. Emmison, *Wills at Chelmsford 1400–1858*, 3 vols. (Chelmsford, 1958–1969)	

ESSEX RECORD OFFICE, COLCHESTER (COLCHESTER AND
NORTH-EAST ESSEX BRANCH)

Colchester Borough Records

Assembly Books, 1655–1725
Depositions relating to Quaker Conventicles, March and May 1664
Examination and Recognizance Book, 1646–1687
Index of Free Burgesses, 1620 onwards
Quarter Session Rolls
    1638–1654, Nos. 36–43
    1654–1659, Nos. 43–8
    1687–1726, Nos. 51–147
    No. 87, D/BM1, Miscellaneous 1572–1709
Session of the Peace, 1630–1663

Order Book
  1677–1684
  1700–1714
  1715–1723
Monday Court Book, 1653–1725
Thursday Court Book, 1650–1725
Monday and Thursday Court Rolls, 1662–1716, Nos. 118–247
Enrolled Deeds, 1670–1713, Nos. 190–229
Tradesmen Recognizances, 1647–89
Oath Book
Foreigners' Fines, 1634–1667

ESSEX UNIVERSITY LIBRARY, COLCHESTER

Quaker Records

Essex Quarterly Meeting, 1711–1754	EQ 1
Supplementary Papers (Quarterly Meeting Minutes, 1690–1711)	EQ 2
Accounts of Suffering in Essex, 1658–1785	EQ 22
Christian and Brotherly Advice given forth by Yearly Meeting in London	EQ 26
Copies of Yearly Meeting Epistles, early days to 1742	EQ 27
Quarterly Meeting Collection for the Poor, 1675–1720	EQ 28
Registers of Properties in Essex and Trustees	EQ 29
Abstract of Titles	EQ 30
Colchester Two Weeks Men's Meeting	
1667–1705	COLTW 1
1705–1725	COLTW 2
Colchester Monthly Meeting	
1672–1718	COLMM 1
1718–1756	COLMM 2
Intention of Marriage, 1676–1794	COLMM 22
Book to Record Sufferings, 1723–1793	COLMM 27
Copies of Yearly Meeting Epistles, 1667–1703	COLMM 34
Birch Monthly Meeting, Accounts of Collections, 1658 onwards, Suffering and other Papers	COLMM 35
Copies of Certificates of Removals, Intentions of Marriage, Condemnation, 1720–1757	COLMM 41
Collection of Letters Written 1662–1777	COLMM 46
Abstract of Titles and Early Properties	COLMM 47
A book of Collections and Disbursements for the Poor,	
1694–1700	COLMM 51
1711–1717	COLMM 52
1717–1763	COLMM 53

Loose Leaf Disbursements for the Poor, 1711–1789	(uncatalogued)
Coggeshall Monthly Meeting Minutes, 1709–1725	COGMM 1
Coggeshall Two Weeks Meeting, 1672–1714 and	
Coggeshall Preparative Meeting, 1713–1789	COGMM 27
Kelvedon Preparative Meeting, 1711–1752	SPM 16
Letters and Correspondence of Stephen Crisp	Crisp MS
Quaker Deeds, 1655–1725	(Black Box)

HARWICH BOROUGH RECORDS, TOWN HALL, HARWICH

Harwich Borough Court Session Papers	Bundle 66/3
Church Book with Vestry Minutes, 1550–1718	Bundle 98/1
Common Council with Apprenticeships	Bundle 98/4
Court of Please with Recognizances	
1662–1688	Bundle 98/11
Session Book, 1649–1695	Bundle 98/15
Chamberlain's Accounts, 1608–1737	Bundle 99/1
Chamberlain's Accounts, 1473–1708	Bundle 99/2
Leases Granted in Great Court, 1610–1659	Bundle 99/6
Rental Book of Borough Property, 1753–1834	Bundle 99/7
Certificate of Quaker Meeting House, 1689	Bundle 126/2
Letter to Mayor Concerning Unlawful Meetings, 1667	Bundle 126/5

FRIENDS' HOUSE LIBRARY, LONDON

Swarthmore MS
Caton MS 3
Crosse MS 3
Portfolio MSS 1–42
The Journal of John Kelsall (MS vol. S, 193–4)
The Journal of Thomas Gwin of Falmouth (MS vol. 77)
Barking Monthly Minutes
    1695–1714
    1715–1724
Plaistow and Barking Women's Meeting Minutes, 1675–1721
Enfield Monthly Meeting Minutes
    1689–1699
    1699–1709
    1709–1718
    1718–1789
Waltham Abbey Monthly Minutes, 1673–1695
London and Middlesex Quarterly Meeting
    1670–1701
    1702–1724
    1724–

The Book of Cases 1, 1661–1695
The Book of Cases 2, 1695–1738
Minutes of Meeting for Sufferings, 1675–1724 (24 vols.)
Six Weeks Meeting Minutes, 1675–1725 (7 vols.)
Yearly Meeting Minutes, 1672–1728 (6 vols.)
The Great Book of Sufferings, 1650–1725 (17 vols.)

THE GREATER LONDON RECORD OFFICE (RECORDS NOW HOUSED
AT THE LONDON METROPOLITAN ARCHIVE)

Bishop of London's Consistory Court

Act Books, 1669–1725	D/LC 31–47
Deposition Books, 1661–1689	D/LC 326–42
Miscellaneous Series, 1629–1640	D/LC 317–25

GUILDHALL LIBRARY, LONDON

Bishop of London's Commissary Court

Churchwardens' Presentments	
1627–1636	MS 9583, Bundle 1
1664–1670	MS 9583, Bundles 2–13
Episcopal Visitation Process	
1664	MS 9583A, Bundle 1
1669	MS 9583A, Bundle 2
1671	MS 9583A, Bundle 3
Episcopal Visitation Books, 1631–1725	MS 9537
St Paul's Archive	
Dean and Chapter of St Paul's Churchwardens' Presentments	Unlisted

PUBLIC RECORD OFFICE, LONDON

Colchester Quaker Association Roll, 1696	C/213/264/3
Essex Hearth Tax, 1674	E179/242/22
Exchequer Decrees and Orders, 1625–1840	E125–7
Depositions taken from the Barons to the Exchequer, Elizabeth 1 to 1841	E133
Depositions taken by Commission, Elizabeth 1 to Victoria	E134
Exchequer Bills and Answers	E112, Bundles 177–84; 396–402; 578–9; 644–50; 799–804; 943–52

Index to Exchequer Bills and Answers	16828–38
Port Books, 1654–1700	E190/606–20
Chancery Proceedings	C6/338/56
Original Registers of Births, Marriages, and Deaths of the Society of Friends,	
Essex	RG6, 1379; 654, 655; 1455, 1345; 1289, 1196; 1800, 1548; 1185, 1189; 1188, 1465; 1573, 1335; 1292, 1382; 1217, 1262; 1396
London and Middlesex	RG6, 1437; 1293, 497; 496, 498–501; 328, 499; 331, 343, 500; 975, 973, 670; 1369, 672; 413, 1095; 1107, 825; 117, 1391; 1297
State Papers, 1642	SP/18/24
Town and County Registers (List of Apprenticeships, May 1710–Jan. 1725)	IR1, 41–8
Wills	Prob 11

BODLEIAN LIBRARY, OXFORD

Rawlinson MS C. 983,
    No. 26, Letter from Sir John Shaw, Recorder of Colchester, to Bishop Compton
    No. 32, Letter from William Shelton to Bishop Compton
Stubbs, John, 'A Primer for Children to Read'

PRINTED PRIMARY SOURCES

Aldam, Thomas, *False Prophets and False Teachers* (1652).
Allen, William, *The Last Word and Testimonies of our Friend William Allen of Earls Colne* (1680).
—— Robert Ludgater, *et al.*, *The Glory of Christ's Light Within* (1669).
The Anti-Quaker; or, a Compendious Answer to a Tedious Pamphlet (1676).
The Autobiography of Richard Baxter, ed. N. H. Keeble (rev. edn., 1975).
The Autobiography of William Stout, ed. J. D. Marshall (Manchester, 1967).
Aylmer, Gerald (ed.), *The Levellers in the English Revolution* (1975).
Bangs, Benjamin, *Memoirs of the Life and Convincement of that Worthy Friend* (1757).

Banks, John, *A Journal of the Life, Labours, Travels and Sufferings (In and for the Gospel) of that Ancient Servant to and Faithful Minister of Jesus Christ, John Banks* (1798).

Barbour, Hugh, and Arthur O. Roberts (eds.), *Early Quaker Writings* (Grand Rapids, Mich., 1973).

Barclay, Robert, *Apology for the True Christian Divinity* (1678; repr. Glasgow, 1886).

Baxter, Richard, *One Sheet Against the Quakers* (1657).

—— *The Quaker's Catechism* (1655).

—— *Reliquae Baxterianae*, ed. Matthew Sylvester (1696).

Bayles, Thomas, *A Relation of a Man's Return* (1677).

—— *A Testimony to the Free and Universal Love of God* (1675).

—— with others, *Some Account from Colchester of the Unfairness and Dis-ingenuity of Two Rectors* (1699).

—— *The Serious Reading and Comfort of Holy Scriptures* (1714).

Benn, Tony (ed.), *Writings on the Wall: A Radical and Socialist Anthology, 1215–1984* (1984).

Besse, Joseph, *A Collection of the Sufferings of the People Called Quakers*, 2 vols. (1753).

Bewick, John, *An Answer to a Quakers Seventeen Heads of Queries* (1660).

Bishop Fell and Nonconformity, ed. Mary Clapinson, Oxfordshire Record Society, 61 (1986).

Blome, Richard, *The Fanatick History* (1660).

—— *Questions Propounded to George Whitehead and George Fox* (1659).

Borke, Henry, *A Few Words* (1659).

Bourne, Immanuel, *A Defence of the Scriptures* (1656).

Bradshaw, Ellis, *The Quakers' Whitest Divell Unvailed* (1654).

Brown, John, *Quakerisme: The Path-way to Paganisme* (Edinburgh, 1678).

Bugg, Francis, *Quakerism Drooping* (1703).

Bunyan, John, *A Vindication of the Book called, Some Gospel-Truths Opened* (1657).

Burford, G. J. (ed.), *Bawdy Verse: A Pleasant Collection* (Harmondsworth, 1982).

Burnet, Bishop Gilbert, *History of his Own Time: From the Restoration of Charles II to the Treaty of Peace at Utrecht, in the Reign of Queen Anne* (1838).

Cadbury, H. J. (ed.), *Letters to William Dewsbury and Others* (1948).

Calendar of State Papers Domestic 1640–1700, xxxix–c (1880–1939).

Child, John, *A Moderate Message* (n.p., 1676).

Christian Discipline of the Religious Society of friends in Ireland (Dublin, 1971).

Clapham, Jonathan, *A Full Discovery and Confutation* (1656).

Claridge, Richard, *The Life and Posthumous Works of Richard Claridge* (1726).

Clarkson, Thomas, *A Portraiture of Quakerism*, 3 vols. (1806).

Coale, Josiah, *The Books and Diverse Epistles of the Faithful Servant of the Lord, Josiah Coale* (1671).

Collier, Thomas, *A Looking Glass for the Quakers* (1657).

Comber, Thomas, *Christianity No Enthusiasm; or, The Several Kinds of Inspirations and Revelations Pretended by the Quakers* (1678).

The Compton Census of 1676: A Critical Edition, ed. Anne Whiteman (Oxford, 1986).

Coxere, Edward, *Adventures By Sea*, ed. E. H. W. Meyerstein (Oxford, 1945).

Crisp, Stephen, *An Epistle to Friends Concerning the Present and Succeeding Times* (1666).

—— *A Memorable Account of the Christian Experiences, Gospel Labours, Travel and Sufferings of that Ancient Servant of Christ, Stephen Crisp* (1694).

—— *Several Sermons or Declarations* (1693).

—— *A Short History of the Long Travel from Babylon to Bethel* (9th. edn., 1778).

—— *Stephen Crisp and his Correspondents*, ed. C. Fell Smith (1892).

—— *A Word of Reproof to the Teachers of the World* (1658).

Crouch, William, *Posthuma Christiana; or, a Collection of Some Papers of William Crouch* (1712).

Davies, Richard, *An Account of the Convincement, Exercise, Travels of that Ancient Servant of the Lord* (1844).

Deacon, John, *The Grand Imposter Examined* (1656).

Dewsbury, William, *The Life of William Dewsbury* (1836).

Diary of Ralph Josselin, 1616–1683, ed. Alan Macfarlane (1976).

Diary of Thomas Burton, ed. J. T. Rutt, 4 vols. (1828).

Dickinson, James, *A Journal of the Life, Travels, and Labour of Love in the Work of the Ministry* (1745).

Duke, Francis, *An Answer to some of the Principle Quakers* (1660).

Dundas, William, *A Few Words of Truth from the Spirit of Truth* (1673).

Eaton, Samuel, *The Quakers Confuted* (1654).

Edmundson, William, *A Journal of the Life, Travels and Sufferings, and Labour of Love in the Work of the Ministry* (Dublin, 1715).

Edwards, Thomas, *Gangraena* (1646).

Ellwood, Thomas, *The History of the Life of Thomas Ellwood* (1714).

Essex Quarter Sessions Order Book, 1652–1661, ed. D. H. Allen (Chelmsford, 1974).

Faldo, John, *A Vindication of Quakerism No Christianity* (1673).

Farmer, Ralph, *The Great Mystery of Godliness and Ungodliness* (1655).

—— *The Lord Craven's Case Stated* (1660).

—— *Satan Inthron'd in his Chair of Pestilence* (1657).

Five Important Queries (1681).

Fowler, Christopher, and Simon Ford, *A Sober Answer to an Angry Epistle* (1656).

Fox, George, *A Collection of Many Select and Christian Epistles, Letters and Testimonies written on Sundry Occasions* (c.1650; repr. Philadelphia, 1831).

—— *Concerning Good-Morrow and Good-Even; the World's Customs* (1657).

—— *George Fox's Book of Miracles*, ed. H. J. Cadbury (1948).

—— *The Journal of George Fox*, ed. N. Penney, 2 vols. (Cambridge, 1911).

—— *The Journal of George Fox*, ed. John L. Nickalls (1952; reissued 1975).

—— *A Warning to All Teachers of Children which are called School-masters and Schoolmistresses* (1657).

—— *The Works of George Fox*, 8 vols. (1831 edn. repr. New York, 1990).

—— *The World's Hypocritical Salutations being out of the Truth are condemned* (1657).

—— Benjamin Furly, and John Stubbs, *A Battle-Door for Teachers and Professors to learn Singular and Plural* (1660).

Fox, George, the younger, *A True Relation of the Unlawful and Unreasonable Proceedings of the Magistrates of Harwich in Essex* (n.p., 1660).

Furly, John, *A Testimony to the True Light* (2nd edn., 1670).

Gaskin, John, *A Just Defence and Vindication of Gospel Ministers* (1660).

Gataker, Charles, *An Examination in the Case of the Quakers Concerning Oaths* (1675).

Gauden, John, *A Discourse Concerning Publick Oaths* (1662).

Gilpin, John, *The Quakers Shaken* (1653).

Glisson, Henry, *A True and Lamentable Relation* (1656).

Gough, Richard, *The History of Myddle*, ed. David Hey (Harmondsworth, 1981).

Gratton, John, *A Journal of the Life of that Ancient Servant of Christ* (1720).

Green, Theophilus, *A Narrative of Some Pasages of the Life of Theophilus Green* (1702).

Grigge, William, *The Quakers' Jesus* (1658).

Grubb, Mollie (ed.), *Quakers Observed in Prose and Verse: An Anthology, 1656–1986* (York, 1993).

—— *Plus Ultra, or the Second Part of the Character of a Quaker, in his True and Proper Colours* (1672).

Hall, Ralph, *Quakers Principles Quaking* (1656).

Hallywell, Henry, *An Account of Familism* (1673).

Hammond, Samuel, *The Quakers' House Built Upon Sand* (1658).

Harris, Francis, *An Answer to Some Queries* (1655).

Haworth, William, *Animadversions* (1676).

—— *The Quaker Converted to Christianity* (1674).

—— *An Antidote Against the Poysonous and Fundamental Error of the Quakers* (1676).

Higginson, Francis, *A Brief Relation of the Irreligion of the Northern Quakers* (1653).

Holme, Benjamin, *A Collection of the Epistles and Works* (1753).

Ives, Jeremiah, *Innocence Above Impudency* (1656).

—— *The Quakers Quaking* (1656).

J. C., *A Skirmish Made Upon Quakerism* (1676).

Jones, William, *Work for a Cooper* (1679).

A Journal of the Life of Thomas Storey, ed. William Alexander, 2 vols. (York, 1832).

Keach, Benjamin, *The Grand Impostor Discovered* (1675).

—— *War with the Devil* (1676).

Kenyon, J. P. (ed.), *The Stuart Constitution, 1603–1688: Documents and Commentary* (1966).

Lampe, Henry, *An Apothecary Turned Quaker* (1895).

Lawrence, Thomas, and George Fox, *Concerning Marriage* (1663).

A Lecture for all Sects and Schismatics to Read (c.1680).

Livingstone, Patrick, *Selections from the Writings* (1847).

Locke, John, *A Letter Concerning Toleration, 1689*, ed. John Horton and Susan Mendus (1991).

Marshall, Charles, *Sion's Travellers Confuted* (1704).

Miller, Joshua, *Antichrist in Man, The Quaker's Idol* (1656).

Moore, Thomas, Jnr., *An Antidote Against the Spreading Infection of the Spirit of Antichrist* (1655).

Osborn, Elias, *A Brief Narrative of the Life, Labours, and Sufferings of Elias Osborn* (1723).

Pagitt, Ephraim, *Heresiography*, 5th edn. (1654).

The Papists Younger Brother; or the Vileness of Quakerisms Detected (1679).

Parnel, James, *Christ Exalted into his Throne* (n.p., n.d.).

—— *A Collection of the Several Writings given Forth—from the Spirit of the Lord, through the meek Patient, and Suffering Servant of God, James Parnel* (1675).

—— *The Fruits of a Fast* (1655).

—— *Goliah's Head* (1655).

—— *A Shield of the Truth* (1655).

—— *A Trial of Faith* (1654).

—— *The Trumpet of the Lord Blown* (1655).

—— *A Warning for All People* (1660).

—— *The Watcher* (1656).

Penington, Isaac, *Memoirs of the Life of Isaac Penington*, ed. J. Gurney Bevan (1831).

—— *The Works of Isaac Penington*, 3 vols. (repr. Glenside, Pa., 1995–6).

Penington, Mary, *Experiences in the life of Mary Penington (written by herself): c.1652–1682* (1911, reissued 1992).

Penn, William, *An Account of William Penn's Travels in Holland and Germany* (1694).

—— *A Brief Account of the Rise and Progress of the People Call'd Quakers* (1694).

—— *No Cross, No Crown*, 2nd edn. (1682; repr. York, 1981).

—— *The Peace of Europe, The Fruits of Solitude and Other Writings*, ed. Edwin B. Bronner (1993).

Penney, Norman, *The First Publishers of Truth* (1907).

Pepys, Samuel, *The Shorter Pepys*, ed. Robert Latham (Harmondsworth, 1987).

Pike, Joseph, *Some Account of the Life of Joseph Pike* (1837).

Price, J., *The Mystery and Method of His Majesty's Happy Restauration* (1680).

Prynne, William, *A New Discovery of Some Romish Emmissaries* (1656).

—— *The Quakers Unmasked* (1655).

The Quacking Mountebanck (1655).

Quakers are Inchanters (1655).

The Quaker's Art of Courtship (1687).

Quakers Confuted (1653).

The Quakers' Wedding Bed (1671).

The Querers and Quakers' Cause (1653).

Rawlinson, Thomas, *Light Sown for the Righteous* (1657).

R. H., *The Character of a Quaker, in his True and Proper Colours* (1671).

—— *Plus Ultra, or the Second Part of The Character of a Quaker, in his True and Proper Colours* (1672).

Rigge, Ambrose, 'A True relation of Ambrose Rigge by way of a Journal', in *Constancy in the Truth Commended* (1710).

Sansom, Oliver, *An Account of many Remarkable Passages of the Life of Oliver Sansom* (1710).

Say and Sele, Lord, *Folly and Madness Made Manifest* (1659).

Semper Idem: or a Parallel Betwixt the Ancient and Modern Phanaticks (1661).

Sewell, William, *The History of the Rise, Increase and Progress of the Christian People Called Quakers*, 2 vols. (1712).

Smith, Humphrey, *To all Parents of Children Upon the Face of the whole Earth* (1660).

Smith, Joseph, *Bibliotheca Anti-Quakeriana: or A Catalogue of the Books Adverse to the Society of Friends* (repr. New York, 1968).

—— *A Descriptive Catalogue of Friends Books* (repr. New York, 1970).

Somersetshire Quarterly Meeting of the Society of Friends 1668–1699, ed. Stephen C. Morland, Somerset Record Society, 75 (1978).

Southey, Robert, *Letters from England by Don Manuel Alvarez*, 3 vols. (1807).

Stalham, John, *Marginall Antidotes* (1657).

—— *The Reviler Rebuked* (1657).

The Substance of a Letter sent to the Magistrates of Colchester, 2nd edn. (1670).

Swift, Jonathan, *A Critical Edition of the Major Works*, ed. Angus Ross and David Woolley (Oxford, 1984).

Thirsk, Joan, and J. P. Cooper (eds.), *Seventeenth-Century Economic Documents* (Oxford, 1972).

Thomas, William, *Rayling Rebuked* (1656).

Toldervy, John, *The Foot Out of the Snare* (1656).

Tom, Mad, *Twenty Quaking Queries* (1659).

Tomkins, John, *Piety Promoted in a Collection of the Dying Sayings of Many of the People Called Quakers*, ed. William Evans and Thomas Evans, 3 vols. (Philadelphia, 1854).

Tomlinson, William, *An Awakening Voice to the Papists* (n.p., 1673).

—— *An Epistle to the Flock* (n.p., 1674).

—— *A Position Concerning Persecution* (n.p., n.d.).

—— *Seven Particulars* (1657).

—— *A Word of Information* (1660).

—— *A Word of Reproof*, 2nd edn. (1656).

Tompkins, Anthony, *A Faithful Warning* (1668).

A True and Faithful Relation of the Proceedings of the Magistrates from the People of God (called Quakers) in Colchester (1664).

Voltaire, *Letters on England*, tr. Leonard Tancock (1734; repr. Harmondsworth, 1980).

W. P., *An Answer According to Truth* (1655).

Wade, Christopher, *Quakerism Slain Irrecoverably* (1657).

—— *To All Those Called Quakers* (1659).

Welde, Thomas, *A Further Discovery* (Gateside, 1654).

—— *The Perfect Pharisee* (Gateside, 1653).

West, Moses, *A Treatise Concerning Marriage* (1707).

Whitehead, George, *The Christian Progress of that Ancient Servant and Minister of Jesus Christ, George Whitehead* (1725).

Whitehead, John, *Persecution Exposed* (1712).

—— *The Written Gospel Labours of That Ancient and Faithful Servant of Jesus Christ* (1704).

Whiting, John, *Persecution Exposed* (1715).

Wylde, Sam, *The Last Legacy of Sam Wylde* (1703).

A Yea and Nay Almanac (1679).

UNPUBLISHED WORKS

Burley, K. H., 'The Economic Development of Essex in the Later Seventeenth and Early Eighteenth Centuries' (University of London Ph.D. thesis, 1957).

Bryson, Anna, 'Concepts of Civility in England *c*.1650–*c*.1685' (University of Oxford D.Phil. thesis, 1984).

Childs, Fenela Ann, 'Prescriptions for Manners in English Courtesy Literature 1690–1760, and their Social Implications' (University of Oxford D.Phil. thesis, 1984).

Cole, W. A., 'The Quakers and Politics, 1652–1688' (University of Cambridge Ph.D. thesis, 1957).

Davies, T. A., 'The Quakers in Essex, 1655–1725' (University of Oxford D.Phil. thesis, 1986).

Forde, H., 'Derbyshire Quakers, 1650–1761' (University of Leicester Ph.D. thesis, 1977).

Glines, T. C., 'Colchester Politics and Government, 1660–1693' (University of Wisconsin Ph.D. thesis, 1974).

Hull, Felix, 'Agriculture and Rural Society in Essex, 1560–1640' (University of London Ph.D. thesis, 1950).

Hurwich, J. J., 'Nonconformity in Warwickshire, 1660–1720' (University of Princeton Ph.D. thesis, 1970).

Nuttall, Geoffrey, F., 'Record and Testimony: Quaker Persecution Literature, 1650–1700' (unpub. typescript, Friends' House Library, London, Box L/32, 17).

Reay, Barry, 'Early Quaker Activity and Reactions To It, 1652–1664' (University of Oxford D.Phil. thesis, 1980).

Spurrier, W. W., 'The Persecution of the Quakers in England, 1650–1714' (University of North Carolina Ph.D. thesis, 1976).

SECONDARY SOURCES: SELECT BIBLIOGRAPHY

The Agrarian History of England and Wales, iv, *1500–1650*, ed. Joan Thirsk (Cambridge, 1967).

Alsop, James, 'Gerrard Winstanley's Later Life', *Past and Present*, 82 (1979), 73–81.

Anderson, Alan B., 'The Social Origins of the Early Quakers', *Quaker History*, 68 (1979), 33–40.

—— 'A Study of the Sociology of Religious Persecution: The First Quakers', *Journal of Religious History*, 9 (1977), 247–62.

Argyle, Michael, *Bodily Communication*, 2nd edn. (1988).

—— (ed.), *Social Encounters: Readings in Social Interactions* (Harmondsworth, 1973).

Aston, Margaret, 'Segregation in Church', in W. J. Sheils and Diana Wood (eds.), *Women in the Church, Studies in Church History*, 27 (1990), 237–94.

'At a Meeting of Midwives in Barbados, 11th 12m 1677', *JFHS* 37 (1940), 22–4.

Ball, Bryan W., *A Great Expectation: Eschatological Thought in English Protestantism to 1660* (Leiden, 1975).

Barbour, Hugh, *The Quakers in Puritan England* (New Haven, Conn., 1964).

—— and J. William Frost, *The Quakers* (Richmond, Ind., 1994).

Barclay, Robert, *The Inner Life of the Religious Societies of the Commonwealth* (1876).

Barker, Eileen, *New Religious Movements* (1989).

Barry, Jonathan, 'Popular Culture in Seventeenth-Century Bristol', in Barry Reay (ed.), *Popular Culture in Seventeenth-Century England* (1985), 59–90.

Bauman, Richard, *Let Your Words Be Few: Symbolism of Speaking and Silence among Seventeenth-century Quakers* (Cambridge, 1983).

Bebb, E. D., *Nonconformity and Social and Economic Life, 1660–1800* (1935).

Beck, William, and T. Frederick Ball, *The London Friends' Meetings* (1869).

Beeman, Richard, R., 'The New Social History and the Search for "Community" in Colonial America', *American Quarterly*, 29 (1977), 422–42.

Bell, Colin, and Howard Newby, *Community Studies* (1971).

Berger, Peter, *The Sacred Canopy: Elements of a Sociological Theory of Religion* (repr. New York, 1990).

Bernstein, Eduard, *Cromwell and Communism: Socialism and Democracy in the Great English Revolution*, tr. H. J. Stenning (1963).

Bitterman, M. G. F., 'The Early Quaker Literature of Defence', *Church History*, 42 (1973), 203–28.

Bittle, William G., *James Nayler 1618–1660: The Quaker Indicted by Parliament* (York, 1986).

Blamires, David, 'Quakers Observed in Verse and Prose', in id., Jeremy Greenwood, and Alexander Kerr (eds.), *A Quaker Miscellany for Edward H. Milligan* (Manchester, 1985), 17–26.

Bossy, John, *The English Catholic Community 1570–1850* (1975).

Bradley, Ian Campbell, *Enlightened Entrepreneurs* (1987).

Brailsford, H. N., *The Levellers and the English Revolution* (repr. Nottingham, 1976).

Braithwaite, William C., *The Beginnings of Quakerism*, 2nd edn. (1955).
—— *The Second Period of Quakerism*, 2nd edn. (1961).
Bremmer, Jan, and Herman Roodenburg (eds.), *A Cultural History of Gesture* (Oxford, 1991).
Breward, Christopher, *The Culture of Fashion* (Manchester, 1995).
Brinton, Howard H., *Friends for 300 Years* (repr. Wallingford, Pa., 1988).
—— *Quaker Journals: Varieties of Experience Among Friends* (Wallingford, Pa., 1972).
Brook, Stephen, *The Club: The Jews of Modern Britain* (1989).
Bryson, Anna, 'The Rhetoric of Status: Gesture, Demeanour and the Image of the Gentleman in Sixteenth- and Seventeenth-Century England', in Lucy Gent and Nigel Llewellyn (eds.), *Renaissance Bodies: The Human Figure in English Culture c.1540–1660* (1990), 136–53.
Burke, Peter, *The Art of Conversation* (Oxford, 1993).
—— *The Fortunes of the Courtier* (Oxford, 1995).
—— *The Historical Anthropology of Early Modern Italy: Essays on Perception and Communication* (Cambridge, 1987).
—— (ed.), *New Perspectives on Historical Writing* (Oxford, 1991).
—— *Varieties of Cultural History* (1997).
Butler, David M., 'Friends' Sufferings 1650–88: A Comparative Summary', *JFHS* 55 (1988), 180–4.
Capp, B. S., *The Fifth Monarchy Men: A Study in Seventeenth-Century English Millenarianism* (1972).
Carroll, Kenneth, 'Early Quakers and "Going Naked as a Sign"', *Quaker History*, 67 (1978), 69–87.
—— 'John Perrot: Early Quaker Schismatic', Supplement 33 *JFHS* (1971), 1–116.
—— 'Martha Simmonds, a Quaker Enigma', *JFHS* 53 (1973), 31–52.
—— 'Quaker Attitudes towards Signs and Wonders', *JFHS* 54 (1977), 70–84.
—— '"Sackcloth" and "Ashes" and other Signs and Wonders', *JFHS* 53 (1975), 314–25.
Carter, Charles F., 'Unsettled Friends: Church Government and the Origins of Membership', *JFHS* 51 (1967), 143–53.
Chartier, Roger (ed.), *A History of Private Life III: Passions of the Renaissance* (1989).
Chu, Jonathan M., *Neighbors, Friends or Madmen: The Puritan Adjustment to Quakerism in Seventeenth-Century Massachusetts Bay* (Westport, Conn., 1985).
Clarke, Peter B., *Black Paradise: The Rastafarian Movement* (Wellingborough, 1986).
Cockburn, J. S., 'Early Modern Assize Records as Historical Evidence', *Journal of the Society of Archivists*, 5 (1975), 215–31.
—— *A History of The English Assizes 1558–1714* (Cambridge, 1972).
Cohen, Stan, *Folk Devils and Moral Panics: The Creation of the Mods and Rockers*, 2nd edn. (Oxford, 1980).
Cohn, Norman, *The Pursuit of the Millennium: Revolutionary Millenarians and Mystical Anarchists of the Middle Ages* (1970).

Cole, Alan, 'The Quakers and the English Revolution', *Past and Present*, 10 (1956), 39–54, repr. in Trevor Aston (ed.), *Crisis in Europe* (5th impression, 1975), 341–58.

—— 'The Social Origins of the Early Friends', *JFHS* 48 (1957), 99–118.

Coleman, D. C., *Industry in Tudor and Stuart England* (1974).

Collinson, Patrick, *The Birthpangs of Protestant England: Religious and Cultural Change in the Sixteenth and Seventeenth Centuries* (1988).

—— 'The Cohabitation of the Faithful with the Unfaithful', in O. P. Grell, J. I. Israel, and Nicholas Tyacke (eds.), *From Persecution to Toleration: The Glorious Revolution and Religion in England* (Oxford, 1991), 51–76.

—— 'Critical Conclusion', in Margaret Spufford (ed.), *The World of Rural Dissenters 1520–1725* (Cambridge, 1995), 388–96.

—— 'The Godly: Aspects of Popular Protestantism', in id., *Godly People: Essays on English Protestantism and Puritanism* (1983), 1–18.

—— *The Religion of Protestants: The Church in English Society, 1559–1625* (Oxford, 1982).

—— 'The Significance of Signatures', *Times Literary Supplement* (9 Jan. 1981), 31–2.

Corns, Thomas N., and David Lowenstein (eds.), *The Emergence of Quaker Writings: Dissenting Literature in Seventeenth-Century England* (1995).

Cragg, Gerald R., *Puritanism in the Period of the Great Persecution, 1660–1688* (1957).

Crawford, Patricia, 'The Challenges to Patriarchalism: How did the Revolution Affect Women?', in John Morrill (ed.), *The Revolution and Restoration: England in the 1650s* (1992), 112–28.

Creasey, Maurice A., '"Inward" and "Outward": A Study of Early Quaker Language', Supplement 30 *JFHS* (1962), 1–24.

Cressy, David, *Birth, Marriage, and Death: Ritual, Religion and the Life-Cycle in Tudor and Stuart England* (Oxford, 1997).

—— *Literacy and the Social Order: Reading and Writing in Tudor and Stuart England* (Cambridge, 1980).

Currie, R., A. Gilbert, and I. Horsley, *Churches and Churchgoers: Patterns of Church Growth in the British Isles since 1700* (Oxford, 1977).

Curtis, T. C., 'Quarter Sessions Appearances and their Background', in J. S. Cockburn (ed.), *Crime in England, 1550–1800* (1977), 135–54.

Dale, Bryan, *The Annals of Coggeshall* (n.p., 1863).

Damrosch, Leo, *The Sorrows of the Quaker Jesus: James Nayler and the Puritan Crackdown on the Free Spirit* (Cambridge, Mass., 1996).

Davidoff, Leonora, *The Best Circles* (1986).

Davids, T. W., *The Annals of Evangelical Nonconformity in the County of Essex from the Time of Wycliffe to the Restoration* (1863).

Davis, J. C., *Fear, Myth and History: The Ranters and the Historians* (Cambridge, 1986).

Davis, J. F., *Heresy and Reformation in the South-East of England, 1520–1559* (1983).

De Gruchy, John W., *Christianity and Democracy* (Cambridge, 1995).

Doncaster, Hugh L., *Quaker Organisation and Business Meetings* (1958).

Douglas, Mary, *Natural Symbols: Explorations in Cosmology* (Harmondsworth, 1973).

—— *Purity and Danger: An Analysis of the Concepts of Pollution and Taboo* (1979).

Durston, Christopher, *The Family in the English Revolution* (Oxford, 1989).

Elias, Norbert, *The Civilising Process: The History of Manners*, tr. Edmund Jephcott (repr. Oxford, 1978).

Emmison, F. G., *Catalogue of Essex Parish Records 1240–1894* (Chelmsford, 1966).

—— *Guide to the Essex Record Office*, 2nd edn. (Chelmsford, 1969).

—— *Wills at Chelmsford, 1480–1858*, 3 vols. (Chelmsford, 1958–69).

—— and I. Gray, *County Records*, Historical Assoc. (1973).

Evans, Eric J., ' "Our Faithful Testimony": The Society of Friends and Tithe Payments, 1690–1730', *JFHS* 52 (1969), 106–21.

Evans, Nesta, 'The Descent of Dissenters in the Chiltern Hundreds', in Margaret Spufford (ed.), *The World of Rural Dissenters, 1520–1725* (Cambridge, 1995), 288–308.

Evans-Pritchard, E. E., *Essays in Social Anthropology* (1962).

Everitt, Alan, 'Nonconformity in Country Parishes', in Joan Thirsk (ed.), *Land, Church and People* (Reading, 1970), 185–97.

Eversley, D. E. C., 'The Demography of Irish Quakers, 1650–1800', in J. M. Goldstrom and L. A. Clarkson (eds.), *Irish Population, Economy and Society* (Oxford, 1981), 57–88.

Firth, Raymond, 'Verbal and Bodily Rituals of Greeting and Parting', in J. S. La Fontaine (ed.), *The Interpretation of Ritual: Essays in Honour of A. I. Richards* (1974), 1–38.

Fitch, S. H. G., *Colchester Quakers* (Colchester, 1962).

Forbes, Anthony H., 'The English Penal Laws: Persecution and Precaution, 1690–1709', *Catholic History Review*, 53 (1968), 556–71.

Forbes, Thomas, 'The Regulation of English Midwives in the Sixteenth and Seventeenth Centuries', *Medical History*, 8 (1964), 238–44.

Forde, Helen, 'Friends and Authority: A Consideration of Attitudes and Expedients, with Particular Reference to Derbyshire', *JFHS* 54 (1978), 115–25.

Fraser, Antonia, *The Weaker Vessel: Woman's Lot in Seventeenth-Century England* (1985).

Frearson, Michael, 'Communications and the Continuity of Dissent in the Chiltern Hundreds during the Sixteenth and Seventeenth Centuries', in Margaret Spufford (ed.), *The World of Rural Dissenters, 1520–1725* (Cambridge, 1995), 273–87.

Frost, J. William, *The Quaker Family in Colonial America* (New York, 1973).

Fussell, Sam, *Muscle: Confessions of an Unlikely Bodybuilder* (1992).

Gay, John D., *The Geography of Religion in England* (1971).

Gillis, John, *For Better, For Worse: British Marriages, 1660 to the Present* (Oxford, 1985).

Gittings, Clare, *Death, Burial and the Individual in Early Modern England* (1984).

Glock, Charles, and Rodney Stark, *Religion and Society in Tension* (Chicago, 1965).

Gooch, G. P., *English Democratic Ideas in the Seventeenth Century*, 2nd edn. (1927).

Greaves, Richard L., *Society and Religion in Elizabethan England* (Minneapolis, 1981).

—— and Robert Zaller (eds.), *Biographical Dictionary of British Radicals in the Seventeenth Century*, 3 vols. (Brighton, 1982–4).

Gummere, Amelia Mott, *The Quaker: A Study in Costume* (repr. New York, 1968).

Halliday, M. A. K., *Language as Social Semiotic: The Social Interpretation of Language and Meaning* (1978).

Harrison, J. F. C., *The Second Coming: Popular Millenarianism 1780–1850* (1979).

Harvey, T. E., 'Quaker Language', Supplement 15 *JFHS* (1928), 1–29.

Hill, Christopher, *Antichrist in Seventeenth-Century England* (Oxford, 1971).

—— *England's Turning Point: Essays on 17th Century English History* (1998).

—— *The English Bible and the Seventeenth Century Revolution* (1993).

—— *The Experience of Defeat: Milton and some Contemporaries* (1984).

—— 'From Lollards to Levellers', in Maurice Cornforth (ed.), *Rebels and Their Causes: Essays in Honour of A. L. Morton* (1978), 49–68.

—— 'Quakers and the English Revolution', *JFHS* 56 (1992), 165–79.

—— *Religion and Politics in Seventeenth-Century England* (1986).

—— *Society and Puritanism in Pre-Revolutionary England* (1969).

—— *Some Intellectual Consequences of the English Revolution* (1980).

—— *The World Turned Upside Down: Radical Ideas During the English Revolution* (Harmondsworth, 1975).

—— Barry Reay, and William Lamont, *The World of the Muggletonians* (1983).

Hill, Michael, *The Sociology of Religion* (1973).

Hobby, Elaine, *Virtue of Necessity: English Women's Writings 1649–88* (1988).

Hoestetler, J. A., *Amish Society*, 3rd edn. (Baltimore, 1980).

Holmes, Clive, *Seventeenth Century Lincolnshire* (Lincoln, 1980).

Horle, Craig, 'Changing Quaker Attitudes toward Legal Defence: The George Fox Case, 1673–5, and the Establishment of the Meeting for Sufferings', in J. William Frost and John M. Moore (eds.), *Seeking the Light: Essays in Quaker History in Honor of Edwin B. Bronner* (Pennsylvania, 1986), 17–39.

—— 'Quakers and Baptists', *Baptist Quarterly*, 26 (1976), 218–38.

—— *The Quakers and the English Legal System, 1660–1688* (Philadelphia, 1988).

Houlbrooke, Ralph, *The English Family 1450–1700* (1984).

—— 'The Puritan Death-bed, *c.*1560–*c.*1660', in Christopher Durston and Jacqueline Eales (eds.), *The Culture of English Puritanism, 1560–1700* (1996), 122–44.

Houston, R. A., 'The Development of Literacy in Northern England, 1640–1750', *Economic History Review*, 2nd ser., 35 (1982), 199–216.

—— *Literacy in Early Modern Europe: Culture and Education, 1500–1800* (1988).

Hufton, Olwen, *The Prospect Before Her: A History of Women in Western Europe*, i, *1500–1800* (1995).

Hull, Felix, 'Early Friends in Central and Northern Essex', *Essex Review*, 56 (1947), 64–72.

—— 'More Essex Friends of the Restoration Period', *Essex Review*, 57 (1948), 60–71.

Hunt, N. C., *Two Early Political Associations: The Quakers and the Dissenting Deputies in the Age of Sir Robert Walpole* (repr. Westport, Conn., 1979).

Hunt, William, *The Puritan Moment: The Coming of the Revolution in an English County* (Cambridge, Mass., 1983).

Hurwich, Judith J., 'Dissent and Catholicism in English Society: A Study of Warwickshire 1660–1720', *Journal of British Studies*, 16 (1976), 24–55.

—— 'The Social Origins of the Early Quakers', *Past and Present*, 48 (1970), 156–61.

Ingram, Martin, *Church Courts, Sex and Marriage in England, 1570–1640* (Cambridge, 1987).

Isichei, Elizabeth, 'From Sect to Denomination among English Quakers', in Bryan Wilson (ed.), *Patterns of Sectarianism: Organisation and Ideology in Social and Religious Movements* (1967), 161–81.

—— *Victorian Quakers* (Oxford, 1970).

James, William, *The Varieties of Religious Experience* (1902, repr. New York, 1985).

Johansson, Egil, *The History of Literacy in Sweden in Comparison with some other Countries*, Education Report, Umea, 12 (Umea, 1977).

Journal of the Friends' Historical Society (1903–).

Keeble, N. H., *The Literary Culture of Nonconformity* (Leicester, 1987).

Kendall, Joan, 'The Development of a Distinctive Form of Quaker Dress', *Costume*, 19 (1985), 58–74.

Kirby, E. W., 'The Quaker Effort to Secure Civil and Religious Liberty', *Journal of Modern History*, 7 (1935), 401–21.

Kraybill, Donald B., *The Amish and the State* (Baltimore, 1993).

Lamont, William M., *Godly Rule: Politics and Religion, 1603–1660* (1969).

—— 'The Left and its Past: Revisiting the 1650s', *History Workshop Journal*, 23 (1987), 141–53.

—— *Richard Baxter and the Millennium* (1979).

Laver, James, *A Concise History of Costume* (1973).

Lidbetter, Hubert, *The Friends Meeting House*, 2nd edn. (York, 1979).

Lloyd, Arnold, *Quaker Social History* (1950).

Lurie, Alison, *The Language of Clothes* (Feltham, 1982).

MacDonald, Michael, and Terence R. Murphy, *Sleepless Souls: Suicide in Early Modern England* (Oxford, 1990).

Macfarlane, Alan, *A Guide to English Historical Records* (Cambridge, 1983).

—— *Marriage and Love in England, 1300–1840* (Oxford, 1986).

—— *Witchcraft in Tudor and Stuart England: A Regional and Comparative Study* (1970).

—— Sarah Harrison, and Charles Jardine, *Reconstructing Historical Communities* (Cambridge, 1977).

Mack, Phyllis, *Visionary Women: Ecstatic Prophecy in Seventeenth-Century England* (Berkeley, Calif., and Los Angeles, Calif., 1992).

MacKinnon, Alison, ' "My Dearest Friend": Courtship and Conjugality in some Mid and Late Nineteenth-Century Quaker Families', *JFHS* 58 (1997), 44–58.

McLeod, Hugh, *Religion and Irreligion in Victorian England* (Bangor, 1994).

Mayo, Janet, *A History of Ecclesiastical Dress* (1984).

Mendelson, Sarah Heller, *The Mental World of Stuart Women: Three Studies* (Brighton, 1987).

Miller, John, *Popery and Politics in England, 1660–1688* (Cambridge, 1973).

Mitterauer, Michael, *A History of Youth* (Oxford, 1992).

Moore, R. I., *The Formation of a Persecuting Society* (Oxford, 1987).

Moore, Rosemary, 'Reactions to Persecution in Primitive Quakerism', *JFHS* 57 (1996), 123–32.

Morgan, Nicholas, *Lancashire Quakers and the Establishment, 1660–1730* (Halifax, 1993).

—— 'Lancashire Quakers and the Oaths, 1660–1720', *JFHS* 54 (1980), 235–54.

—— 'The Social and Political Relations of the Lancaster Quaker Community 1688–1740', in Michael Mullett (ed.), *Early Lancaster Friends*, Centre for North West Regional Studies, University of Lancaster Occasional Paper, 5 (1978), 22–32.

Morrill, John, 'The Church in England, 1642–1649', in John Morrill (ed.), *Reactions to the English Civil War* (1982).

Morris, W. D., *The Christian Origins of Social Revolt* (1949).

Mortimer, Jean E., 'Quaker Women in the Eighteenth Century: Opportunities and Constraints', *JFHS* 57 (1996), 228–59.

—— 'Thoresby's "poor deluded Quakers": The Suffering of Leeds Friends in the Seventeenth Century', *The Thoresby Society: The Leeds Historical Society*, 2nd ser., 1 (1990), 35–57.

Morton, A. L., *The World of The Ranters: Religious Radicalism in the English Revolution* (1970).

Mullett, Charles F., 'The Legal Position of English Protestant Dissenters 1660–1685', *Virginia Law Review*, 22 (1936), 495–526.

Mullett, Michael (ed.), *Early Lancaster Friends*, Centre for North-West Regional Studies, University of Lancaster, Occasional Paper, 5 (1978).

—— 'From Sect to Denomination? Social Development in Eighteenth-Century English Quakerism', *Journal of Religious History*, 13/2 (1984), 168–91.

'Notes and Queries', *JFHS* 21 (1924).

Nuttall, Geoffrey F., *The Holy Spirit in Puritan Faith and Experience*, 3rd edn. (Chicago, 1992).

—— 'Overcoming The World: The Early Quaker Programme', in Derek Baker (ed.), *Sanctity and Secularity: The Church and the World, Studies in Church History*, 10 (Cambridge, 1973), 145–64.

—— 'Reflections on William Penn's Preface to George Fox's Journal', *JFHS* 57 (1995), 113–17.

O'Day, Rosemary, *Education and Society 1500–1800: The Social Foundations of Education in Early Modern Britain* (1982).

O'Dea, T. F., *The Mormons* (Chicago, 1957).

—— and Janet O'Dea Aviad, *The Sociology of Religion*, 2nd edn. (Englewood Cliffs, NJ, 1983).

Olsen, V. N., *John Foxe and the Elizabethan Church* (Berkeley, Calif., and Los Angeles, Calif., 1973).

O'Malley, Thomas P., 'Defying the Powers and Tempering the Spirit: A Review of Quaker Control over their Publications, 1672–1685', *Journal of Ecclesiastical History*, 33 (1982), 72–88.

—— 'The Press and Quakerism, 1653–1689', *JFHS* 54 (1979), 169–85.

Ormsby-Lennon, Hugh, 'From Shibboleth to Apocalypse: Quaker Speechways during the Puritan Revolution', in Roy Porter and Peter Burke (eds.), *Language, Self and Identity: A Social History of Language* (1992), 72–112.

Owen, Dorothy M., *Records of the Established Church in England*, British Record Association (1970).

Pestana, C. G., *Quakers and Baptists in Colonial Massachusetts* (New York, 1991).

Petegorsky, David W., *Left-Wing Democracy in the English Civil War: Gerrard Winstanley and the Digger Movement* (repr. Stroud, 1995).

Polhemus, Ted, *Street Style* (1994).

Porter, Roy, *The Enlightenment* (1990).

Pullan, Brian, 'Catholics and the Poor in Early Modern Europe', *Transactions of the Royal Historical Society*, 5th ser., 26 (1976), 15–34.

Raistrick, Arthur, *Quakers in Science and Industry* (Newton Abbott, 1968).

Ramsay, G. D., *The English Woollen Industry 1500–1700* (1982).

Reardon, Bernard M. G., *Religious Thought in the Reformation* (Harlow, 1981).

Reay, Barry, 'Quaker Opposition to Tithes, 1652–1660', *Past and Present*, 86 (1980), 98–120.

—— *The Quakers and the English Revolution* (1985).

—— 'The Social Origins of Early Quakerism', *Journal of Interdisciplinary History*, 11 (1980), 55–72.

Robertson, Roland (ed.), *Sociology of Religion* (Harmondsworth, 1969).

Roodenberg, Herman, 'The "Hand of Friendship": Shaking Hands and other Gestures in the Dutch Republic', in Jan Bremmer and Herman Roodenberg (eds.), *A Cultural History of Gesture* (Oxford, 1991), 152–89.

Rowntree, J. S., *Quakerism: Past and Present* (1859).

Schlatter, Richard B., *The Social Ideas of Religious Leaders* (repr. New York, 1971).

Schofield, Roger S., 'The Measurement of Literacy in Pre-Industrial England', in Jack Goody (ed.), *Literacy in Traditional Societies* (Cambridge, 1975), 311–25.

Scott, David, *Quakerism in York, 1650–1720*, University of York, Borthwick Paper, 80 (1991).

Sennett, Richard, *The Fall of Public Man* (Cambridge, 1974).

Sharpe, J. A., *Crime in Seventeenth-Century England: A County Study* (Cambridge, 1983).

—— 'Enforcing the Law in the Seventeenth-Century English Village', in V. A. B. Gatrell, Bruce Lenman, and Geoffrey Parker (eds.), *Crime and the Law: The Social History of Crime in Western Europe Since 1500* (1980), 97–119.

Sheils, W. J., 'Oliver Heywood and his Congregation', in id. and Diana Wood (eds.), *Voluntary Religion, Studies in Church History,* 23 (Cambridge, 1986), 261–77.

Simpson, Charles R., 'Benjamin Furly, and his Library, *JFHS* 11 (1914), 70–4.

Smith, Harold, *The Ecclesiastical History of Essex under the Long Parliament and Commonwealth* (Colchester, n.d.).

Smith, Nigel, *Perfection Proclaimed: Language and Literature in English Radical Religion, 1640–1660* (Oxford, 1989).

Smout, T. C., 'Born Again at Cambuslang: New Evidence on Popular Religion and Literacy in Eighteenth-Century Scotland', *Past and Present*, 97 (1982), 114–27.

Snell, K. D. M., *The Annals of the Labouring Poor: Social Change and Agrarian England, 1660–1980* (1985).

Sommerville, C. John, *The Secularisation of Early Modern England: From Religious Culture to Religious Faith* (New York, 1992).

Speck, W. A., *Reluctant Revolutionaries* (Oxford, 1988).

Sprawson, Charles, *Haunts of the Black Masseur: The Swimmer as Hero* (1992).

Spufford, Margaret, 'Can We Count the "Godly" and the "Conformable" in the Seventeenth Century?' *Journal of Ecclesiastical History*, 36 (1985), 428–38.

—— *Contrasting Communities: English Villagers in the Sixteenth and Seventeenth Centuries* (Cambridge, 1974).

—— 'First Steps in Literacy: The Reading and Writing Experience of the Humblest Seventeenth-Century Spiritual Autobiographers', *Social History*, 4 (1979), 407–35.

—— 'The Quest for the Heretical Laity in the Visitation Records of Ely in the late Sixteenth and early Seventeenth Centuries', in G. J. Cuming and Derek Baker (eds.), *Schism, Heresy and Religious Protest, Studies in Church History*, 9 (Cambridge, 1972), 223–30.

—— *Small Books and Pleasant Histories: Popular Fiction and its Readership in Seventeenth Century England* (London, 1981).

—— 'The Social Status of Some Seventeenth-Century Rural Dissenters', in G. J. Cuming and Derek Baker (eds.), *Popular Belief and Practice, Studies in Church History*, 8 (Cambridge, 1972), 203–11.

—— (ed.), *The World of Rural Dissenters, 1520–1725* (Cambridge, 1995).

Stark, W., *The Sociology of Religious Sects,* 2 vols. (1967).

Stevenson, Bill, 'The Social and Economic Status of Post-Restoration Dissenters, 1660–1725', in Margaret Spufford (ed.), *The World of Rural Dissenters, 1520–1725* (1995), 332–59.

—— 'The Social Integration of Post-Restoration Dissenters, 1660–1725', in Margaret Spufford (ed.), *The World of Rural Dissenters, 1520–1725* (Cambridge, 1995), 360–87.

Stone, Lawrence, *The Family, Sex and Marriage in England 1500–1800* (1977).

—— 'Literacy and Education in England, 1640–1900', *Past and Present*, 42 (1969), 69–139.

Sutherland, Stuart, 'What's in a Smile?', *Falmer*, 18, University of Sussex (1991), 4–5.

Taylor, Lou, *Mourning Dress: A Costume and Social History* (1983).

Thirsk, Joan, *The Agrarian History of England and Wales*, iv, *1500–1650* (Cambridge, 1967).

Thomas, Keith, *Age and Authority in Early Modern England* (1976).

—— 'Cleanliness and Godliness in Early Modern England', in Anthony Fletcher and Peter Roberts (eds.), *Religion, Culture and Society in Early Modern Britain: Essays in Honour of Patrick Collinson* (Cambridge, 1995), 56–83.

—— *Man and the Natural World: Changing Attitudes in England, 1500–1800* (Harmondsworth, 1983).

—— 'The Meaning of Literacy', in Gerd Baumann (ed.), *The Written Word: Literacy in Transition* (Oxford, 1986), 97–131.

—— *Religion and the Decline of Magic: Studies in Popular Beliefs in Sixteenth and Seventeenth Century England* (Harmondsworth, 1973).

—— 'The Utopian Impulse in Seventeenth-Century England', *Dutch Quarterly Review of Anglo American Letters*, 15 (1985), 162–88.

—— 'Women and the Civil War Sects', *Past and Present*, 13 (1958), 42–62, repr. in Trevor Aston (ed.), *Crisis in Europe* (5th impr., 1965), 317–40.

—— 'Yours', in Christopher Ricks and Leonard Michaels (eds.), *The State of the Language: The 1990s Edition* (1990), 451–6.

Tillyard, E. M. W., *The Elizabethan World Picture* (Harmondsworth, 1972).

Tolles, Frederick B., 'The Atlantic Community of the Early Friends', Supplement 24 *JFHS* (1952), 1–40.

Transactions of the Essex Archaeological Society, 20 (1930–1).

Trevitt, Christine, *Women and Quakerism in the Seventeenth Century* (York, 1991).

Tual, Jacques, 'Sexual Equality and Conjugal Harmony: The Way to Celestial Bliss. A View of Early Quaker Matrimony', *JFHS* 55 (1988), 161–73.

Tyacke, Nicolas, *Anti-Calvinists: The Rise of English Arminianism, c.1590–1640* (Oxford, 1987).

—— 'Puritanism, Arminianism and Counter Revolution', in Conrad Russell (ed.), *The Origins of the English Civil War* (1973), 119–43.

Underwood, T. L., 'Early Quaker Eschatology', in P. Toon (ed.), *Puritans, the Millennium and the Future of Israel* (1970), 91–103.

—— *Primitivism, Radicalism, and the Lamb's War: The Baptist–Quaker Conflict in Seventeenth-Century England* (New York, 1997).

Vaisey, D. G., 'Probate Inventories and Provincial Retailers in the Sixteenth-Century', in Philip Riden (ed.), *Probate Records and the Local Community* (Gloucester, 1985), 91–111.

Vann, Richard T., 'Quakerism and the Social Structure in the Interregnum', *Past and Present*, 43 (1969), 71–91.

—— 'Rejoinder', *Past and Present*, 48 (1970), 162–4.

—— *The Social Development of English Quakerism, 1655–1755* (Cambridge, Mass., 1969).

—— 'Wills and the Family in an English Town: Banbury, 1550–1800', *Journal of Family History*, 4 (1979), 346–67.

—— and David Eversley, *Friends in Life and Death: The British and Irish Quakers in the Demographic Transition, 1650–1900* (Cambridge, 1992).

Van Beek, E. A. (ed.), *The Quest for Purity* (Berlin, 1988).

Victoria County History of Essex, vols. ii–vii (1907–78).

Vigarello, Georges, 'The Upward Training of the Body from the Age of Chivalry to Courtly Civility', in Michel Feher, Ramona Naddaff, and Nadia Tazi (eds.), *Fragments for a History of the Human Body, Part II* (Cambridge, Mass., 1989), 148–99.

Wales, T., 'Poverty, Poor Relief and the Life-Cycle: Some Evidence from Seventeenth-Century Norfolk', in Richard M. Smith (ed.), *Land, Kinship and Life Cycle* (Cambridge, 1984), 351–404.

Walker, Andrew, *Restoring the Kingdom: The Radical Christianity of the House Church Movement* (1985).

Wallis, Paul E., *The Profane Culture* (1978).

Walvin, James, *The Quakers: Money and Morals* (1997).

Watkins, Owen C., *The Puritan Experience* (1972).

Watts, M. R., *The Dissenters*, i. *From the Reformation to the French Revolution* (Oxford, 1978).

Webb, Maria, *The Fells of Swarthmoor Hall* (Philadelphia, 1896).

Whiteman, Mary, *Friends in Saffron Walden* (n.p., n.d.).

Whiting, C. E., *Studies in English Puritanism from the Restoration to the Revolution, 1660–1689* (1968).

Wildeblood, Joan and Peter Brinson, *The Polite World: A Guide to English Manners and Deportment from the Thirteenth to the Nineteenth Century* (1965).

Williams, J. A., *Catholic Recusancy in Wiltshire, 1660–1791*, Catholic Record Society (1968).

Wilson, A. N. (ed.), *Church and Clergy* (1992).

Wilson, Bryan, *Religion in Sociological Perspective* (Oxford, 1982).

—— (ed.), *Religious Sects* (1976).

—— *The Social Dimensions of Sectarianism; Sects and New Religious Movements in Contemporary Society* (Oxford, 1990).

Woodhouse, J. R., *From Castiglione to Chesterfield: The Decline in the Courtier's Manual* (Oxford, 1991).

Worley, G., *Essex: A Dictionary of the County Mainly Ecclesiological* (1915).

Wright, L. M., *The Literary Life of Early Friends 1658–1725* (New York, 1932).

—— 'Literature and Education in Early Quakerism', *Humanities Studies* (University of Iowa), 5/2 (1933), 1–60.

Wrightson, Keith, *English Society, 1500–1680* (1982).

—— 'Love, Marriage and Death', in Lesley M. Smith (ed.), *The Making of Britain: The Age of Expansion* (1986), 101–12.

—— 'Two Concepts of Order: Justices, Constables, and Jurymen in Sixteenth-Century England', in John Brewer and John Styles (eds.), *An Ungovernable People: The English and the Law in the Eighteenth Century* (1980), 21–46.

—— and David Levine, *Poverty and Piety in an English Village: Terling, 1525–1700* (1979).

Wrigley, E. A., and R. S. Schofield, *The Population History of England, 1541–1871: A Reconstruction* (Cambridge, 1989).

INDEX